THE
TEN CHALLENGES

OTHER BOOKS BY DR. LEONARD FELDER

LEARNING TO LOVE FOREVER
(*with Adelaide Bry*)

MAKING PEACE WITH YOUR PARENTS
(*with Harold Bloomfield, M.D.*)

MAKING PEACE WITH YOURSELF
(*with Harold Bloomfield, M.D.*)

A FRESH START

WHEN A LOVED ONE IS ILL

DOES SOMEONE AT WORK TREAT YOU BADLY?

THE TEN CHALLENGES

Spiritual Lessons from
the Ten Commandments
for Creating Meaning,
Growth, and Richness
Every Day of Your Life

LEONARD FELDER, Ph.D.

HARMONY BOOKS/NEW YORK

Grateful acknowledgment is given to reprint the following:
From *Birdsong: 53 Short Poems by Rumi,* translated by Coleman
Barks. Published by Maypop Books in 1993. Reprinted by
permission of Coleman Barks.
From *The Essential Rumi,* translated by Coleman Barks with John
Moyne. Published by HarperCollins in 1995. Reprinted by
permission of Coleman Barks.
From *When Bad Things Happen to Good People* by Harold S.
Kushner. Copyright © 1981, 1989 by Harold S. Kushner. Preface
copyright © 1989 by Harold S. Kushner. Reprinted by permission
of Schocken Books, published by Pantheon Books, a division of
Random House, Inc.

Published by Harmony Books, a division of Crown Publishers, Inc.,
201 East 50th Street, New York, New York 10022.
Member of the Crown Publishing Group.

HARMONY and colophon are trademarks of Crown Publishers, Inc.

Random House, Inc. New York, Toronto, London, Sydney, Auckland

http://www.randomhouse.com/

Printed in the United States of America

Library of Congress Cataloging-in-Publication Data
Felder, Leonard.
The ten challenges : spiritual lessons fron the Ten Commandments
for creating meaning, growth, and richness every day of your life /
by Leonard Felder.—1st ed.
p. cm.
Includes bibliographical references and index.
1. Spiritual life. 2. Conduct of life. 3. Spiritual healing.
4. Mental healing. 5. Psychology and religion. I. Title.
BL624.F44 1997
241.5′2—dc20 96-32429
CIP
ISBN 0-517-70505-2

10 9 8 7 6 5 4 3 2 1

First Edition

This book is dedicated to my maternal grandparents, Pauline and William Rothenberg, who taught me the delicious foods, sounds, and feelings of our heritage;

To my paternal grandparents, Johanna and Leopold Dingfelder, who perished with the six million and whose story taught me the importance of building bridges with others who want to repair this broken world;

And to my wife, partner, lover, and best friend, Linda Schorin, whose insights and suggestions added an enormous amount to each chapter of this book and whose warmth and wisdom helps us to treasure each day.

AUTHOR'S NOTE

Some of the issues addressed in this book can stir up intense feelings and memories. Anyone who has a history of psychiatric disorder, feels emotionally unstable, is taking tranquilizers, or is on antianxiety or antidepressant medication should not do the exercises in this book without first consulting a qualified mental health professional.

CONTENTS

THE
TEN CHALLENGES

INTRODUCTION

During many years of counseling men and women from all walks of life, I've seen repeatedly that most people hunger for something that can't be satisfied just by surviving or going through the motions of daily living. Most human beings have a profound desire for meaning and connection in a world that sometimes feels cold or indifferent. If you, too, have felt this hunger for a sense of something more meaningful in your life, you know it's not an easy thing to satisfy. It often feels like an anxious, almost hollow sensation in the pit of your stomach, a feeling that seems to ask: "Why am I here? Do I have a purpose? Is there a good reason for all the struggle and pain I'm going through? How can I make each day more worthwhile and fulfilling?"

As we approach the year 2000, I'm noticing that more and more of my friends, clients, and adult students are asking these deeply spiritual questions about how to create a life that feels worthwhile and that also makes a difference for others. We are living in an exciting time, yet the more fast-paced and technological our society becomes, the more our souls long for a chance to step back and gain a clearer perspective on what really matters in life. Often, we seek this perspective by returning to time-tested and honored writings that have provided a context for meaning through many centuries.

The book you are about to read focuses on one highly respected source of guidance on how to live a meaningful and satisfying life. In the chapters that follow, I will describe a series of ten spiritual lessons that are among the most important pieces of wisdom ever revealed. They are the ten statements found in the twentieth chapter of the Book of Exodus, which most people are familiar with as the Ten Commandments.

REDISCOVERING A PROFOUND SOURCE OF USEFUL KNOWLEDGE

When I was first introduced to the Ten Commandments as a child, they sounded rather intimidating and inaccessible, especially with all those "Thou shalt not"s ringing out. I remember worrying, What if I broke one of the commandments? What if I couldn't live up to some of them? Would God be angry or patient and forgiving? Eventually, I barely thought of them at all until, when I was a senior in college, they suddenly took on new meaning. I began to study them not as ancient artifacts or angry warnings but as useful psychological insights about how to have a fulfilling life.

This approach was first suggested to me by Dr. Rowland Shepard, my faculty adviser and a professor of clinical psychology at Kenyon College, a small liberal arts school in Ohio. It was twenty-three years ago that Dr. Shepard and I had a memorable conversation after class one afternoon, in which he said, "Maybe the Ten Commandments are misnamed. They ought to be called the ten hardest things we try to do in life—honoring our parents, dealing with adultery, attempting to get off the treadmill for one day each week, and not feeling jealous about what other people have. These topics aren't ancient history— they are the core issues that most of us struggle with in our personal lives."

Several years later, after I had become a practicing psychologist, I continued to be fascinated by spirituality. I began to study on my own and with various teachers just how much the issues raised by the Ten Commandments are ten of the most essential challenges we face in our lives. For example, most people don't realize that the Ten Commandments address topics such as:

• How do you decide what you believe about God and how you want to practice your spirituality? (The First Commandment: "I am the One who is and will always be, Your God, who brought you out of enslavement.")

• How do you make sure you don't get distracted or trapped by addictions and other seductive habits, like workaholism, that eventually leave you burned out and dissatisfied? (The Second Commandment: "You shall not worship false idols or images.")

• How do you deal with self-righteousness and anger when you're in an argument with a romantic partner, a family member, or someone at work? (The Third Commandment: "You shall not take God's name in vain.")

• How do you unhook each week from the stresses of life

and find a way to reconnect with people you care about and with a sense of inner peace? (The Fourth Commandment: "Remember the Sabbath day and keep it holy.")

• How do you honor a parent who has been difficult, insensitive, or abusive and make sure you heal enough from that relationship so that you can be your best with your own children and your own adult responsibilities? (The Fifth Commandment: "Honor your father and mother.")

• How do you make sure you don't inadvertently crush someone's spirit or let yourself become defeated or self-destructive during life's most difficult moments? (The Sixth Commandment: "You shall not murder.")

• How do you respond when you or your loved one feels attracted to someone else, and how do you rebuild a relationship when trust has been broken? (The Seventh Commandment: "You shall not commit adultery.")

• How can you accomplish what you want in life while still maintaining your integrity? (The Eighth Commandment: "You shall not steal.")

• How do you make sure you don't hurt people by lying, gossiping, or saying harmful things? (The Ninth Commandment: "You shall not bear false witness against your neighbor.")

• How do you stop wanting what other people have or wishing you could be like someone else? (The Tenth Commandment: "You shall not covet.")

Clearly these issues are as challenging today as they were in ancient times. With so many pressures and distractions today, it's even harder to find one's sense of spirituality, to live with integrity, and to set aside quiet time in our hectic schedules.

THE COMMON THREAD OF MANY SPIRITUAL TRADITIONS

The more I studied the various commentaries and interpretations of the Ten Commandments, the more I realized that the spirit of these lessons are the foundation of the world's major religions. In Judaism, the stone tablets of the Ten Commandments are visible in the sanctuaries of most temples and synagogues along with an eternal flame of light. For Jews around the world, these ten spiritual teachings are part of a continually evolving set of guidelines on how to build a life that has a deeper meaning and a higher purpose. For thousands of years, devoted Hebrew scholars as well as passionate teachers have interpreted and reinterpreted these ten spiritual lessons to explore how each new generation can benefit from their usefulness.

In the Sermon on the Mount, Jesus of Nazareth reinforced the Ten Commandments: "Anyone who infringes even one of the least of these commandments and teaches others to do the same will be considered the least in the kingdom of Heaven; but the person who keeps them and teaches them will be considered great in the kingdom of Heaven." As Jesus sought to clarify the teachings and their observance, he frequently stressed their importance; he said at one point, "If you keep my commandments you will abide in my love, just as I have kept my Father's commandments and abide in his love." He also said about the Commandments, "I have come not to abolish but to complete them. . . . Not one dot, not one little stroke, is to disappear from the Law until all its purpose is achieved." The purpose of the Law (the Commandments) is to guide each new generation.

In Islam, the Ten Commandments are respected and included as part of the highly developed guidelines given to Muslims on how to live a spiritual life, which are outlined in great detail in the Quran, the holy teachings of the prophet Muhammad. In Buddhism, the Five Precepts that form the basis of Right Behavior are almost identical to several of the Ten Commandments from Judaism: Do not kill, do not steal, do not lie, do not take drugs or drink intoxicants, and do not be unchaste.

The more I have learned about these ten spiritual lessons from the Book of Exodus, the more powerful, useful, and intriguing they have become. No matter what type of religious background you have, or even if you have none at all, the questions raised in these ten chapters will make you think about your life in a new and constructive way. My goal in this book is to make the ancient wisdom of the Ten Commandments accessible to everyone interested in spiritual meaning, growth, and change. That means you will find this book relevant and helpful to living your life whether you are spiritual, religious, or whether you identify with one particular tradition (such as Judaism, Christianity, Islam, or Buddhism) but are not religiously observant most of the time. If you are somewhat or very religious and want to deepen your understanding of the psychological aspects and hidden levels of wisdom in the Ten Commandments, you will find these chapters inspiring as well.

WHY IS A PSYCHOLOGIST WRITING ABOUT SPIRITUAL ISSUES?

In my work as a psychotherapist, I have seen how clients benefit most when both their spiritual and their psychological concerns are addressed in counseling. This approach of combining the scientific with the spiritual was first developed by a Viennese psychotherapist, Dr. Viktor Frankl, who broke from Freud in the 1940s and whose books I admired in college and graduate school before I finally had the opportunity to meet and study with him personally.

Viktor Frankl's approach to psychological healing came out of his experiences during World War II, where he was a concentration camp survivor and was able to maintain his sense of meaning and purpose in life despite losing his wife, his brother, his mother, and his father to the Nazis. Frankl started a radically new approach to therapy after the war and wrote several inspiring books about his life and his therapy work, including *Man's Search for Meaning* and *The Doctor and the Soul.* *

Briefly summarized, Dr. Frankl's research and counseling showed that one of the most important factors in restoring psychological well-being, especially during traumatic times, is finding a sense of meaning and purpose. Only by addressing a person's spiritual concerns can a counselor get to the core issues that affect this individual's daily struggle for fulfillment. Frankl has helped thousands of clients and influenced numerous psychologists and spiritual counselors with his techniques for asking the important questions and searching with the individual client for answers that bring meaning, direction, and well-being to one's life.

* For details on this or any other work I mention, please see the Sources section at the back of this book.

I felt drawn to Frankl's theories and techniques not only because of their effectiveness for my clients, but also because I felt a personal connection to Frankl and his search for healing and meaning after the Holocaust. My own father barely escaped from Nazi Germany, several close relatives were concentration camp survivors, and I grew up with unforgettable stories of how my paternal grandparents and many other relatives were killed in the death camps.

Both Frankl's approach and the therapy techniques I have developed over the years emphasize the strong connection between psychological healing and spiritual healing. For example, I have found repeatedly that the exact same spiritual issues named by the Ten Commandments offer profound clues for helping us regain our emotional health and psychological well-being. Quite often when I'm counseling someone or facing a difficult challenge in my own life, using the Ten Commandments' guidance has led to healing and personal growth. I have seen hundreds of individuals and couples benefit from their essential wisdom.

THE REASON FOR CALLING THEM "CHALLENGES" AS WELL AS "COMMANDMENTS"

While the topics explored in this book are from the Ten Commandments, I've called my approach "The Ten Challenges" for some specific reasons. According to many scholars, the original Hebrew term *Ahseret Ha-deebrot* literally means "The Ten Words" or "The Ten Things" but was mistranslated into Greek and later into English as "The Ten Commandments." While many people prefer the word "commandment," an even greater number of individuals would be open to appreciating the wisdom of these ten insights if they were presented in a less authoritarian fashion.

I've found over the years that "challenge" is the word that most accurately describes how these ten lessons function for most people. The word "commandment" implies you must either obey or disobey the rules in chapter 20 of the Book of Exodus, while the word "challenge" describes the *voluntary, ongoing process* of what actually occurs when you start to apply these important spiritual principles to your daily life. This *process* of taking the Ten Words and attempting to live according to them includes the following steps:

• Understanding the deeper meanings and original Hebrew words that are at the root of each of these spiritual lessons. In each chapter I will explain what the actual Hebrew words suggest and how some of these words have been mistranslated and misinterpreted over the centuries.

• Defining the obstacles and difficulties that come up for most people when they try to abide by the Ten Words. For the vast majority of individuals, it's a question not of whether to obey or disobey, but rather how to make these useful principles a part of their life despite the distractions of modern living.

• Developing the internal strength as well as the resources and external support to follow through on each of these ten spiritual lessons. In each chapter I will recommend specific steps you can take to increase the likelihood that you will be able to live up to these spiritual goals.

• Experiencing the satisfaction of knowing that your life has taken on a new sense of meaning and purpose. *The Ten Challenges* is not a theoretical book about unattainable visions of perfection, but rather a psychological and pragmatic exploration of how to apply these useful ideas to your everyday decisions and your most important relationships.

TRYING OUT THESE PRINCIPLES ON THE MOST STRESSFUL PARTS OF YOUR LIFE

To illustrate how the ten challenges can be extremely useful for healing and growth, let's look at an example. When Jenny and Bill* were first referred to me for counseling, they said they wanted to stop fighting so often. They needed help in reestablishing a more satisfying and less volatile marriage.

Witty and intelligent, Jenny was a hardworking lawyer. Bill

---

* Names and identifying details in cases throughout this book have been changed to protect confidentiality.

was the media director at an advertising agency and a very creative, strong-willed individual. They both seemed committed to improving their marriage, in part because they were concerned about their two young daughters (ages eight and five), who'd had recent troubles in school almost certainly linked to the tensions at home.

"Bill and I can't have a conversation anymore without it turning into a fight," Jenny said in their first session. "The more we argue, the more our daughters suffer—it's got to stop."

Even though I was able to improve Jenny and Bill's communication and defuse their tensions somewhat during the first few counseling sessions, it became clear there was a deeper pain in their marriage. In Jenny's words: "There's a frustration Bill and I both bring home from work each day. I hate my job, even though I've worked my whole life to get to where I am today. And Bill hates the office politics and the unrelenting pressures where he works."

Bill added, "We both come home each night edgy and exhausted. We usually take out our unhappiness on each other."

At this point, I began to look at how I might use the issues raised by the Ten Challenges to identify why Jenny and Bill had become so disillusioned with their lives, as well as what they could do to put new energy into their home life.

Like so many career-focused people, Jenny and Bill had believed that if they gave their all to their jobs, they'd feel happy and fulfilled. But when I asked Jenny to talk about her work life and what it meant to her, she said, "I feel like I made it so important, more important than anything else in this world." Bill had also believed his career would make him feel complete, yet he feels spiritually empty. He explained, "It's frustrating to devote my life to my job, and yet it doesn't seem to mean much at all."

Jenny and Bill's descriptions of their unhappiness are exactly the issues addressed by the Second Challenge, which in the Book of Exodus says, "Don't worship false gods or false images." I refer to it as "Breaking free of unfulfilling paths and habits."

In order to defuse their frustration and stop taking out their unhappiness on each other, Jenny and Bill needed to find a deeper sense of what they wanted their lives to be about and to stop looking to their careers as their only source of identity and satisfaction. For the next few sessions, we discussed several specific ways of reducing their overemphasis on work and bringing a new sense of meaning and purpose to their busy lives.

First, Jenny and Bill realized that even though they were unhappy with their careers, neither of them felt it was the right time economically to initiate a major career change. As Bill put it, "Our mortgage and the job market are telling us to hang in there a while longer."

But that didn't mean they had to keep *worshiping* their jobs. Instead, they needed to see their careers more realistically for what they can provide—income, a sense of structure, and a chance to be creative—but not as the "key to happiness." This first step became an exercise in substituting realism for false hope.

Second, both Jenny and Bill decided it might be possible to add greater meaning to their lives by volunteering just one afternoon a month with an organization that gives workshops on goal setting, career planning, and interview skills for teenagers from low-income neighborhoods.

A few months after they began volunteering, Jenny reported, "Each month when we've participated in these miniworkshops, there are always a few of these teenagers who I get to know personally, and we've stayed in touch on the phone. It feels good to know we've made a small difference in their lives."

Bill adds, "Helping these young people develop the skills to become self-supporting feels a lot more meaningful than just doing my job in advertising day after day."

As an additional healing step, Bill and Jenny began to try out some creative ideas contained in the Fourth Challenge, which in the Book of Exodus says, "Remember the Sabbath day and keep it holy." I describe it as "The struggle to unhook from your everyday pressures and connect with something profoundly joyful."

Neither Jenny nor Bill was raised in a religious household, and both had assumed that keeping the Sabbath was nothing more than a bunch of restrictive rules. They both became interested, however, when I began to discuss with them the calmness and family closeness that might occur if they started to take one day a week to unhook from work activities. This day would be devoted to spending special time together with their daughters and would also allow for some quiet time on their own.

Jenny was enthusiastic from the start. "The idea of spending a day each week with Bill and the girls, taking walks and discussing our lives," she said, "that's what we've needed to improve our marriage and our home life."

Bill was a little more skeptical at first, admitting, "I like the concept of a weekly sabbatical, but the reality is that I tend to plunk myself down in front of the TV and I would hate to give up watching my usual megadoses of football, basketball, golf, and tennis."

But after several weeks of experimenting with a weekly sabbatical that included family fun, extended conversations, and walks together, Bill commented, "It does feel great to unhook. I still grumble a bit if I miss some TV sporting event, but now I just tape it and watch it later, without all the commercials. Or I limit my television sports to one game I absolutely don't want to miss."

Bill concluded, "If I have to choose between connecting with my wife and daughters or spending the whole weekend watching television and doing meaningless stuff, I'd rather be with my family. Our home life is a lot less crazy now as a result."

THE PEOPLE YOU WILL MEET

In each chapter of this book, you will be introduced to a variety of interesting women and men who are wrestling with the same questions and concerns that you and I face in our daily lives. Their stories will give you ideas for your own search for meaning, and you will discover creative ways to apply the wisdom of the Ten Challenges to your most pressing concerns.

Some of the people whose stories you will discover come from my psychotherapy practice, in which clients seek ways to handle depression, anxiety, difficult decisions, grief, loss, divorce, separation, and family conflicts. Underneath these issues there is often a deeper questioning of "What is my life about?" and "Where am I going?" that crosses over into the spiritual search for meaning and purpose.

In addition to stories from my practice, many come from other settings where I was fortunate to be able to discuss the Ten Challenges with couples and individuals who were grappling with important psychological and spiritual concerns. These settings include:

• For seven years I facilitated dialogue programs between Jews and Christians on religious and personal issues. Sponsored by the National Conference of Christians and Jews, these dialogue series were not about converting anyone or judging anyone's way of practicing (or not practicing) their religion. Rather, these were fascinating and unusual conversations between women and men of different backgrounds to find out more about how each of us seeks meaning, community, and connection to a higher power in ways that are similar and divergent. We would meet once a week for six to ten weeks and discuss very personal concerns about how we deal with our spiritual lives and how we handle the issues raised by the Ten Commandments and other important works of our common heritage.

• For nine years I was a staff member for a multiracial, multiethnic summer workshop called Brotherhood-Sisterhood USA, in which two hundred high school students from various parts of southern California (ranging from affluent suburban kids to gang members) would get together for a weeklong series of small-group discussions on their lives. We explored in depth how to develop a sense of community, greater self-worth, and purposeful goals despite all the pressures these teens face. I found myself listening more than talking each summer as these passionate and intense young people described how they deal with the challenges in their lives. Some of their stories of how they respond to the issues in this book will surprise and inspire you.

• For more than twenty years I have been researching how various religious and spiritual traditions deal with the topics raised in the Ten Commandments. I have studied with and interviewed people from many different belief systems on how they find their sense of meaning and purpose, and in this book you will hear some of the insights I obtained from people who are agnostic, atheist, Bahai, Buddhist, Catholic, Protestant, Eastern Orthodox, Hindu, Jewish (including Orthodox, Conservative, Reconstructionist, Reform, Renewal, and Secular), Muslim, Native American, Religious Scientist, Taoist, and Unitarian. (Note: If any of the words in this book are unfamiliar to you, please look them up in the Glossary of Terms located in the back. There is also a Sources section in the back that lists where various opinions come from, along with suggestions for additional reading.)

A COLLECTION OF VIEWPOINTS

You also will meet in each section of this book a diverse group of spiritual and psychological teachers and writers who have some unique things to say about the Ten Commandments. I have selected from many centuries of scholarly and practical insights to give you the most useful ideas and suggestions to apply to the stresses and dilemmas in your life.

For example, in the chapter about the Tenth Challenge ("You shall not covet," or "The way to feel good about what you have"), you will hear from several psychological experts on the physical and emotional problems that can arise when day after day a person keeps desiring what others have or wishes he or she were more like someone else. You will also learn about the different ways that Judaism, Christianity, and Buddhism deal with this important challenge of how to break free of the painful longing for what you don't have. By the end of Chapter 10, you will have specific tools and techniques for the next time your spirits decline because of someone who is younger, better looking, more creative, or more successful. Instead of feeling powerless to change the habit of wishing you could be like someone else, you will know exactly how to turn these jealous feelings into an inspiration for reviving the most fulfilling parts of your own life.

My hope is that in each chapter of *The Ten Challenges* you will recognize a part of yourself and learn not only what the commandment means intellectually but, more important, how to make your life richer and more satisfying by taking the steps toward living up to that particular challenge. Of course, I can't guarantee that everything will flow smoothly once you start applying these ten spiritual lessons to your daily life, but I can assure you that how you deal with life's ups and downs will be dramatically improved. With these ten sources of guidance in mind, you will be able to approach each day with a much greater sense of mastery and fulfillment.

1

THE FIRST CHALLENGE

Discovering the Still Small Voice Within

Deciding what you believe about God and how you want to practice your spirituality is for most people a lifelong process of questioning and discovery. Many people—including your relatives, teachers, friends, and even the preachers on cable TV—may try to influence your thinking or twist your arm about how to be a spiritual human being. But ultimately the decision is your own to make.

"I AM THE ONE WHO CARES"

While reading this chapter on the First Commandment, you will have the opportunity to look at your own feelings about the beliefs others have tried to force upon you as well as the beliefs that you've been wrestling with in your own mind. This questioning and searching for a direct personal experience of God's support is exactly what the First of the Ten Words is about. Briefly stated, the First Commandment is a request from God for each of us to decide whether we believe in and want to be partners with the Infinite One. The Hebrew words in Exodus 20:1, which we'll explore in detail later in the chapter, say essentially, "I am the One who is and will always be, your God, who has helped you in the past and who cares about your freedom."

THE CHOICE BETWEEN SKEPTICISM
AND CURIOSITY

As a psychologist who has discussed spiritual issues with thousands of women and men, I have learned repeatedly that decent and intelligent people often disagree with one another about whether there is a God who cares about us and who is involved in our daily lives. Even among psychologists, there is great disagreement and controversy about spiritual issues. For example, more than sixty years ago three of the most prominent psychologists who ever lived (Sigmund Freud, Carl Jung, and William James) each attempted to define the "ultimate truth" about God and the role that spirituality plays in our lives. As you might expect, the three experts came to three substantially different conclusions.

The Austrian physician and founder of psychoanalysis, Sigmund Freud, wrote in a book called *The Future of an Illusion,* "Religion is an obsessional neurosis . . . a childish illusion to defend oneself against the crushing superiority of nature." A fervent nonbeliever, Freud hoped spirituality and religion would be replaced by what he called "objective science and pure reason."

The Swiss psychiatrist Carl Jung was fascinated by religious symbols and archetypes, which he viewed as clues that reveal our soul's deep quest to connect with the Divine. Jung wrote several books on the benefits and dangers of the human search for religious meaning and viewed spirituality as a courageous part of being alive.

The American psychologist and Harvard professor William James wrote a classic study called *The Varieties of Religious Experience,* in which he described how one small part of the brain focuses on rational issues while a more substantial part of the mind is capable of mystical experiences, spiritual exploration, and the pursuit of wholeness. A careful observer of human behavior, James described many people who dramatically changed their lives through opening up to a deep faith in God or by following a spiritual practice. James argued that ignoring our spiritual need to connect with a higher form of consciousness is the equivalent of limiting one's mind to a small percentage of its potential.

If you had to choose between the skepticism of Sigmund

Freud or the curiosity of Carl Jung and William James, which would you pick? On most days, do you find yourself feeling somewhat distant and skeptical about God and religion? Or do you sometimes feel a desire to learn more, become closer to your sense of God, or become more active in your practice of spirituality?

THE SEARCH FOR SPIRITUAL VIEWS AND PRACTICES THAT MAKE SENSE TO YOU

As you look back at your own spiritual life thus far, has it been an easy or a difficult path? For example, have you felt criticized or ostracized for your way of viewing spiritual and religious issues? Or have you found books, teachers, and a positive sense of community to help you move toward a deeper understanding of your spiritual concerns? Have you sometimes felt guilty for questioning things that others accepted more easily, or have you felt supported by people who wanted you to find your own way toward a sense of spiritual meaning and purpose?

Almost fifteen years ago I participated in a workshop where Christians, Jews, and Muslims all talked about their childhood imaginings about God and their adult questions and beliefs. The need to rethink one's earliest sense of God happens not just to people of one religion but to people of all religions. Sooner or later, most people feel the need to sort out for themselves an adult sense of God and spirituality.

In some families and congregations, religious questioning is encouraged and thoughtfully guided, but for others it is viewed as shameful or evil. In my psychotherapy practice and from talking with friends, I have seen that quite often individuals carry emotional scars for much of their lives because certain relatives, friends, or religious authorities rejected or scorned them for questioning and rethinking what the majority accepted as "ultimate truth." Sometimes an important part of our spiritual lives is to recover and start again after being "psychologically beaten up" for believing differently from those around us.

For instance, here's how one workshop participant described her own recovery and her search for a God that makes sense to her as an adult:

"As a child, I blindly accepted what my elders told me about

God and religion. But as I grew into my late teens, I couldn't truthfully pray to a harsh, judgmental, and angry old man with a long white beard. I'd grown up with that image of God, and when I stopped believing it, my parents were furious with me. For several years I kept running into dogmatic people who were threatened by my questions and my search for a different, less patriarchal sense of God. So I pulled away from religion for a while, but the longing to understand my spiritual side continued. Fortunately I came across a few teachers, books, and a more progressive congregation, in which God is discussed in a more complex and intelligent fashion. I'm glad I found my way back to a sense of God and spirituality that I can believe once again."

WHAT IMAGE OF GOD DID YOU GROW UP WITH?

Even though no one really knows what God looks like, many of the people I interviewed for this book told me that when they were younger they believed God to be a male humanlike Being who lives up in heaven. Even if no one directly tried to tell you what God looked like, you may have picked up the notion of an "old man with a long white beard" from illustrated Bible stories or paintings. Possibly you tried to replace this childhood image of a distant or inaccessible God with a different sense of spirituality, but you may still be praying to a deity like the one pictured in many paintings, sitting on a throne in heaven or hurling bolts of lightning, especially when your life is difficult and you ask God for help. Reflecting on the notion you have of God or a higher being can help you clarify your view of yourself, your life, and your purpose.

UNDERSTANDING WHAT THE FIRST WORD IS SAYING

In opening up your imagination to other views of what God might be, a good place to start is the First Commandment. According to most scholars and theologians, the first of the Ten Commandments offers us a chance to experience a God who cannot be seen with the eye nor heard with the ear. These scholars and clergy members suggest that the God who offers the Ten Words to Moses and the gathered multitudes in the desert is more like an energy that dwells among us or a mysterious internal sense of guidance.

This sense of a Divine Presence dwelling among us or expressing through us corresponds to an interpretation of receiving the Ten Commandments, which I've heard several times over the years from various rabbis and scholars, as having come from God in a silent, intuitive way. Some of the gathered multitude heard these words in their hearts, much like when you have an inner sense of knowing, or as when a dream, an emotion, or a piece of music comes into your awareness. God's mind spoke to the people from deep within their own minds and spirits.

So when you think about the specific words of the First Commandment, imagine yourself to be wandering in the desert and receiving an intuitive sense—a quiet moment of wisdom that seems to arise from deep within you. Imagine that the still small voice of your soul is giving you an important message.

According to the Book of Exodus, chapter 20, verse 1, the actual Hebrew words people heard in their hearts as they waited for Moses to come down the mountain with guidance from God were, "Anokhee [I am] Yud-Hei-Vov-Hei [the mysterious and unknowable name of God, best translated as 'the One who is and will always be'], Eloheykha [your God], Asheyr hohtseitikha mei-eretz mitzrayim [who brought you out of Egypt], me-beit avadeem [out of the house of bondage]."

Many rabbis and Hebrew scholars translate this First Commandment differently because the word *mitzrayim* can refer to not only the actual place Egypt but also anything that is narrow, restrictive, or limiting. The root of *mitzrayim* is the word *tsur,* as in *tsuris,* which means troubles or worries.

So these translators recommend hearing the words of the First Commandment not just as a statement about God who is the One who freed the ancient Hebrews from slavery in Egypt. Rather, they suggest the First Commandment can be translated, "I am the One who is and will always be, your God, who can bring you out of a narrow way of seeing things, out of your enslavements and worries."

WHAT WOULD HAVE BEEN YOUR REACTION IN THE DESERT?

To consider what this First Word means to you personally, let's imagine for a moment that you were one of the many thousands of wanderers in the Sinai desert following Moses out of slavery and across the Red Sea with Egyptian soldiers pursuing you. After a period of wandering, you stood at the foot of a cloud-enshrouded mountain while your leader was unavailable for forty days because he went up to look for what he hoped would be a closer connection to God.

Imagine that either during a quiet moment or right in the middle of your daily chores, you sensed inside your heart an almost silent voice that felt like God reaching out to you and saying essentially, "I know about your worries and I can help you find your way out of them. I am the One who has helped before."

You probably weren't sure if anyone else heard the same message—or even if you truly heard it yourself. Maybe it was a hallucination or just the wind playing tricks on you. But then you talked to several of your fellow wanderers and found they, too, had sensed something about God wanting to connect with us humans.

Soon after, Moses came down from the mountain with these same ideas on tablets of stone. What would have been your reaction? If you were there in the desert, struggling to make sense of the message you felt in your heart, which of the following would you have thought in response (based on how you are today):

A. I don't know who you are or what you want from me. Is this some kind of magic trick?

B. OK, maybe I accept there is an energy calling to me, but I'm not so sure You really helped. It seems like I did all that trudging through the desert by myself and there were plenty of times when I called out to You for help and You didn't answer.

C. Yes, You are a powerful and helpful force, but I get the feeling You want something in return and I'm not sure I can agree to most of the terms You might ask of me.

D. I'm curious to know more. You seem to care about me, and when I open up to Your support I feel a lot better than when I stay stuck in my narrow, anxious mind.

Which of the above choices feels most like how you are today: the person who feels skeptical about whether there's a voice calling? The person who hears it but who isn't sure if God really helps because so often God seems to be silent? The person who accepts God as a helpful and powerful force but who isn't sure about agreeing to what God wants in return? Or the person who is curious and open to exploring what a closer relationship might entail?

I realize these are not simple choices. But I hope you give these or any other responses you might come up with on your own some serious thought. In this chapter and throughout this book, I offer traditional and nontraditional interpretations of the Commandments, which I hope will help you formulate a new, more positive, less constricting view of the Ten Commandments and the guidance they offer us.

WHAT THE SCHOLARS SAY

Among thousands of interpretations of the First Commandment, most scholars agree on a few key points that can help you sort out your own feelings about there being a God, a Divine Presence who is reaching out for connection:

- Exodus 20 begins not with God the powerful force saying, "I created the universe and I can destroy it as well," but rather with God the caring source of support saying essentially, "I need a partnership with you, based on a history of my love for you, and I'm committed to working together to repair this broken world. I can't do it without you."
- The First Commandment is an offer of partnership or a proposal of marriage of spirit. The silent, intuitive voice of the Holy One is saying, "I've cared about you and come through for you, but now I need a commitment from you as well." The biblical scholar Benno Jacob explains the warmth and caring of this statement as, "The opening words of the Decalogue engage

God in an eternal covenant of love. 'I am yours' is the counterpart of 'You shall be mine.' "

• God is reaching out to all future generations, not just to the gathered multitudes at the foot of Mount Sinai. One Talmudic scholar explained that the reason these Ten Words were given in the wilderness and not within any one country's borders is that they are intended for all peoples, not just for one nation, and for all generations, not just those who were alive during the Exodus from Egypt.

HOW DO YOU WANT TO ANSWER?

Whether you are a strong believer, a strong nonbeliever, or somewhere in between, these first words from Exodus 20 present quite a challenge. There's something intriguing and appealing about the idea of a still small voice beckoning us to help complete the creation of the world by joining with God to repair it. But the idea of being God's partner in fixing even your own small corner of the world may feel like too much of a burden. Or you might be saying to yourself, "What is all this talk about God wanting a partnership with human beings? Where was God during the Holocaust? Where was God recently when I called out and didn't see or hear a response?" Many people feel reluctant to engage in a partnership with God because they blame God for the death of many millions of people around the world and for other tragedies that happen to us or to people about whom we care.

I remember having these feelings myself. When I was ten years old and my mother was diagnosed with cancer, I began to pray each night for God to help her recover. I desperately wanted a sign from God that my prayers were being received and that my mother was going to be helped. But when I was fourteen years old, my mother died painfully at the age of forty-six, and I stopped praying. I felt betrayed and for quite a while kept my distance from the world of believers. It took several years of reexamining how I viewed God before I began to find explanations that made sense to me about why bad things happen to good people. It took a while before I could pray again and longer still before I could feel trust and warmth toward the One to whom I was praying.

If you currently are feeling angry or distrustful about God for allowing terrible things to happen in this world, I urge you to talk with friends, clergy members, or a counselor who can help you sort out your feelings. I also recommend several books that can expand your idea of what God might be and why God doesn't intervene every time humans mistreat one another, nature erupts in a devastating disaster, or the fragile human body becomes ill:

For Jews or for anyone who wants to understand the many ways that Judaism looks at God, there is an outstanding book called *Finding God,* which was written in 1986 by Rifat Sonsino and Daniel Syme. It describes ten different, highly intelligent ways of understanding God while still calling yourself a religious person. If you thought the only way to envision God is what you were taught when you were in grade school, this book can help you discover how God is described differently by the biblical writings, the later oral rabbinic tradition, the eleventh-century teachings of Moses Maimonides, the sixteenth-century mysticism of Isaac Luria and the Kabbalistic writers, as well as the twentieth-century views of Martin Buber, Erich Fromm, and others.

For Catholics, there are at least two books that have helped many believers and nonbelievers understand why God doesn't always intervene or answer our prayers in the way we would like. One is a guidebook to traditional Catholicism called *Christ Among Us: A Modern Presentation of the Catholic Faith for Adults,* by Anthony Wilhelm. The other is a more mystical and contemplative guide to faith by Henri Nouwen entitled *The Way of the Heart.*

For Protestants, there is an excellent book for rethinking what you learned as a child and coming to an adult understanding of Christian faith and practices. Entitled *To Begin at the Beginning,* by Pastor Martin Copenhaver of Phoenix, Arizona, it goes deeply into many issues of faith without resorting to the divinity school terminology that makes most religious books so difficult to read.

For Muslims, one of the finest modern interpretations of the Islamic view of God's way of connecting with human beings is contained in *Reading the Muslim Mind,* by Dr. Hassan Hathout of the Los Angeles Islamic Center, and in two books by Annemarie Schimmel: *Islam: An Introduction* and *Mystical Dimensions of Islam.*

Finally, if you want to learn more about how various traditions connect with God and deal with the mystery of a God whose ways are not always perceptible to humans, I strongly recommend the classic work on the subject, *The Illustrated World's Religions,* by Huston Smith. In this highly readable book, you will recognize the similarities and differences in how Judaism, Christianity, Islam, Hinduism, Buddhism, Taoism, Confucianism, and other traditions experience a sense of the Infinite One.

"HUMAN BEINGS ARE GOD'S LANGUAGE"

Yet to answer the questions raised earlier—"Where was God during the Holocaust?" and "Where was God when I called out and my loved one still suffered?"—there are two other books. I have recommended these two to people of many different faiths, including those who have felt alienated from God or religion, and they are the best resources I have found to explore the possibility of believing in a God who cares about us—even when there is so much human cruelty and unexplainable suffering in the world.

The first book, entitled *When Bad Things Happen to Good People,* was written in 1981 by Harold Kushner, who was trained as a religious counselor but had his faith challenged when his three-year-old son Aaron was diagnosed with a rare illness called progeria, which led to the child's rapid aging and death at the age of fourteen. In his book, Harold Kushner describes how he came to terms with his son's terminal illness and found a renewed sense of faith and purpose. Several passages are particularly helpful to many people who are feeling confused or angry about their own spirituality as a result of an innocent person dying or being killed. Kushner writes,

"I believe in God. But I do not believe the same things about God that I did years ago when I was growing up or when I was a theological student. God does not cause our misfortunes. Some are caused by bad luck, some are caused by bad people, and some are simply an inevitable consequence of our being human and being mortal, living in a world of inflexible natural laws. The painful things that happen to us are not punishments for our misbehavior, nor are they in any way part of some grand design on God's part.

"Because the tragedy is not God's will, we need not feel hurt or betrayed by God when tragedy strikes. We can turn to God for help in overcoming it, precisely because we can tell ourselves that God is as outraged by it as we are.

"How does God make a difference in our lives if God neither kills nor cures? God inspires people to help other people who have been hurt by life, and by helping them, they protect them from the danger of feeling alone, abandoned or judged. God, who neither causes nor prevents tragedies, helps by inspiring people to help. As a nineteenth-century Hasidic rabbi once put it, *'Human beings are God's language.'* God shows opposition to cancer and birth defects not by eliminating them or making them happen only to bad people (God can't do that), but by summoning forth friends and neighbors to ease the burden and to fill the emptiness. God may not prevent the calamity, but God gives us the strength and perseverance to overcome it."

FINDING AN INNER PRESENCE

The other book I like to recommend to clients and friends who are struggling with spiritual questions is *She Who Dwells Within* by Rabbi Lynn Gottlieb. Published in 1995, this inspiring and thought-provoking book for people of all faiths presents traditional and modern views of God that you may have experienced personally but not known how to describe. For instance, Gottlieb explains how one aspect of God is our internal sense of longing for wholeness. Another way to experience God's Presence is as the Being who connects all life. Yet another way to feel God's Spirit is in the deeply intuitive sense of justice and compassion we feel in our hearts.

In other words, instead of thinking of God as "out there" or "up in heaven," you may share ideas of God's Presence that many scholars and teachings have maintained and described for centuries. In Hebrew the in-dwelling Presence of God is called the Shekhinah, which can be found within our hearts and within our passion for healing, justice, and caring.

Looking for a sense of God *deep within your own being* may

seem controversial to some people. But in fact the mystical and contemplative traditions of Judaism, Christianity, and Islam have explored this inner sense of God for many centuries and have offered much guidance on how to find a deeply intuitive connection to the Divine Presence.

For example, if you read the tradition-based guide called *Jewish Meditation,* by Aryeh Kaplan, you will find techniques for connecting with the aspect of God that exists within the deepest part of your subconscious mind. Or if you read Rodger Kamenetz's recent book *The Jew in the Lotus,* you will hear Orthodox, Conservative, Reconstructionist, Reform, and Renewal rabbis discuss the various Jewish meditative paths to finding God. *The Jew in the Lotus* is the true story of a series of conversations in 1990 between the Dalai Lama and several American rabbis about how to keep one's spirituality alive while in exile from one's homeland. Both the Jewish teachers and the Buddhist monks discuss how to experience a deep sense of oneness with the Eternal through various spiritual practices.

Many priests, ministers, and Christian theologians have also explored similar ways to find God's Spirit deep within one's heart. One such theologian is Henri Nouwen, who has taught for many years at Yale Divinity School. He writes, "Prayer is standing in the presence of God with the mind in the heart; that is, at that point of our being where there are no divisions or distinctions and where we are totally one. There God's Spirit dwells and there the great encounter takes place. There heart speaks to heart, because there we stand before the face of the Lord, all-seeing, within us."

As far back as the fourteenth century, a German priest and influential teacher named Meister Eckhart spoke in a similar fashion, saying, "As long as a person holds himself unto God, you will receive the Divine inflowing. How does the soul receive from God? The soul receives from God not as something foreign, as happens when the air receives light from the sun. The soul receives from God as light receives from light, where nothing is foreign or distant."

In the Islamic mystical tradition, which is called Sufism, the brilliant thirteenth-century scholar and writer Jalad ad-Din Rumi wrote love poetry for God that has inspired people of various faiths for centuries. In one of his poems, Rumi describes the inner sense of God's Presence as:

You dance inside my chest,
where no one sees you,
but sometimes I do,
and that sight becomes this art.

WHAT MIGHT BE YOUR WAYS OF EXPERIENCING GOD'S PRESENCE?

Quite often when I am counseling someone I ask a question such as, "Have you ever had a sense of God's Presence guiding you or supporting you?" I find that most people have had such experiences but are reluctant to call it spiritual guidance. Many people fear that they will be mocked or criticized if they admit to spiritual experiences. Other people underestimate their own capacity for spirituality. Fortunately, many traditions' teachings can help reduce this insecure feeling. These supportive teachings tell us that there is one God but many different personal experiences for sensing a connection with that one God.

As an example, the Amidah or Standing Prayer in Judaism, which is recited several times each weekday and on the Sabbath, begins with the statement, "Blessed are You, Eternal One, God of our ancestors, God of Abraham, God of Isaac, God of Jacob, God of Sarah, God of Rebecca, God of Rachel, and God of Leah." * In the rabbinic literature that discusses this prayer, one scholar asked, "Why do we repeat the words 'God of' this person and 'God of' that person so many times? Wouldn't it be simpler and more grammatical to say just one time: God of Abraham, Isaac, and Jacob?"

After much discussion the rabbinic commentary answers that even with one God, each human being has a different personal experience of God and a different way of expressing his or her sense of God's Presence. So the God of Abraham might be a different experience from the God of Jacob or the God of Rachel, even though there is only one God. In other words, each of us has to find our own individual way of opening up to our particular spark of the Divine Presence.

* The egalitarian version of the Amidah prayer I am using here, which includes the matriarchs Sarah, Rebecca, Rachel, and Leah, can be found in some Conservative and most Reform, Renewal, and Reconstructionist congregations.

According to the Catholic theologian Anthony Wilhelm, "Many seek God and find God in the depths of their being without realizing it. Some through their unrelenting pursuit of truth and justice, or the good of the community, or another humanitarian ideal. And many through their insatiable thirst for love. Through their total commitment to a transcendent idea they are reaching the absolute we call God."

The diversity of spiritual practices within each religion also suggests there are many ways to experience the Infinite One and that each of us must choose our particular ways of feeling God's Presence. For example, some people feel ecstatic and connected to God during moments of deep meditation, prayer, or singing, while others report feeling bored or unmoved during these activities. Some have moments of peaceful transcendence when they fast, take spiritual walks in nature, or go on a religious or spiritual retreat, while others would rather do anything but fast, be in nature, or go on a retreat.

What I am suggesting is that if we stop judging ourselves and other people for our different ways of being spiritual, we will find there are a great many viable paths to the Divine. As the Buddhist expression says, "There is one moon and many reflections."

As you think about your own personal style of spiritual practice, I want you to take note of the ways in which you have most often experienced deep moments of connection with God or Spirit. For a moment, please look over the following brief and highly incomplete list of possibilities. Notice which experiences sound like you, which sound like something you would rather avoid, and which might be something you would like to try out in the future. My goal is not to tell you how to practice your spirituality but to help you reawaken inspiring memories and also to offer you the possibility of new experiences that may feel right to you.

Please take a moment to note which ways of attaining a sense of connection with God you have experienced or would like to experience:

- A deep moment of prayer, meditation, or song in which you truly broke free of the mind's noisy chatter to find a stronger sense of inner peace and oneness with God or the universe

- A warm and meaningful gathering of friends or family to celebrate a religious holiday or an important life-cycle event
- A sermon, book, class, or teaching on a spiritual topic that not only stimulated your mind but also improved the way you live
- A spiritual or religious retreat that took you out of your everyday routine and gave you ideas about your higher purpose in life
- A brief or ongoing volunteer experience or paid job in which you felt you helped another human being and did some of "God's work"
- A ritual or spiritual ceremony that moved you emotionally and made you feel connected to a higher consciousness
- A visit you made to a place you consider holy or inspiring
- Noticing during the illness or death of a loved one that you were able to feel a strong connection to God's love and to the support of caring people
- A moment when you treated a stranger or a person in need with dignity and respect, or when you saw the godliness in someone and it made a difference in how you related to each other
- Moments in which a sunrise, a walk in nature, a piece of music, the birth of a child, or a deep connection with someone you love made you feel open to the Divine Presence

IS SOMETHING HOLDING YOU BACK?

As you look at this brief list of spiritual and religious possibilities, what do you think holds you back from having more of these peak experiences in your life? Is it a lack of time, a lack of interest, or some pressing demand or priority you can't seem to get away from? Do you have some hesitation about religion because you grew up when for many people it was unfashionable to care about God and spirituality? Or do you have some emotional baggage from the past because someone betrayed you, belittled you, or hurt you regarding spiritual or religious issues?

As a psychotherapist I have seen repeatedly that when people uncover and begin to resolve what has been blocking their spiritual or religious life from developing, it can lead to an enormously positive phase of personal growth and healing. I hope you will take some time, either on your own or with a friend or counselor, to sort out your positive and negative feelings about this important part of life. Reenergizing your spiritual self and reconnecting with a sense of meaning and purpose can be one of the most life-affirming steps you ever take.

TAKING ACTION ON YOUR SPIRITUAL BELIEFS

For many people, living a spiritual or religious life entails much more than just clarifying your beliefs about God and how the universe operates. Many teachings in Judaism, Christianity, and Islam, as well as those of other religions, suggest that being spiritual encompasses how you treat other people, how you treat nature, and how you deal with the daily stresses and responsibilities of your life.

So in a very practical sense, the First Commandment isn't just about resolving your feelings regarding God and religion. It also challenges us to decide on a daily basis, "How do I want to conduct my life so that it's consistent with my spiritual beliefs?"

If all of us woke up each day and remembered the First Statement from chapter 20 of the Book of Exodus, "I am the One who is and will always be, your God, who brings you out of a narrow way of seeing things, out of your worries and enslavements," how would that change the way we live our lives? Would it make us feel more in partnership with God? Would it make us more aware of the responsibility of being "God's language" doing good deeds here on earth? Would it remind us to be loving to our children, to be careful with nature, to treat other people with dignity, and to do whatever we could to repair this broken world?

In studying many of the world's major religions, I have found that this theme of conducting one's life so that it makes this world a better place is an important part of every spiritual tradition. For instance, in the mystical tradition in Judaism, as described by the sixteenth-century Kabbalist Rabbi Isaac Luria, God pulled back from completing the creation of the world in order to allow humans to be free and to make their own choices. Luria explains that during this painful process of God's pulling back, the divine light broke into millions of tiny fragments from the intensity of God's restraint. Each individual carries some of the broken shards of light that must be put back together if the world is to be repaired.

This concept of Tikkun Olam, of repairing the world and becoming closer to God through good deeds, is at the core of Christianity as well, especially in the sense of mission or calling to do service to humanity on behalf of one's faith. When a Christian seeks to emulate the ways of Jesus, Mary, the Disciples, or the Saints, it is said that an aspect of God is being expressed through his or her good deeds. According to the Book of James (2:14), Jesus taught, "What good is it if a man claims to have faith but has no deeds? Can such faith save him? Suppose a brother or sister is without clothes and daily food. If one of you says to him, 'Go, I wish you well; keep warm and well fed,' but does nothing about his physical needs, what good is it? In the same way, faith by itself, if it is not accompanied by action, is dead."

Islam also focuses on moral action as a key pillar of faith. The Quran says that giving alms or charity, working for justice, and helping others are as important as prayer and other rituals. Similarly, in Buddhism, Hinduism, Taoism, and Zen, there are the concepts of Right Livelihood and Karma-Yoga, which can be defined as the union of all things being expressed through doing good work or helpful service in a mindful way. According to Buddhist tradition, when the Buddha was asked how a person can enter the heavenly realm of Brahma, the Buddha explained, "The doorways to the realm of Brahma are right here on earth and they are four in number: through loving kindness (metta), compassion (karuna), sharing joy (muditha), and equanimity (upekha). It is through service in this world, not by abandoning this world, that we attain to heavenly realms or spiritual fulfillment."

CAN YOU BE SPIRITUAL ON YOUR OWN OR DO YOU NEED A SENSE OF COMMUNITY?

One more crucial decision that most people struggle with when they are sorting out their feelings about God and religion is whether or not to be active in a spiritual or religious community.

For many people who've had painful or boring experiences in a religious setting, this can be an especially difficult issue. On the one hand, you realize it's hard to deepen your spirituality and repair the world on your own. On the other hand, you may have had frustrations, clashes, or an empty feeling at the places where you've gone to services or joined as a member.

What is your current position regarding whether or not to join and be active in a spiritual or religious community? For centuries, the nonjoiners have accused the joiners of "using organized religion as a crutch." The joiners have responded by saying, "It's not a crutch, it's just a more positive and less isolated way to live."

While I've met good people and heard reasonable viewpoints on both sides of this debate, as a social scientist I need to let you know that several recent research studies seem to side with the joiners on this controversial issue. While I am in no way saying that every religiously active person is emotionally healthy or even morally upright, or that every noninvolved person feels isolated or lacking in spirituality, I have found that there is some interesting scientific evidence suggesting a *moderately positive correlation* (but not necessarily a cause-and-effect relationship) between people's involvement in spiritual or religious communities and several specific health factors.

Regarding psychological health, in one study of 1,650 men and women, researchers found that religious involvement positively correlated with overall well-being, a stronger sense of community, and increased marital satisfaction for both men and women. A second study found that people's religious involvement had a statistically significant correlation with a sense of meaning and purpose, while attendance at religious services correlated with reduced anxiety levels. Several other studies showed that attendance at religious services correlated positively with duration of marriage, satisfaction with family life, and overall happiness.

Regarding physical health, researchers have found a slightly positive correlation between being active in a religious community and having a reduced rate of certain physical illnesses, as well as an improved ability to cope with serious ailments and family tragedies. The researchers suggested this was *not* necessarily due to religion itself preventing or curing illness, but rather that one's active involvement in a supportive religious or spiritual community can provide:

- a stronger sense of ethnic or cultural identity
- a stronger sense of meaning and purpose
- ways of overcoming feelings of helplessness and isolation
- systems of support and mutual aid
- meaningful rituals and group support for coping and comfort in the face of difficulties, disasters, and triumphs

Unfortunately, many people find that not all religious settings feel welcoming or supportive, and some individuals don't feel comfortable joining or being active in religious communities. In watching how people relate to churches, synagogues, temples, mosques, and other spiritual groups, I've noticed that these communities tend to bring out the best *and* the worst in people. Sometimes a spiritual community can be the most comforting and inspiring place to be for religious events, community activities, social-action projects, study groups, or *havurot* (a Hebrew word for friends who meet regularly for prayer, study, or holiday gatherings). At other times, a spiritual community can be painfully cliquish, judgmental, or conformist. Yet finding the one group that feels right to you and that helps you deepen your spirituality is one of the most important adult research projects you'll ever do.

A few years ago, I counseled a somewhat shy, private woman named Gabriela. She described herself as someone who "never fits in very well in large groups." In searching for a place to feel spiritually connected, Gabriela kept finding herself isolated or too unlike the people around her. A few times it was something about the clergy that turned her off. Most other times the sense of exclusivity or self-righteousness among the congregants made her feel unwelcome and apart. But I urged her to keep looking. I remember telling Gabriela, "When you finally find a congregation that feels like home to you or doesn't make you feel as much like an outsider, it will be worth all the searching and disappointments."

It took Gabriela several months of trying out different congregations before she finally came upon one that did feel more like home to her. She told me, "Even though this congregation has a few people I don't agree with and a few tacky qualities that make me want to cringe at times, I think I've found enough of what I'm looking for. The people, the services, and the activities are usually inspiring. I come home feeling a lot more positive about my life and more motivated to follow through on some of my most cherished goals. Even if I'm still not completely comfortable in groups, at least here I've found a place where people are intelligent, accepting, and warm."

YOUR NEXT STEPS

After reading this chapter, you probably have identified a few of the places where your spiritual life has gotten stuck or derailed. For instance, the problem might be:

A. You would like to develop a deeper relationship with God or a stronger sense of spirituality, but you still seem to be caught up in fear or rebellion against childhood views of God. If so, your next steps might be to begin reading and talking with supportive people about other, more adult approaches to God and spirituality.

B. You would like to develop a stronger sense of meaning and purpose in your daily life, but it's not easy with all the competing priorities, stresses, and time pressures you face each day. If so, your next steps might be finding ways to set aside a little more time each week to develop and nurture a more spiritual perspective on your life. You might start with just a few hours a week for stepping back and taking a fresh look at your priorities and your direction in life, but even a small beginning can help you develop a much stronger sense of meaning and purpose if you keep at it for weeks or months.

C. You would like to find a community that will help you deepen your spiritual life and support your efforts to live with passion and purpose, but you haven't been able to find the right setting yet. If so, then your next steps might be to ask around and sample other congregations, or to make a renewed effort to find the good teachers, projects, and friends at the congregation where you are currently.

As I mentioned earlier, deciding what you believe about God and how you want to practice or not practice your spirituality is a lifelong process of questioning and discovery. Because the First Commandment offers you the challenge of determining if you want to be partners with the mysterious Divine Being who can be found deep inside you, there's a moment of silence in which the world awaits your response. Choose carefully—the spark of divine light you carry inside needs to be shared in order for the world to improve.

2

THE SECOND CHALLENGE
Breaking Free of Unfulfilling Paths and Habits

When most people read the Second Commandment from the Book of Exodus, they see it as an outdated warning against worshiping idols. The commandment says not to build idols and not to bow down to false images or false prophets. The immediate response of most people today would be "Why does this concern me? I certainly don't build statues of other gods, and I don't bow down to any modern-day false prophets who promise instant holiness for a donation check." Most people these days do not see themselves as idolators, so they tend to think that the Second Commandment is an irrelevant relic.

Fortunately, the wisdom and usefulness of the Second Commandment are a lot more substantial. I call this Second Challenge "Breaking free of unfulfilling paths and habits," and it is a central issue in personal and spiritual growth. First, it helps to determine the various meanings of the biblical phrase "Don't bow down to idols."

"WHEN WE FORGET WHO WE ARE"

Many scholars and spiritual teachers throughout the centuries have interpreted the Second Commandment in ways that you and I can apply to our daily lives today. As you look at each of the following viewpoints, see which you agree with and which you find to be different from your own sense of spirituality:

In traditional Judaism, the warning against bowing down to idols says essentially that you are capable of having a direct and personal *relationship* with the Divine Presence deep inside your own consciousness, so do not settle for a visible, external imitation. The subtle but invisible sense of God's love is violated by stand-ins because in the Bible, the Talmud, and many other Jewish writings, the special bond between God and us humans is like a marriage partnership. Putting your faith in rigid images of God means betraying the marriage, not taking your partner seriously, limiting the full expression of the relationship.

In addition, a number of Jewish scholars and teachers have elaborated on this definition of bowing down to idols to include several other ways we get sidetracked from our spiritual essence. In the twelfth century, a Jewish philosopher from Muslim Spain, Bahya ben Joseph ibn Paguda, wrote a fascinating book on the steps toward spiritual fulfillment entitled *Duties of the Heart,* in which he warned against becoming spiritually distracted and entrapped by uncontrolled bodily appetites and excessive material pursuits. Bahya ben Joseph commented that "people make their bellies into their gods, their fine clothes into their law, and their home maintenance into their ethics." In his book *Psychoanalysis and Religion,* the twentieth-century Jewish humanist Erich Fromm wrote, "Words and machines can become idols. Putting too much faith in science and the opinions of others can become idolatrous."

One of my favorite modern rabbis, the mystic storyteller Ted Falcon of Seattle, explains idolatry as "the moments when we forget who we really are and instead of remembering that we are sparks of the Divine, we start giving up our power to a guru, an ideology, a romantic obsession, a stressful job that begins to define us, or an unhealthy habit we think we can't live without. Even if we no longer build or worship physical idols like in ancient times, we have modern-day addictions and pressures that cause us to forget that our purpose here is to be a vehicle for Divine energies."

"THE THING WE'VE GRABBED ON TO TURNS OUT TO BE AN ILLUSION"

In Christianity, similar discussions over the centuries address how people lose touch with their inner compass and become distracted by idolatrous substitutes. For example, in the Book of Matthew, chapter 6, verse 24, Jesus is quoted as teaching, "No one can serve two masters, God and money." In the nineteenth century, the Catholic archbishop Ullathorne wrote, "Whatever a man seeks, honors or exalts more than God, that is the god of his idolatry."

A contemporary Protestant minister explained to me recently at an interfaith dialogue conference another similar view on how idolatry works. She offered, "If we think something is going to make us feel better more quickly than God can, then we're tempted to grab on to it. It might be a drug, a get-rich scheme, or some fringe group that seems to have a shortcut to salvation. But sooner or later the thing we've grabbed on to turns out to be an illusion and we need to slow down again to find our way back to God."

In the Quran of Islam, to give your primary allegiance to material pursuits or to put complete trust in something other than God is considered to be *shirk,* or idolatry, which is the greatest sin a Muslim can fall into. In the Zen Buddhist tradition, idols and illusions of every sort are to be overcome— whether they include one's dependence on the ego, one's ambitions, too much adherence to a rigid doctrine, or even too much reliance on the Buddha himself. In the ninth century, a Buddhist master named Tan-hsia T'ien-jan was so intent on breaking free of any idolatry that, as the story is told, on a cold night he warmed his bare backside at a fire which he made with a wooden image of the Buddha. This story has been repeated for centuries to remind people that not the external objects but the sincerity of one's spiritual practice brings fulfillment.

THE DIFFICULTY OF SAYING NO TO QUICK FIXES

Even though several of the major religions speak forcefully against idolatry, it is a very common human tendency to get distracted from your higher purpose or spiritual path and go off on detours and escapes. The most frequent detour or escape seems to occur when people feel anxious or impatient, at which time they tend to be more susceptible to false promises of a quick fix or a way to feel better immediately.

This normal tendency to fall away from one's beliefs, values, and spiritual practice is described vividly in the biblical story most people associate with the Second Commandment, the well-known tale of the Golden Calf. To many, it sounds like ancient history, but you can read the incident as though you are a part of it, wandering in the desert after fleeing slavery in Egypt, searching for but not yet finding the promised land of true freedom.

The mixed multitude of Hebrews and others had journeyed through the desert after their escape from Egypt. They felt a strong sense of God's Presence at moments, especially when they crossed the Sea of Reeds safely and saw the Egyptian soldiers swallowed up minutes later by the shifting winds and currents. But after many additional setbacks and triumphs, the wanderers came to the foot of Mount Sinai, where they waited day after day for Moses, who had gone up the mountain to obtain a clearer sense of God.

According to various scholars, Moses' mysterious connection with the unseen God must have been a source of constant discussion and doubt among many of the people. As the several hundred thousand women and men waited at the foot of the mountain with no word from their leader, some became anxious and restless. Days passed. Windstorms and fierce afternoon heat, along with chilly desert nights, made daily survival difficult. Weeks passed. Rumors began to circulate: Maybe Moses is dead. Maybe Moses has abandoned or betrayed us. Maybe we were wrong to believe in the invisible God that Moses felt so strongly about.

This feeling of uncertainty among many of those waiting in the desert is described by the philosopher and religious scholar Martin Buber, who wrote, "And now, to cap it all, the man Moses has vanished completely. He said that he is going aloft to the God up there, when we need the God down here just where we are; but he has not come back, and it must be supposed that this God of his made away with him, since something or other between them was clearly not as it should have been. What are we to do now? We have to take matters into our own hands. An image has to be made, and then the power of the God will enter the image and there will be proper guidance."

Some of the more vocal members of the large gathering of people insisted that they needed to build a tangible image of God, one that was more reassuring and solid than mere belief in a mysterious and invisible source of support. Soon they had built a statue of a Golden Calf out of the rings, necklaces, and other precious items they had taken with them when they hurriedly escaped from Egypt. This new sculpture not only contained their most treasured earthly possessions but it held out the promise of giving them the strength and support they longed for as they searched for a new life in a land that God had promised to their ancestor Abraham.

As described in the Book of Exodus, chapter 32, while many of the people worshiped and danced around the Golden Calf, up on the mountain God and Moses argued about the ability of human beings to be faithful and reliable. God said it was infuriating to trust a group of anxious individuals who could forget so quickly the parting of the Sea of Reeds and all the other ways God had shown caring and support. Moses tried to reassure God that the people deserved another chance, that they were simply worried and impatient but still capable of doing God's work on Earth. God and Moses argued heatedly until Moses convinced God that the people deserved another opportunity to be faithful. God's forgiveness of the people tells us that when we, too, wander and lose faith or misplace our faith, we, too, will have another chance.

ASKING THE HARD QUESTIONS

Two important questions arise from this story. First, if you were waiting in the desert and there had been no visible sign from Moses for forty days, would you have gotten impatient and started doubting your belief in a caring and supportive God that you had felt so strongly about not too long ago? When you want something important in your life and it eludes you day after day, month after month, are you able to maintain your focus and your faith? Or do you give up and say, "This is never going to happen" and turn instead to the first good offer that comes along with what looks like a quick fix? If so, you might have been drawn to the Golden Calf, this huge and stunning substitute that intelligent and articulate people were saying could ease your pain of waiting for a new life of freedom that had begun to seem hopeless and out of reach. In other words, based on what you know about yourself, how well-developed is your tolerance for frustration? Are you able to say no to impulsive detours when times are tough?

The second question is whether you feel, like Moses, that it's important and permissible to argue with God and to speak your truth forcefully and passionately. Or do you, like most people, feel so uncomfortable with arguing or confronting that you'd keep silent, wait for a good excuse to exit the relationship, and go off with the first available spiritual path or substitute direction you could find?

Wrestling and arguing with God is a tradition that goes back to the Book of Genesis. Yet most people today who feel disappointed or upset with God or religion simply withdraw and flee. Or they mistakenly feel guilty for arguing with God because someone told them it's sacrilegious, when in fact the very word *Israelite* means "the one who wrestles and strives with God."

According to Conservative rabbi and theologian Harold M. Schulweis, "Religious tradition validates the right of the believer to challenge authority on moral grounds. God isn't angered by Moses' defense of the people even against God's initial judgment. Far from being considered acts of insubordination, these acts of dissent testify to the high status accorded to human conscience."

This story of the Golden Calf reminds us that developing a deeper sense of spirituality is *not* a polite, docile exercise. In fact, the daily ups and downs of wrestling with your doubts and breaking free of seductive idols and distractions requires tremendous perseverance and resilience. The Second Commandment is more than an outdated preaching against idolatry. It is a compassionate, useful warning that says as you seek to deepen your spirituality, you *will* have plenty of chances to give up, get distracted, or feel drawn to illusions and paths that leave you feeling empty.

CHOOSING BETWEEN TWO WAYS OF LIVING

The Second Commandment and the story of the Golden Calf also teach an important but difficult spiritual lesson, namely that we sometimes get impatient waiting for God or our spiritual practice to show us some results. During those moments of anxiety, loneliness, or impatience, we are very susceptible to seductive idols or things that distract us from our true purpose and direction in life.

If you don't want to be seduced or distracted by things that leave you feeling empty, then you may need to find a way to quiet your anxious mind and help it return to a path that can actually bring fulfillment. According to many scholars and interpreters, the Second Commandment is about waking up your soul each day so that you will connect with your true spiritual essence and not be so easily sidetracked by certain things and activities that distract you. The underlying message in the warning "Don't succumb to idols or false paths" is the encouraging statement *"Do* find ways to awaken your true self each day so that you can stay on track toward your essential purpose in life."

This urging to wake up and reach for your true potential each day is at the core of many sacred traditions. Judaism, Christianity, Islam, Buddhism, and many other faiths teach that there are two contrasting ways of living your life. On one path, you can become fully awake, alive, and in touch with the hidden truth that you are carrying a spark of Divine Light or universal oneness deep within your soul. On the more well-traveled path, you become distracted, numbed out, or spiritually asleep as you go through the motions of life day after day.

If you ask most people which they would prefer, the vast majority say they'd choose the path of aliveness and awareness. But that's an extremely challenging way to live and, as many spiritual teachers from a variety of traditions have pointed out, we barely reach a small percentage of our potential to be conscious and awake. As described by the early-twentieth-century spiritual teacher G. I. Gurdjieff, "Moments of consciousness are very short and are separated by long intervals of completely unconscious, mechanical living . . . you can think, feel, act, speak and work without being conscious."

If you sincerely want to take on the challenge of the Second Commandment to become more spiritually awake and alive, you need to develop some specific methods for firing up your deeper consciousness each day and reducing your susceptibility to false paths and empty pretenses. Each of the major spiritual traditions addresses this human tendency to be numb, complacent, or mechanical in the way we live our lives, and each offers profoundly useful but somewhat different approaches for helping us to awaken. For example, in Judaism, on the holiest days of each year, Rosh Hashanah and Yom Kippur, the blaring sound of the shofar, or ram's horn, helps wake people up and give them the clarity of mind necessary to pursue the deep self-examination and personal growth that are essential to these holidays. In a quieter way, a daily prayer is also designed to awaken our souls and help us refocus on what's important in life; read it carefully and slowly: "Elohai neshamah shenatatah beeh, tehorah heeh—O God, the soul You have given me is a pure one. You have created it and formed it, breathed it into me, and within me You sustain it. So long as I have breath, therefore, I will give thanks to You."

In Christianity, various Catholic, Protestant, and Eastern Orthodox churches make changes to enliven the prayer services and wake up the congregations to the enthusiasm of living a spiritual life. In fact, the word enthusiasm has *theos,* or "God," as its root. Many Christian scholars and preachers have pointed out that to wake up the Divine energies within people seems to be the true meaning of being alive and enthusiastic.

Numerous Christian clergy members also discuss the difficulty in waking up and not getting distracted by our anxious and neurotic tendencies. For instance, in a chapter he wrote explaining the Second Commandment, the famous novelist, social scientist, and Catholic priest Father Andrew Greeley of Chicago offered the following description of the challenge of waking up and saying no to distractions and false paths.

Father Greeley explained, "Each of us has inclinations of personality both genetic to the human race and specific to our own experience that make us hesitant about the leap of faith and commitment required to surrender ourselves to the loving tenderness of a passionate God. Our fight against these tendencies does not end when when we make an intellectual commitment to that God. On the contrary, the fight [against these hesitancies and distracting inclinations] has just begun."

According to the spiritual traditions of Buddhism, Hinduism, Taoism, and Zen, one of the major false paths or obstacles that keep us from being fully awake and aware is something called "monkey mind." In his book *The Heart of Stillness: The Elements of Spiritual Discipline,* meditation teacher David Cooper gives an excellent description of how "monkey mind" can interrupt our connection to God or to our true purpose in life. Cooper explains, "When we begin to pray or meditate, we quickly realize how much the mind is chattering. We have all experienced active, nervous minds, when our thoughts seem to jump rapidly from one branch to another, just like monkeys we see in a zoo. Fortunately, there is a remedy. Monkey mind holds power over us only to the extent that we believe it is the normal flow of our life process. It is not. Many spiritual teachers have transmitted to us that we live far below our potential, miss most of what is going on around us, and exist in a world of illusion. They teach that peace of mind is our natural heritage and that we can awaken this potential within us at any time."

THE SPIRITUAL STEPS FOR BREAKING FREE

It's no easy task to let go of the habits that keep us numb, distracted, or held back from our true potential in life, but there are creative spiritual steps we can take to become more attuned to our soul's path and less thrown off track by the idols and illusions that get in the way. Whether you consider yourself not very spiritual, somewhat spiritual, or deeply spiritual, you probably have days when your mind races with things to do or unresolved feelings. You may have wished there were some way to quiet down your noisy brain to focus on what's really important.

Listed below are several ways to wake yourself up spiritually each day and live more fully. Examine them and decide for yourself which can be most useful for putting greater meaning and purpose in your daily life, as well as for building up your psychological immunity to false paths and self-destructive habits that can distract you from your true purpose.

Step #1: *Find a way to confess or confront what's been distracting you or holding you back.*

One of the great contributions of many spiritual traditions has been to design confession rituals that allow us to be *completely honest* when confronting our bad habits, so that we can seek personal growth *without being cut off* from the Divine love and support we will need for making those changes. In Judaism, through daily prayers, Sabbath prayers, and High Holiday prayers you can have a one-on-One conversation with God about where you have missed the mark recently. When confessing or baring your soul to a God who understands, there is no sense of distance or separation. In fact, one of the Hebrew words for God's loving compassion that you will find in many prayers is *rakhaman. Rakhaman* means compassion, but also it can mean "womb" or "womblike." So, in essence, when you bare your soul to God you are surrounded by warmth and caring, much like the kind of nourishment you find in the womb.

In most Catholic and some Protestant churches, this same sense of receiving God's love when you engage in confession occurs in a formal procedure of ritual confession. In other congregations, the practice of confessing the ways you have fallen short of your spiritual goals is a more personal ritual. Asking God or Jesus for forgiveness is an intimate process. One of my close friends who was raised in a Catholic congregation where confession was extremely important says, "I found that as a kid I resented being told I had to go to confession. But as an adult, I view it as a remarkable tradition that feels cleansing and motivating. There I am, pouring out my feelings and shortcomings to a God who is rooting for me to do well. It's very moving to feel such support and love."

Some Native American traditions also have cleansing and purifying rituals for changing or improving a part of ourselves. One type is described by the Native American healer and teacher Bear Heart of Albuquerque, New Mexico, in his recent book *The Wind Is My Mother:* "If we really want to know ourselves, at some point we're going to have to surrender to a Higher Wisdom who knows all about us—our weaknesses, our mistakes, and our potentials. Many Native American tribes do that through our meditation known as the 'Vision Quest'—the setting aside of a time and place, alone out in nature, to communicate with a Higher Being and explore that which is within. A Vision Quest entails many hours of meditation and fasting and doing without everyday comforts as vision questers empty themselves of attachments to become ready to receive. Somewhere in that space of time as we are questing, answers come. It's an opportunity to know more about ourselves and the options that we have to choose from in life."

Instead of Trying to Hide from God

If someone in your upbringing gave you the idea that God would abandon you or refuse to care about you if you admitted where you were falling short of your potential, then you may need to talk to other clergy members and scholars within your own spiritual tradition to find a more loving and forgiving sense of God. Instead of trying to hide from God or ignore your spiritual side when you are going through a hard time or doing things you know aren't right, most spiritual traditions suggest that *those are precisely the moments when you need to open up and let a higher sense of guidance and support give you added strength and clarity.*

Opening up and being completely honest about some imperfect aspect of one's life is extremely difficult. We are far more likely to deny, minimize, or rationalize. One of my favorite lines from the 1983 film *The Big Chill,* written by Lawrence Kasdan and Barbara Benedek, comes when one of a group of friends asks, "Which is more important—sex or rationalizations?" Another character answers, "When was the last time you went for a week without a rationalization?"

In most traditions, the first spiritual step for breaking free of a habit or situation that is holding you back from your potential is to sit down and have a talk with God or the still small voice inside you. Depending on your spiritual beliefs and practices, you might do this alone in your room; or in a church, synagogue, temple, or mosque; at a Twelve Step meeting or personal-growth seminar; or out in nature or at a special sacred place in which you tend to feel the presence of God. Regardless of how you do it, choose to address at least one false path or distraction that you want to begin changing. I've found in my therapy practice that most people feel a lot more motivated and committed to their goals for self-improvement when they've made a sacred vow to God and they feel accountable to a higher wisdom that cannot be tricked or fooled.

ARE THERE ANY IDOLS OR DISTRACTIONS YOU WOULD LIKE TO BREAK AWAY FROM?

To help you address some possible Second Commandment–related issues, I have compiled a brief list of questions about some of the most common idols and distractions that cause many people today to hold back from living up to their potential and thereby diminish their aliveness. As you look at each of the following possibilities, notice which ones sound like you and which sound like someone you know. Then decide which of these you are willing to discuss with God as a first step toward changing the habit that has been holding you back.

- Do you have trouble following through on some of your most purposeful dreams and goals because of a desire to be "perfect" or a fear that whatever you do won't be "good enough"?
- Does your constant focus on making a living sometimes dictate your life and prevent you from giving time or attention to the other people and priorities you care about?
- Have you ever given up your power to a charming or seductive lover, guru, or business partner who turned out to be a fraud?
- Have you ever gotten so enamored with an idea, a political cause, or a spiritual group that you began to feel contemptuous of anyone who didn't share your viewpoint?
- Have you ever been so sure that you were doing God's will that you unfortunately did something cruel or insensitive that hurt someone else and therefore was probably not God's will?
- Do you sometimes idolize people too much for their looks, status, intellect, or ability to express themselves?
- Do you sometimes fall into the habit of being so skeptical and "playing the devil's advocate" that you are unable to surrender to intangibles like love, satisfaction, or faith in God?
- Do you tend to lose motivation or fail to complete im-

portant goals because you sometimes get numbed out by drugs, alcohol, or binge eating?

- At the end of a hard or stressful day, do you find yourself tuning out people who care about you or who need you because you'd rather be consumed by watching television, playing a video game, or spending hours on the Internet?

"A Part of Me Was Saying, 'Why Not Stay Home and You Won't Get Disappointed by Anyone.'"

Anita's case is an example of what can happen when you talk to God about the ways you've been distracted or lost your sense of purpose in life. An award-winning journalist in her late forties who writes on scientific topics for a major newspaper, Anita had always stayed away from organized religion because, in her words, "As a journalist I tend to be somewhat skeptical and inquisitive about everything. When I was a child my family and the congregation they belonged to were not open to my questions. Especially since I tend to focus on the scientific and rational view of things, I've had very little tolerance for some of the hard-to-prove leaps of faith that are so common in religion. So I've never thought of myself as a spiritual or religious person."

But recently Anita went through a series of painful events. Her best friend died of ovarian cancer. Anita's five-year relationship with a man she'd hoped to marry had broken up. Most recently, Anita was diagnosed with carpal tunnel syndrome, a painful hand and wrist ailment that afflicts many people who spend a great deal of their time working at a computer keyboard. In addition, Anita had begun binging on snacks each night and watching more television than usual.

As Anita explained to me, "At first I just let myself overeat a little and watch some mindless TV, since I figured I'm depressed and I deserve to tune out the world a bit. But after several months of isolating myself each night in front of the TV with a lot of unhealthy snacks, it's starting to become more of a demanding habit. Last week I thought about going out to dinner and having a good conversation with a close friend, but I could hear a part of me saying, 'Why go out? Why not stay home and you won't get disappointed by anyone.'"

When Anita first came in for therapy, it was to deal with the depression and loss she felt from the death of her friend, the breakup of her relationship, and the frustration of having carpal tunnel syndrome. But during her first session, it became clear that Anita was also dealing with a spiritual crisis. When I asked her, "What would you truly want if this counseling is successful?" Anita replied, "I want to regain my old sense of hopefulness and fire that's gotten knocked out of me these past few months. There's a part of me that wishes I could feel some support from God or that I could pray for my health to get better. There are days when I'm in so much discomfort and I wish I could turn to a sense of love or support that would inspire me to keep going. But my skeptical side just won't allow it."

I asked Anita, "Is your skeptical side one hundred percent convinced there is no such thing as a loving or supportive God?" At that moment her expression changed from that of the hard-edged journalist she presented most of the time to one that was open and vulnerable. She admitted then what I have heard from many intelligent men and women who seem at first to be strongly opposed to spiritual ideas but in fact have a deep longing inside. Anita said, "If you want to know the truth, I cry sometimes at night because of how lonely it feels with no person in my life who's there for me and no sense of a God who cares about me. I'm comfortable being the skeptic during the day, but at night when I'm alone I wish more than anything that I could trust there is something I can lean on."

To help her explore this longing for "something to lean on" I recommended that Anita read a few books and talk to two clergy members from the religious tradition she grew up with about how a skeptical person can talk to God and confess his or her doubts and concerns. It took several weeks before Anita was ready, but eventually she had a one-on-One conversation with a God she could neither see nor hear but to whom she confided her deepest longings and hopes.

During her next counseling session, Anita told me, "It was such an unusual experience for me. There I was crying and pouring out my feelings to an invisible Being I neither understood nor fully believed in. But the simple act of opening up my heart like that was so healing for me. It hasn't made me devout or a zealot or anything, but I feel an openness and curiosity I've carried with me ever since."

At that moment, I asked Anita, "What was your sense of

God's reaction to your doubts and skepticism?" Anita smiled as she told me, "That was the most interesting part. As a child I used to be afraid, probably because of my parents' view of God, that I would be punished or rejected for voicing my doubts. But during the conversation I had with God a few nights ago, I had a sense of some Divine Wisdom seeing right through me and saying, 'Don't worry about it, Anita. You make your living from being skeptical and rational. We don't need to change that and it doesn't scare Me a bit because we both know there's another side to who you are, a side you don't show in public but that we've always known is there in your private moments.' It felt like exactly the kind of loving and accepting God I had never been exposed to as a child, but that I want to continue to connect with as an adult."

After that initial conversation with God, Anita gradually began to cut back on her nightly snacking and TV watching. She began reaching out again to friends and she also signed up for a class on spirituality, where she met a man whom she has begun to date regularly. As she admitted to me recently, "It's scary to be open and somewhat optimistic again, but it feels a lot better than living with that depressing 'Don't trust anyone' attitude that I've slipped into at several difficult times in my life. I don't think I'll ever be a bubbly cheerleader or a person who has no moments of doubt or skepticism, but I hope I never become as jaded and unhappy as I was those several months, shutting out the world, all cooped up in front of my TV with bags of junk food."

Step #2: Set up daily reminders and inspirational supports to help you keep living up to your potential

Even if you are successful in changing a bad habit when you confess your detours and distractions to God, you are still highly likely to be tempted again soon to slip back into a less conscious state and repeat some of the same behaviors. Each of us needs daily routines and periodic wake-up calls to stay on any path, especially one as intangible as the development of your spirituality or your purpose in life. Just as some of the desert wanderers who built the Golden Calf forgot the earlier help of God, who shifted the winds and parted the Sea of Reeds, so do the rest of us tend to become anxious and susceptible to idols and false paths when we've gone a few months, a few weeks, or even a few days without a strong reminder of God's Presence.

That's why nearly every spiritual tradition offers daily and weekly sources of support. As you think about your own spiritual practice and the ways in which you give yourself periodic doses of positive energy, consider whether you want to add some of the following to your personal routines:

• Do you have a morning ritual or routine that inspires you to do good each day? Or do you feel so rushed and half-asleep in the morning that your day often slips by without your being able to check in with your higher self?

• Are you able to stop for a moment before each meal to slow down and remember the source of the food and nourishment you take into your body? Or do you feel it's embarrassing, tacky, or a waste of time to have a prayer or a silent moment of meditation before each meal?

• Are there inspiring books, affirmations, and quotes that you have available to give you a dose of support and refocusing when your life becomes stressful or discouraging? Or do you try to make it through hard times without looking at any sources of inspiration?

• Are there religious services, volunteer activities, classes, or study groups that can spark your sense of what matters in life at least once a week? Or do you find yourself trying to maintain your spiritual center entirely on your own?

• Do you have a ritual or routine that helps you unwind and feel a sense of gratitude at the end of each day? Or do you feel so worn out that you simply collapse or shut off your mind with little or no awareness of the progress you're making on a daily basis?

THE MANY VARIETIES OF MORNING INSPIRATION
While each of the daily reminders listed above can help you reduce your susceptibility to idols and false paths, I have found that for many of my therapy clients, as well as for close friends and myself, the morning ritual seems to be the most crucial factor in making each day a lot more purposeful and satisfying. Each spiritual tradition seems to have its own creative rituals

and practices for waking up the soul each morning and helping a person focus on what's important.

For instance, if you visit China or if you watch the morning rituals in most Chinese-American neighborhoods, you will see a variety of Taoist physical-movement exercises that wake up not only the body but also the Chi, or the vital energy and breath of life that exists in each of us. In Hebrew the somewhat equivalent words for Chi energy are Yah (the Divine breath of life) or Ruakh (the wind or Spirit of God). In Christianity it is usually called Holy Spirit.

Whatever you call this life-force energy, you can sense it moving and coming alive when you watch or engage in Tai Chi Chuan, a series of soft, flowing movements that shift the energy in the body and coordinate the body, mind, and breath into a harmonious state. Tai Chi Chuan is an ancient body-movement ritual that is still practiced widely in many parts of the world today. Tai Chi, aikido, and other spiritual-energy techniques have a gentle power to connect the internal breath of life with the vital energy all around you. They are not easy disciplines to master, but you can learn movements that can easily awaken your spirit each morning with great aliveness and focus.

Yoga is another spiritual way to awaken the soul each morning. More than just stretching the creaky bones and muscles as they slowly awaken in the morning, yoga in its spiritual sense is a profound system for balancing the Divine and personal energies of life. In Hinduism the word *Yoga* literally means to harness oneself to God, seeking union with the Divine.

In traditional Judaism, a similar sense of harnessing oneself to God occurs daily in the saying of morning prayers and the wearing of braided tefillin (two small black boxes with black straps attached to them, one for the arm and one for the head). This practice stems from the passage in the Book of Deuteronomy, chapter 6, verses 5–9, in which we are asked to love God with all our hearts, souls, and minds, and to "bind these words as a sign upon your hand and let them be a symbol between your eyes."

Many nontraditional Jews have a variety of other ways they wake up their souls and focus their energies each morning. When, for this book, I interviewed numerous people about their morning rituals, I discovered the following:

- A woman who reads the traditional prayers in English from her congregation's prayer book each morning on her patio while facing east, toward Jerusalem
- A man who sits in silent meditation with the words *Baruch Yah* ("Blessed is the Breath of Life") as his mantra, as he waits for clarity and direction on how to do good that day
- A teenager with nonreligious parents who recites several of the traditional prayers each morning in English and in Hebrew before getting dressed and going to school
- A man who quiets his mind each morning and says, "Dear God, help me to grow and learn today on how to be helpful and not harmful to myself or anyone else."
- A woman who writes in her journal each morning, which she describes as her best method for getting in touch with her daily purpose and her spiritual strength
- A man who sings a *niggun,* a wordless Hasidic melody that bypasses the verbal mind and wakes up the soul for higher purposes
- A busy parent who told me, "I only have time for a few sentences each morning before my ten-month-old child is screaming. So I take a breath and quickly say the Shehekhiyanu prayer, which thanks God for the newness of each moment by saying, "Blessed are You, Eternal One, who sustains us, who keeps us in life, and who brings us to this moment for good. Amen."
- A woman who recently recovered from a nearly fatal gastrointestinal disorder and who found new meaning in the traditional morning prayer that says, "Blessed is the Eternal God, creator of the universe, who has made our bodies with wisdom, combining veins, arteries, and vital organs into a finely balanced network. If but one of the openings and cavities of the body were to be ruptured or blocked it would be impossible to survive and to stand before You. Blessed are You, Eternal One, source of our health and our strength."

In Islam, an observant Muslim chants the morning call to prayer in a haunting and melodic tune with the words "Allahu akbar, God is most great [repeated four times], Ashhadu an ilaha illa Allah, I testify to you that there is no god but God [repeated twice], Ashhadu anna Muhammadan rasul Allah, I testify that Muhammad is the Messenger of God [repeated twice], Hayya 'ala al-salat, Hurry to prayer [repeated twice], Hayya 'ala al-falah, Hurry to betterment [repeated twice], Allahu akbar, God is most great [repeated twice], La ilaha illa Allah, I testify that there is no god but God."

A daily prayer that wakes up the Muslim to break free of false paths is the Opening Prayer, or Fatihah, which has been called the very essence of the Quran: "In the name of God, the merciful Lord of mercy, praise be to God, the Lord of all being, the merciful Lord of mercy, Master of the Day of Judgment. You alone we serve and to You alone we come for aid. Guide us in the straight path, the path of those whom You have blessed, not of those against whom there is displeasure, nor of those who have gone astray."

Most of the American Muslims I interviewed for this book told me they felt strongly that these two prayers were an essential part of their morning routine. Many Muslims also read various passages from the Quran each morning to guide them toward making that day holy and purposeful. I also found a woman who does Sufi dancing from the Islamic mystical tradition each morning and a man who meditates in silence as part of a Sufi belief to get beyond the illusory words to the Divine connection underneath. Another woman reads from the mystical love poems to God by Rumi and some of the other great writers of the Sufi tradition each morning.

Christianity has numerous inspiring prayers and rituals that help people focus on doing good each day. For example, I found while researching this book:

- A female corporate executive who sits for a half hour each morning while holding and counting the rosary beads as she says prayers for various people in her life
- Several people who frequently recite the prayer attributed to Saint Francis, which says, "Lord, make me an instrument of Thy peace. Where there is hatred, let me sow love. Where there is offense, pardon. Where there is discord, unity. Where there is doubt, faith. Where there is error, truth. Where there is despair, hope. Where there is sadness, joy. Where there is darkness, light."

- A man who walks in nature each day and says to Jesus, "Please guide me today to see the good in people and be of service."
- A teenager who lives in a tough neighborhood and prays each morning, "Please God, surround me today with your love so that no one tries to mess with me."
- A woman who rides on her exercise bicycle each morning and thinks about how to emulate one or more of the Disciples
- A man who tapes the inspiring Sunday sermon at his church each week and then listens to it in his car on the way to work for several days afterward
- A woman who reads one page each day from a book of 365 meditations, as a way of giving focus to each day
- A man who puts Gregorian chants on the stereo and meditates in his living room
- A woman who looks at her two children each morning and thanks God that they are alive and well
- Several people who start each day with the well-known prayer from Protestant minister Reinhold Niebuhr, also known as the Serenity Prayer, which says, "God, give us grace to accept with serenity the things that cannot be changed, courage to change the things which should be changed, and the wisdom to distinguish the one from the other."

What kind of wake-up call would you like to include in your morning ritual? Although you may have a hard time doing anything in the morning except getting dressed and out the door, with possibly a quick bite to eat, an extra ten to thirty minutes each morning can dramatically change the way you live each day, and keep you from losing track of your spiritual essence.

THE MAN WHO DIDN'T KNOW THE WORDS

If you have been held back from setting up a morning prayer or meditation routine because you worry about "doing it wrong" or that your prayers might not be profound or substantial enough, I want to offer you an old Hasidic story that might give you a new perspective. According to the legend, there was once a man who had not been to a religious service for many years and who feared that he wouldn't be able to pray properly to God because he didn't know how to read the Hebrew words. But this man's heart was filled with things he wanted to talk about with God—prayers for the health and well-being of his loved ones, concerns about the way the world is, and worries about his own daily struggles.

The man entered a nearby synagogue one morning and was afraid to speak. He heard the other worshipers reciting the traditional prayers, but all he knew how to say was "Amen." Finally the man got his courage up and decided to talk from the heart directly to God and to say "Amen" at the end of the prayers recited by others. He waited for the right moment and said in a quiet but sincere voice, "Amen."

The legend has it that not only were this man's prayers received lovingly by God but his words were said with such truthfulness that they deeply touched the Divine Presence. I'm assuming that you will be able to say a lot more than "Amen" during your morning ritual to help you focus on doing good. But even if you say nothing more than a heartfelt "Amen," I'm hoping you will experience a profound sense of connection and awakening each day.

Step #3: Open up to ways you can share your gifts and live with greater purpose

Most people deeply desire to live with a sense of purpose, but many are unclear about what that is or how to make it happen. Quite often, other people try to impose on you what *they* think your sense of purpose should be. From the time you are born, people are forever trying to distract you from your inner purpose and assign you what their values and needs would want you to do with your life. Unfortunately, many individuals use up so much energy rebelling against or being sidetracked by the expectations of others that they don't follow through on their own heartfelt sense of purpose and direction.

Now is a good time to take a fresh look at what your inner sense of purpose and meaning might be. The Second Commandment not only warns against false paths but implicitly says to each of us, "Make sure you find and follow through on your own unique path in life." The more you understand about your special gifts and your daily opportunities to live a life of meaning, the more likely you are to find a sense of being on the right path. Here are some techniques to consider:

A. Ask a most unusual question. There are many creative ways to uncover a stronger sense of meaning and direction for your own life. One way, suggested by the psychotherapist and writer Viktor Frankl, is simply to ask yourself, "Why haven't I committed suicide?" Even if the question sounds morbid or absurd, when you think about it seriously you will discover there are specific reasons your being here is important and worthwhile.

Maybe the reason you don't end it all is your love for your children, your work, your creativity, your sense of discovery, or your commitment to a cause or a volunteer activity. Maybe you just have a sense of wanting to follow through on the hard work you've done to become a person capable of love and sharing your special gifts of insight and compassion. Possibly you are waiting to be used for a higher purpose and your moment hasn't arrived yet. Probably you know there are ways you contribute to specific individuals, even if those efforts are not often acknowledged or appreciated.

B. Work backward from a future point. Another creative method for recognizing your deeper purpose is to write your own obituary, looking back from a point in the distant future. Try to find the important elements of your life that in hindsight will allow you or others to say, "That was a worthwhile person. This person had something to share and will be missed." Quite often when you do this exercise, it stimulates ideas of how to make your life more purposeful while there's plenty of time left. If you're not satisfied with the contribution you've made thus far, you still have a chance to build a life that makes a loving impact on your corner of the world.

C. Look for moments of passion and purpose that keep showing up in your life. Yet another way to explore your meaning in life is to take note of the different ways you have been called to be of service to others. Here are some questions that can help you refocus on your sense of purpose:

What are the moments in your life when someone has come to you for help and you were able to give something valuable?

What recent opportunities have presented themselves for you to get involved?

What are the strengths, life lessons, and experiences you've acquired over the years that might be useful to others if you found a way to share your insights with them? What are the special gifts and talents you've developed that you can now offer to help others, whether it's for income or as a volunteer?

What are the injustices and serious problems you've encountered that need your ideas and your energy? What situations could you help improve so that others won't be forced to suffer in ways you, your loved ones, or your ancestors were forced to suffer?

This technique of constantly asking yourself, "How can I be useful?" could be the source of many rewarding ideas and meaningful projects. Clearly you will need to make sure you don't overcommit yourself or become burned out. Yet you will never be lacking for meaning and purpose if you remember to face each difficult moment in your life with the attitude "How can I turn this into something that will be useful to others?"

For example, Nina is a divorced woman in her late forties with two teenage children and a job working as an office manager for a large company. Recently, Nina kept hearing from her children and from other parents at their school that there was a shortage of quality computers for the students to learn with. Normally, Nina does not consider herself a political individual or an activist. In fact she said to me, "I'm one of those people who is so busy with my work, my kids, and the other responsibilities in my life that I rarely have time to read the paper or keep up with what's going on."

But the idea of her kids and lots of other kids being at a disadvantage because their schools couldn't afford quality computers upset Nina enough that she decided to get involved. At first she simply called up a few executives at her own company and discussed whether or not they would be interested in getting a tax write-off for the firm if they donated some of the older computers that they no longer used. These machines were only two to five years old, which meant the corporation saw them as obsolete but the schools would love to have them.

Working only a half hour each day on this volunteer project,

Nina began to explore other companies that weren't using their slightly aged computers. Pretty soon she was able to get more than twenty-five machines donated to her kids' school. She thought about stopping there, but when a principal from a nearby school asked her for help, Nina kept devoting a half hour a day to her phone inquiries to various companies. Within a year she had managed to arrange for more than two hundred computers to be donated to budget-strapped schools.

Anthony's story is a second example of how to step back from a frustrating situation and ask yourself, "How can I turn this experience into something that will help others and increase my sense of purpose?" A sensitive and intelligent man in his late thirties who has worked in a number of fields, Anthony recently thought he had finally found his career direction. Working as an account executive for an advertising agency, Anthony felt he at last had a job with a future and some security. Then an industry-wide slump in the advertising business put the firm Anthony worked for into bankruptcy. Anthony was devastated. For several weeks, he berated himself that this once again proved he was irresponsible, a flake, someone who would never find a worthwhile direction.

However, when Anthony turned his setback into the question "How can I use this experience to be useful to others?" several constructive ideas came to mind. He thought about forming a consulting business to help retrain people who had lost their jobs. He considered writing a book about how to take care of your doubts and critical voices when you're out of work. He also looked into volunteer activities that would give him a sense of purpose and satisfaction while he was looking for another job. Choosing carefully from several volunteer opportunities, Anthony decided to work for free while he sent out résumés and waited to hear from employers.

Working two afternoons a week at a local hospital as a volunteer, Anthony rediscovered a sense of self-worth that had been taken from him when he'd lost his job. He says, "Even though it was frustrating applying to ad agencies and getting rejected, when I'd go to my volunteer job each week I felt like a useful human being again. Working with people who care about what they're doing and helping people who really appreciate a responsive person can make all the difference. I stopped second-guessing myself and started feeling once again I was here for a purpose."

After six months as a volunteer, Anthony was asked to take on a new position as the coordinator of volunteer services. Even though he had thought his future was in the advertising field, he discovered his satisfaction came from working with people in the helping professions. What began as a career setback had turned into a rewarding opportunity. Anthony admits, "I don't know if this is a forever position, but I do know that I've learned a lot about myself and what I'm capable of accomplishing if I trust my instincts and keep focusing on things that feel worthwhile."

In your own life, what are some of the unexpressed creative ideas, untapped passions, and hidden gifts or talents that you might want to begin thinking about? Brainstorm with a friend, relative, or counselor about various options you have that would give your life more meaning and fulfillment. You don't have to turn up an immediate project. Sometimes you may respond to a current situation that needs your help; other times you may recall a heartfelt interest that you had to postpone or ignore a while ago but that you now could renew successfully. There is no greater satisfaction than to be used for a higher purpose. There is no richer way to live than to know you are being of service to others. We all know the world needs repair; finding a purposeful way to do whatever you can in your own corner of the world is important and worthwhile.

3

THE THIRD CHALLENGE

*Learning to Control Anger, Insecurity, and
Self-Righteousness*

A few years ago a dynamic and insightful spiritual teacher in Los Angeles named Rabbi Mordecai Finley told his congregation, "If you want to find out how well you are living up to your spiritual values and higher principles, pay close attention to how you behave in the middle of an argument or a tense moment involving someone you live with, work with, or are in love with."

Finley and many other spiritual teachers from different faiths have suggested that interactions in relationships are the most common and most frequent challenges we face. In nearly every important relationship, there are moments when what you want and what the other person wants seem to be in direct conflict. At those moments of tension or conflict, you'll discover just how far you've come on your spiritual path. You will find out whether you are too rigid, self-righteous, or quick to anger. Or on the other hand, you'll see whether you are too flexible, eager to please, or easily swayed by someone else's pushiness or anger.

As you think about your own life for a moment, when was the last time you felt tense or frustrated about an important relationship? It could be a marriage or long-term relationship that has its moments of tension and disagreement, or a creative or business partnership in which you and the other person see things differently. Even your relationship with God has moments of tension and disagreement, especially when you start to feel separate from God or conflicted about living in the everyday world but still following your spiritual beliefs.

AN UNEXPECTED SOURCE OF WISDOM ABOUT RELATIONSHIPS

The Third Commandment from the Book of Exodus offers some extremely useful and practical ways to overcome the obstacles to behaving with compassion and integrity in any relationship. If you ask most people what's meant by the words of the Third Commandment—"You shall not take God's name in vain"— they will answer what many of us were taught as children: that the commandment tells us not to swear or curse. In fact, that's only a small part of its real meaning.

In this chapter I will explore the various interpretations of the Third Commandment as a key to dealing with one of the most essential challenges we face in our lives: how to build and maintain quality relationships, day to day, in a world where most people are guarded or defensive and the majority of business and romantic partnerships don't last.

There are four major interpretations of the Third Commandment that can help you in your most important relationships with your loved ones, business partners, and clients or customers, as well as with your connection to God. As you read each of these four explorations of the meaning of "Don't take God's name in vain," notice which ones speak directly to the relationship issues you've been facing in your own life.

Interpretation #1: The Third Commandment can be seen as a helpful reminder not to make promises you won't be able to keep, especially promises in which you say "I swear to God I'll do it" and then you don't.

To most scholars of the Bible, including the great eleventh-century French-Jewish teacher and commentator Rashi, the essence of the Third Commandment is not about cursing but rather about not making false promises or extravagant statements like "I swear to God" when we don't really mean it. These traditional commentaries explain that when people insist self-righteously, "I swear to God my word is good on this" and then don't follow through on their word, it's a misuse of God's name.

For example, it's hard to sustain a love relationship if one or both partners are constantly promising things or saying "I swear to God I'll do this for you" and then not coming through. A business partnership can't survive if one partner keeps saying, "I'll take care of this important task, I swear, let me do it," and then doesn't get it done. Similarly, in families it's quite painful for a child to be let down by a parent's unfulfilled promises such as "I'll be there"—at your recital, or your soccer game, or your birthday party.

The twelfth-century Jewish scholar Moshe ibn Ezra described this common human tendency to make shaky promises when he wrote, "So many people do not realize they use idle oaths like 'I swear to God' countless times every day until it has become subconscious, and they do not even know what is meant when someone reprimands them with the words 'Why do you swear on God's holy name so much?' Then they will swear that they have not sworn at all, not realizing that they're swearing again."

To understand how unfulfilled promises can negatively affect everyday relationships, think about your own life for a moment. When you were young do you recall one or both of your parents promising you something they never followed through on? Have you ever felt a loss of trust when a loved one promised to be more considerate but repeatedly ignored or broke that promise? Or have you ever done business with someone who declared self-righteously, "I swear to God I sent it on time" or said confidently, "No problem," "Trust me," or "Don't worry about a thing"—and then let you down?

As a psychologist, I suggest that you do *not judge or condemn* anyone for saying things like "I promise" or "I swear to God." Instead, find out what causes someone to make false oaths using God's name. When do you yourself make promises you know in your heart you probably aren't serious about keeping? What are the deeper reasons people feel pushed to guarantee something they probably can't fulfill? We need to ask ourselves and the people who let us down, "What were you thinking when you said 'I swear to God I'll do it'?" We need to be patient and sort out the underlying psychology of why people say one thing and do another.

THE PRESSURE TO OVERSTATE WHAT YOU CAN DO

I have observed over the years that people who promise more than they can deliver are usually insecure and afraid of being found inadequate, incompetent, or unlovable. For instance, I once counseled a man named Jim who most people viewed as handsome and successful in his sales career. Whenever Jim was dating, however, he would exaggerate his achievements and make fatuous promises, such as "I swear you're never going to meet anyone who'll be as good to you as I will." Even though many women were attracted to Jim at first, the relationships rarely lasted, because sooner or later they discovered that Jim frequently promised things he couldn't deliver. Each breakup was long and painful, as Jim would promise more things to win the woman back until eventually she would get fed up and leave for good.

One afternoon during a counseling session, I asked Jim, "Do you know why you feel so much pressure to exaggerate your achievements and make promises you won't be able to fulfill?" His answer reflected the insecure feelings that most of us carry inside. Jim explained, "If I didn't stretch the truth a little, no one would have anything to do with me."

Have you ever felt that same insecure sense that unless you pretended to be a little more than you really are, no one would have anything to do with you? At a job interview, on a first date, in a business negotiation, or even when you're sitting in prayer or meditation, have you ever felt, "I'm just not going to be taken seriously as I am. Maybe I need to fake it a little and promise more than I'm likely to deliver?"

It took several months of counseling to change the way Jim viewed himself and how he presented himself to others. Like many people, Jim had grown up with harsh, critical parents; he worried that no one would truly love him as he was. As a result, he had fallen into the habit of trying too hard to influence people with excessive promises. Only when he began to accept that someone could love him for just being decent and hardworking did he stop pushing so aggressively. If you met Jim today you would no longer hear any false bravado or manipulative statements. His balanced perspective on his own self-worth has also allowed him to find a marriage partner with whom he doesn't make false promises. To this day, Jim does battle with a few deep insecurities from his painful childhood, but for the most part he has those feelings under control and has learned to be extra careful about not acting self-righteous or making inflated promises. He and his wife have one of the most caring and honest relationships I've ever seen.

"I Just Wish There Were More Hours in the Day"

Bernice's case shows a different version of the pressure many of us feel to make promises we aren't sure we'll be able to keep. When Bernice first came to me for counseling, she was extremely worn down from the stressful demands in her life. She has a high-pressure job, three children between the ages of nine and seventeen, and an unemployed husband who is recovering more slowly than expected from a serious back problem.

Like most of us, Bernice says she often feels a great deal of pressure to come through for all the people who are depending on her. As a result, she sometimes finds herself promising more than she can deliver and feeling drained by all the demands on her time.

Bernice explained, "I noticed recently that when my boss or an important client asks me to hurry up and finish a project that absolutely needs more time to get done right, I don't seem to be able to stand up for what I know is best. Sometimes I'll hear myself saying, 'I promise I'll have it done as quickly as you need it,' and then it becomes a frantic race to meet an absurd and often unnecessary deadline."

Bernice also told me, "I have so much trouble sticking to what I know is best when it might disappoint someone. For instance, I've said far too often to my kids, 'I'll be home by six tonight so we can go over your homework.' But even as I'm saying it I know in my gut there's a good chance I'm going to have to work late. Why don't I ever speak up and tell my husband that he and the kids have to arrange dinner without me and start on the homework before I get there? I just wish there were more hours in the day so I could come through on all the things that people are counting on me to do."

If you notice that you or someone you know is a lot like

Bernice, trying hard to keep up with all the demands on your time, then it's extra important for you to take seriously the words of the Third Commandment. Do not make unreasonable promises when your gut is telling you that you need to appreciate your limits or admit that you need additional time or assistance.

I urge therapy clients to do an exercise that you can try on your own to break the habit of feeling insecure and making unrealistic promises to people you care about. Keep a daily notebook or computer log of your promises and verbal agreements for an entire week. Notice when you're feeling pressured or overstating what you can do. Be aware of when you say yes to something that you should have said no to or when you are more realistic and offer a qualified yes instead. A qualified yes is when you say, "Yes, I can do it, but I will need some additional time and assistance, which will lead to a better result."

If you simply begin to take note of whenever your insecurities are pushing you to pretend past your capacity for love, work, or strength, then you will make the first step toward avoiding false or unrealistic promises. You will become a person of your word.

When Bernice used this exercise, her list included several unrealistic promises at first. She promised her husband and kids she would be able to get the groceries one night after work, but in her gut she knew she might be held up by a late meeting that threatened to drag on until the evening. She also made an unfortunate promise to an important client to have a presentation ready sooner than she knew was possible.

It took several days of writing down these unrealistic promises in her notebook before Bernice began to start slowing herself down and asking herself each time, "What exactly is realistic in this situation and what will be unnecessarily stressful?" Bernice needed a few weeks of counseling to improve her ability to stand up for herself, but eventually she learned how to tell her boss and her clients in a calm, warm, and managerial tone, "I would love to give you what you want, but it's going to take a little more time and assistance. I'm pretty sure, though, that it will be worth the extra time and care." On nights when it seemed unrealistic to promise to be home by six, Bernice began to tell her kids and her husband, "I love you and I'll be home late tonight. So take out the frozen leftovers I saved from last weekend and I'll see you as soon as I can get there."

As Bernice told me on the day she completed her counseling, "Speaking up for my needs was never comfortable for me. My habit was to act like a self-righteous martyr and try to do it all without letting anyone know how stressed I was becoming. So I'd get sick a lot or I'd get resentful, but I never stopped and said to anyone clearly, 'This is what I can do and this is what will require more time and more help from others.'

"After years of jumping whenever someone said jump," Bernice commented, "now I'm slowly beginning to realize that they're not going to hate me or fire me for giving them a realistic sense of my limits as a human being. So far, even with a few grumbles from my boss, my husband, and my kids, it's clear they still know they can rely on me and that I haven't really let them down. In fact, I think I'm doing a much better job now that I'm not promising too much and getting as stressed as I did for so many years."

As you think about your own life, are there times when you felt pressured to promise things or impress someone, even though a wise voice inside you was saying, "Who are you kidding?" I see this first interpretation of the Third Commandment as a healthy guide for making your word, your promises, and your assurances more conscious and more reliable. Instead of being pushed into saying automatically, "I swear I'll do it," you will have the freedom to say, "Let me take a moment and think realistically about what I can do and what I may need help with."

Interpretation #2: The Third Commandment can be seen as a reminder not to become rigid or self-righteous when you disagree with someone.

A few years ago, when I began to explore the various scholarly writings about the phrase "Don't take God's name in vain," a second useful theme emerged. Not only does the commandment teach us to avoid making false promises (as discussed above), but it also tells people that if you want your personal and work relationships to be successful you need to watch out for the common human tendency to become rigid, self-righteous, and inflexible during an argument or a disagreement. You have to stop assuming that God or logic is *on only your side* and realize instead that in most cases the person with whom you are disagreeing might also have some integrity, some validity, and some humanity as the basis for his or her point of view.

This warning against self-righteousness appears in several scholarly interpretations of the Third Commandment. For example, the eighteenth-century Moroccan Hasidic master Hayyim ben Moses Attar, whose book *Ohr Hahayyim* (The Light of Life) is a highly regarded Kabbalistic commentary on the Five Books of Moses, said the essence of taking God's name in vain is to pretend to be more correct, more righteous, and more holy than in fact you really are. It's what people today would call "having an attitude" or what many would refer to as "acting holier-than-thou."

Think about the different ways you have seen that sense of self-righteous rigidity occur in your daily life. As you look at the following brief list of examples of self-righteous behavior, see if you can recall any of the judgmental and holier-than-thou people you've encountered over the years as well as those instances in which *you might have become a bit rigid or self-righteous yourself* during an argument or a disagreement with a spouse, a friend, a co-worker, or a relative. Consider for a moment:

- Have you ever been around a religious or spiritual person who talked about loving people unconditionally but who in fact was extremely rigid, close-minded, or insulting about the "right way" or the "wrong way" to practice religion or spirituality?
- Have you ever been in an argument with someone who not only felt you were "wrong" for seeing things your way but said or implied you were "evil," "immoral," or "likely to go to hell" for having a different perspective?
- Have you ever been in a creative, business, or academic setting in which the people who held one point of view called the people who had a different point of view "morons," "idiots," or "pigs"?
- Have you ever been in a political discussion (for example, about abortion, the environment, gun control, welfare policy, gay rights, or affirmative action) in which one side acted as if the other side was inhuman or evil for having a different point of view?

- Have you ever been in a family argument in which some family members belittled or said vicious things about the family member who was doing things differently?

- Have you ever been in a disagreement with a spouse, lover, or close friend in which one or both of you acted as if the other person were your "enemy" because he or she saw things differently from you?

In psychology, this process of believing you are 100 percent right and the other person must be bad or evil is referred to as overidentification. Specifically, we human beings are very identified with our own ideas and our own point of view. As a result, it can be extremely threatening and frustrating when someone else, especially someone you care about, holds a different point of view from your own.

At the same time, that's what makes life so challenging and fascinating—how you find a way to live in peace with someone who sees an important issue differently from you!! Can the two of you come up with a healthy way to respect your differences and to work together toward creative solutions that are satisfying to both of you? Or will you, like most people, resort to calling each other names, resenting each other, and drifting apart?

Maintaining Awareness of the Other Person's Humanity

The Third Commandment is crucial in our everyday lives, because *most relationships sour* when one or both partners are unable to overcome the natural human tendency to objectify anyone who holds an opposing viewpoint, and often, to demonize him or her. I have found repeatedly with my therapy clients and in my own life that it takes a conscious and deliberate effort to snap out of the trap of self-righteousness and see deeper into the humanity of the other person. It requires an almost unnatural willingness to be open to an opposing viewpoint when our more "natural" instinct is to stick with the self-righteous idea that we are 100 percent right and the other person is either stupid, out to get us, or just "being difficult."

A married couple who feels deeply in love one minute can hate each other the next minute if they get into an argument in which one or the other of them acts self-righteous or holier-than-thou. Two colleagues at work on an important project can suddenly feel like enemies if one or the other becomes rigid or inflexible on an important decision. The same is true when political groups, ethnic groups, or religious groups disagree vehemently and fail to see the God-given humanity of the people on the other side. It is far more "normal" for human beings to get self-righteous than to imagine that the other person has some good reason for holding a viewpoint different from their own.

As you think about your own marital fights, business disagreements, and political or religious arguments, can you recall feeling self-righteous and 100 percent correct? If so, don't be embarrassed. It's a natural human reaction. Hopefully, as you read on, you'll see ways to "break out of the trap of self-righteousness." Here's one example:

I volunteered for nine summers at a weeklong workshop for two hundred high school students in Los Angeles. Part of the schedule called for African-Americans, Asian-Americans, Latinos, and whites to engage in uncensored dialogues with one another about their racial and cultural differences. Invariably, each summer the conversations would start out sounding self-righteous and accusatory, but eventually there would be a desire in the room for some path toward healing.

One summer there was a terrible impasse between the African-American and the Korean-American groups at the workshop. One member of the Korean-American group insisted, "I don't know why you people act so rude and disrespectful when you come into my father's grocery store. In my culture, respect is very important."

In response, one member of the African-American group said, "Why should I treat you with respect? You look at me like I'm an animal and you don't give a shit about my culture, my values, or respecting who I am."

It went back and forth like this for almost an hour until one of the African-American teenagers stood up and said, "I don't think we can work together unless we can see a higher purpose to all this. And I'm wondering right now what it means that most of us in this room, blacks and Koreans, are Christians. I don't think Jesus would want us to be in each other's faces like this."

After a few minutes of brainstorming, one of the staff members, a part-time minister, offered the following suggestion. She said, "Instead of tearing each other down or trying to compete as to whose pain is worse, I'd like us to spend a few moments giving some thought to what Jesus meant when he said, 'Judge not, lest ye be judged.' "

For the first time that afternoon the room became quiet. Dozens of teenagers, some of them gang members and others who had grown up fearing that they would never be accepted by the other race, sat in silence for several minutes and then began discussing what they thought the words 'Judge not, lest ye be judged' could mean to them personally.

Those moments of deep inner searching broke the impasse and the two groups began to treat each other with a great deal more respect for and curiosity about who they were as human beings. It didn't solve all the deep conflicts between the two groups, but for the teenagers in that room a major shift had occurred.

Another illustration of how difficult and important it is for people to break out of their self-righteousness occurred in my therapy office one afternoon when a mom and her teenage son were struggling to find a way to live together. They had both become so rigid and defensive with each other that neither of them felt much hope for their relationship.

Right in the middle of the session, the mom asked the son for the thousandth time when he was going to clean up his room. The fourteen-year-old son stood up and said, "That's it! I'm outta here!"

But before he could leave I made him an offer. I said that if he could spend five minutes imagining himself to be his mother, walking into his room and seeing the mess, and then tell us how that felt, he would then be free to leave the session.

So the son, who was quite gifted dramatically and had a great imagination, spent the next five minutes brilliantly imitating his mom, telling us exactly how it felt to walk into his messy room and how frustrating it was that he wouldn't clean it up. After the five minutes, the mom applauded and the son's rigid demeanor began to melt. For the first time, he had been able to appreciate his mother's frustration, and for the first time his mom had appreciated and applauded something about him. That was the beginning of an improvement in their relationship. Once again, it didn't resolve all the tensions and parent-teenager conflicts, but it opened up the possibility that they might see each other in a new light.

In one of the final scenes of Richard Attenborough's award-winning film *Gandhi,* starring Ben Kingsley, the Hindu and Muslim factions are close to civil war and Gandhi, near death, is well into a prolonged fast to bring attention to the need for peace.

A Hindu man approaches Gandhi and asks, "What can I do to get you to stop fasting?" Gandhi replies, "If as a Hindu you would be willing to adopt an orphaned Muslim child and raise that child as a Muslim, then I will stop fasting and there can be peace."

That leap of consciousness, to think carefully about the pain and the humanity of someone who has felt like an enemy to you, is one way to overcome the self-righteousness that the Third Commandment suggests is a violation of God's holiness. In each of our lives, whether we disagree with a spouse, a family member, a colleague, a friend, or a stranger, we all will have moments in which we must decide to recognize the humanity of the other person.

Interpretation #3: ***The Third Commandment can be seen as a warning against using hurtful words, against the common human tendency to use God's name as a weapon to get back at someone, especially your loved ones, when you're upset or angry.***

When we're feeling misunderstood or unappreciated, we're tempted to lash out in anger. These flashes of anger are even more instinctual and automatic in some cases than the self-righteous response described earlier.

When human beings feel attacked, criticized, or belittled, a "fight or flight" response is triggered in our hypothalamus, adrenal glands, respiratory system, autonomic nervous system, and muscles. We feel agitated and impatient, ready to say things like "Damn you," especially to the people we care about the most and whose love we are most afraid of losing.

When married partners, work colleagues, and family members say "Goddamn you" to each other during an argument, they shatter the closeness and trust that has been built up. These flashes of anger and hurtful words can leave a lasting scar on other people and damage important relationships. Quite often, loved ones become distant or emotionally estranged when they've heard the words "Damn you" one too many times.

In traditional Judaism, the Third Commandment is not the only warning against using God's name as a weapon and lashing out in anger at other people. The Book of Leviticus (chapter 19, verse 14) says, "do not curse a deaf person," which later rabbis explained to mean that the gift of speech is for blessing and uplifting our lives, not for degrading ourselves or other people. Even if a deaf person can't hear the hurtful words, the *basic misuse of our own gifts* is wrong. We should employ our minds and tongues not to hurt but to heal and to connect with others.

Over eight hundred years ago, Maimonides, a physician as well as a great Torah scholar, took this explanation further, saying, "Cursing is prohibited not because of what it can do to the victim, but because of its effect on the individual who pronounces it. Jewish law seeks to keep the individual from acquiring the damaging habit of ventilating anger and frustration on others."

THE TRUTH ABOUT ANGER

Unfortunately, one of the biggest modern sources of encouragement for the habit of swearing and unloading one's anger on other people has come in the past few decades from my own profession of psychology. Thousands of therapists urge clients to vent their angry feelings, saying, "You've got to let it all out. Tell people exactly how you feel. Let them know you're angry."

This belief that "dumping your anger on someone must be a good catharsis" comes from earlier Freudian theory, which said that repressed anger is the root of many ailments while anger expressed in a dramatic release can alleviate the pent-up tension in a cathartic breakthrough. This notion became extremely popular during the 1960s and 1970s when encounter groups, marathon weekends, primal-scream therapy, and other approaches suggested that the "only way" to heal fully from old emotional wounds was to yell, scream, and pound.

Fortunately, a good amount of solid scientific research and healthier options have emerged in the past few years. In her insightful book *Anger: The Misunderstood Emotion,* Carol

Tavris denounces the myth that unloading anger on loved ones is healthy. She offers several other constructive ways you can clear up conflicts and assertively express your needs and your anger *without* resorting to name-calling, swearing, or hurtful words that escalate the warfare between spouses, relatives, co-workers, or feuding friends.

In addition, Dr. Murray Mittleman at Harvard Medical School has documented research that shows that angry outbursts actually add to the physiological tensions of the cardiovascular system and that "letting it all out" on people can more than double the risk of a heart attack in some individuals.

These and other studies suggest that the supporters of the "let it all out" approach may have been incorrect. Screaming at your loved ones usually adds to the problems at home, while screaming at important colleagues and customers at work may be effective once in a while but overall will have long-term negative consequences on your career and your physical health. For physiological and psychological reasons, there is a great deal of wisdom in meeting the biblical challenge of not using God's name to curse or belittle your kids, your partners, your family members, or anyone else who gets on your nerves. Please note that I am *not* suggesting people should stuff their anger inside or rationalize it away. The idea is to develop healthy ways of letting off steam and resolving conflicts in personal and work relationships. These other solutions can include therapy, meditation, and counseling.

You can learn more about healthy uses of anger from reading books on the subject (see the Sources section at the back of this book) or from working with a counselor who specializes in managing anger. The following exercise might help you establish good communication and appropriate anger release. The steps are:

1. Pay attention to your body's signals. Start to notice the early warning signs that your blood is beginning to boil. Most people are unaware that they are building up tension or anger, so they have no control over the "fight or flight" process. Pay attention to when your thoughts start becoming hostile or negative, when your hands, shoulders, neck, or stomach begin to tighten, or when your adrenaline has given you a "keyed-up

feeling." By listening to your body's messages, you will provide yourself more time to avoid exploding in an angry tirade.

2. Breathe slowly in and out. Focus on your breathing. Say calming things to yourself. Stop yourself from "building a case" against the other person in your mind. Take a few moments to breathe slowly and evenly, inhaling and exhaling gently and calmly. Count to ten or twenty if that helps. Remind yourself that this person in front of you is *not* your enemy. Even if he or she is being rude, defensive, or stubborn, focus on your breathing and ask yourself two questions: "What do I need in order to stop feeling so angry?" and "Can I ask for what I need without blaming, attacking, or belittling this other person?"

3. Take a brief time-out. If you find that your mind is racing with hostile thoughts or it continues to "build a case" against the other person, you definitely should take a ten-minute break from each other. When asking for this ten-minute time-out, be sure to tell the other person that you are not running away from the situation but rather you need ten minutes to calm yourself and be able to approach the situation from a more positive and constructive frame of mind.

4. Work as partners, not adversaries. After the breathing or the time-out has relaxed you a bit, see if you feel calm enough to be open to a healthy resolution of the conflict. If not, take another ten-minute time-out. Then when you're a little less agitated, tell the other person, "Let's work together to see where we both got hurt and what we can do in the future to make sure this doesn't keep happening."

"I Can't Seem to Stop Myself"

Jerry and Gwen's case is a good illustration of how painful it can be when two people who love each other start tearing each other down with swearing and verbal digs. Jerry is a screenwriter and Gwen is an actress. They came for counseling because their marital fights had become more frequent and more vicious.

Gwen described their problem: "Jerry and I used to argue occasionally about money, the kids, and other issues, but never like this. Recently Jerry's been unable to sell his scripts and I've been getting a lot of turndowns every time I go on an audition. So we're both extratense, and when he starts talking down to me or trying to control the conversation, I can't seem to stop myself. I've always had an explosive temper and I say things to Jerry that I wish I hadn't said."

Jerry adds, "It's not just the fact that we've been hurting each other with these screaming matches. For me the bigger concern is that our kids get so worried and almost depressed when they see us fighting. I grew up in a household where my parents had some real awful arguments, so I know what they must be going through."

As we worked in counseling for a few sessions, it also became clear that not only were Jerry and Gwen saying hurtful things to each other during some of their marital fights, they were both caught up in the common habit of saying harsh and painful things to themselves. Gwen admitted, "Whenever I have another disappointment in my career or when things are going badly with Jerry or the kids, I can be so brutal on myself. It's not just the swearing I do, but also the discouraging remarks. I'll hear myself saying things like, 'You'll never find another job. No one wants you. Nothing you do turns out right anyway.' After listening to that litany day after day, all Jerry has to do is say one condescending remark and I go off on him real fast."

Like many people facing hard times, Gwen and Jerry were feeling a lot less patient and hopeful than they might have been in better economic circumstances. It took several weeks in counseling before they could begin using the four-step exercise for resolving angry conflicts without name-calling. Jerry confessed, "At first I didn't even want to do those steps because I had no desire in the middle of an argument to say things to myself like 'Gwen is *not* my enemy' or to ask her to 'work together to see where we both got hurt and what we can do in the future to make sure this doesn't keep happening.' There was this other, much stronger urge inside me to blame her, to make her feel guilty, and to let out all my frustrations on her because in the past she used to just take it, at least for a while."

As I've found with many couples, it took a few weeks of practicing these four anger-management steps before Gwen and Jerry began to snap out of their chronic habit of dumping their frustrations on each other. But when they did successfully begin to take ten-minute time-outs and work together in a less attacking way, it made a big difference not only for them but also for their children.

Gwen explained the process during their final session. "Once we learned to calm ourselves down and talk about issues as though we're partners instead of screaming at each other, my whole attitude about things began to change. The kids seem to be a lot less moody now that Jerry and I are arguing hardly at all, and even when we do have a disagreement we can stay partners and not attack each other. The improvement in my relationship with Jerry has also translated into my being a lot more creative and positive when I'm out doing auditions. I've landed two great roles in the past few months, partly because I'm no longer walking around with as much anger and bitterness as I was a few months ago."

This technique for managing anger allows for hurt feelings to get expressed and resolved by people working as partners instead of as enemies. Without becoming prudish or uptight, you can gain some control over your swearing and your reactions to your kids, your spouse, your co-workers, or anyone else who triggers your anger. Instead of using God's name as a weapon, you'll have better ways to communicate.

Interpretation #4: The Third Commandment tells us not to take others for granted.

Certain relationships are so special and important that it would be tragic to take them for granted. Who in your own life has been a friend, teacher, mentor, relative, or loved one and brought tremendous joy, assistance, or wisdom to you? Do you have a heart connection with one or more of your children that you would miss terribly if it were to end? Do you have a spiritual connection to God or to a certain clergy member, teacher, author, or sacred ritual that has added a great deal of meaning and warmth to your life? We all would like to honor these relationships as fully as possible.

Unfortunately, the human brain is a problem-oriented machine that tends to focus more on what we don't have than on what we do have. Our minds like to chase after goals that are often beyond our reach more than they like to appreciate a relationship that has been part of our lives for many years. We all take some people for granted.

What then can we use to wake us up and remind us not to take for granted the important heart connections that are so crucial in our lives? What can we use to remind ourselves that our most important relationships need just as much time, energy, and creativity as the other goals for which we are reaching?

Regaining a Sense of Specialness

In the Kabbalistic Jewish book called the Zohar, the Third Commandment, "Don't take God's name in vain," is discussed as a reminder to wake up and remember the sacred intimacy of our relationship with God and with the people in our lives who, because of their specialness and warmth, help us appreciate the depth of love we are capable of feeling.

The Zohar says that since God's Presence is such an amazing blessing and so filled with love, we need to be extremely careful not to utter God's name in any thoughtless or empty phrases. In essence, the Zohar is saying that unless we pay attention to the sacredness of our relationships, especially the one with God, we will quickly slip back into taking them for granted and losing the specialness.

Just listen closely for a day to yourself and others for how many times we speak the awesome name of God in the most negative and trivial ways. We don't just frequently use "God" next to the word "damn"; we also employ dozens of other throwaway phrases. Think, for example, about how you respond when someone walks into the room with a garish outfit or a strange hairdo. It's uncommon not to mutter to yourself, "Oh, God!" Or when we feel disgusted about something or impatient with someone's incompetence, it's almost automatic to say, "Oh, for God's sake," or "For the love of God!"

The famous nineteenth-century German writer Goethe described vividly this human challenge of whether or not to speak God's name thoughtlessly. Goethe said, "People treat the name of God as if that incomprehensible and most high Being, who is beyond the reach of thought, were just another trivial thing. Otherwise they would not say 'Oh God,' 'for the love of God,' 'good God,' and other such comments. These expressions become an empty phrase for most people, a barren name to which no thought is attached. If people were impressed by the sublime greatness of God, they would be silent; honor would keep them from mentioning God's name hardly at all."

So the next time you hear yourself or someone else saying

"Dear God" or "Oh, my God" in a thoughtless way, you might want to ask yourself, "Is that how I would like to relate to the Divine Source? Do I want to continue to be thoughtless and trite about something as profound and deep as the Infinite One?"

Making the Words Heartful Again

This problem of saying God's name thoughtlessly occurs not only in secular settings; some would argue that it happens in synagogues and churches as well. For example, the eighteenth-century rabbi and founder of the Hasidic movement, Israel Baal Shem Tov (whose name translates into English as the Master of the Good Name), once visited a community where he was urged to go into the fine new synagogue. Everyone talked about its majestic architecture, its beautiful Torah, and its striking sculpture of the Ten Commandments.

So finally the Baal Shem Tov decided to visit the synagogue, but when the door was opened he looked inside and without a word turned around to go back to the inn where he was staying.

"Rabbi," the leaders of the congregation complained, "why aren't you going to enter this beautiful synagogue of which we are so proud?"

"There is no room," the Baal Shem Tov explained.

"No room? There are plenty of empty seats. It's a huge synagogue, the largest for hundreds of miles," they persisted.

"There was no room for me," the great rabbi said. "All the thoughtless words filled it up. All the prayers that people utter without thinking or feeling are like dead words, which have no heart or soul in them. They do not soar up to heaven, but they lie there like dead leaves from a tree. They fill up the synagogue to overflowing and there's no room left for heartful words in that building."

This often-told story about the Baal Shem Tov has always touched me deeply, because for many years I had a similar feeling of not knowing how to find a deep, heartful experience in many religious services that seemed performed by rote and overcrowded with formality. Several years ago, however, I began studying what the prayers actually mean and the passion with which they were first written. I was fortunate to find several classes and some excellent teachers who profoundly changed the way I experience the formal prayers today.

For instance, one of the most frequently repeated prayers in Judaism is the Sh'ma, which in Hebrew gets recited as "Sh'ma Yisroel Adonai Eloheynu Adonai Ekhad." I'd said it thousands of times, but neither the Hebrew verse nor the translation— "Hear O Israel the Lord our God the Lord is One"—ever felt like a deeply heartful prayer. Then one particular rabbi taught a passionate translation of the Hebrew words and I began to experience a more personal connection to this commonly repeated prayer:

Sh'ma: listen, or wake up. Yisroel: you who seek to understand and connect with God. Adonai: the Eternal One who has been present since the beginning of time and who expresses love and wisdom by entering our hearts and our world as Eloheynu: our God. Adonai Ekhad: this Eternal energy is the unity within and between all things.

The next time I said that prayer, I felt a much stronger sense of curiosity and connection to this loving energy that expresses Itself through our lives and unites all beings. Nearly every time I've said the Sh'ma prayer since then has been much more heartful for me. Like many other people, I've realized I'm not comfortable praying in a thoughtless or formalized way, which feels like taking God's name in vain. But I would rather say things to God from the heart, which means that sometimes I need to go back and find teachers, classes, or books that can help me get to the passion and the depth of meaning that are underneath most psalms, blessings, and formal prayers.

This process of learning and deepening how to pray in both formal and informal settings is an ongoing part of my spiritual life that I expect will be a challenging journey for as long as I live. Just as I've learned from experience that I need to devote time and energy to avoid taking my marriage and my close friendships for granted, so do I need to put time and energy into my relationship with God so that it doesn't become rigid or lifeless.

A Christian colleague of mine named Teresa told me a similar story of her own struggle to find the heart and soul in the prayer words she had repeated thoughtlessly so many times. Teresa recently found out that her former best friend Janet was in the hospital recovering from surgery.

Teresa explained, "I had these mixed feelings about whether

or not to visit Janet. We'd been best friends for many years until six years ago, when her husband and my husband got into a disagreement over a business deal that went bad. So Janet and I drifted apart, but I still have a lot of love for her, and I wanted to be there with her in the hospital."

Teresa was in church that week when she heard the priest say the traditional words "Go in the name of the Father, the Son, and the Holy Spirit," only he wasn't consciously talking about Teresa's decision about whether or not to visit Janet in the hospital.

Teresa recalls, "I'd heard those words thousands of times and they always felt distant, formal, and a little too male-oriented for me. But later that day I did go to see Janet in the hospital, and as I was sitting by her side and holding her hand, I felt a tremendous sense of Spirit there with us. My eyes filled with tears and I said a prayer of thanks that God was there for us—not only for Janet's physical healing but also for the healing of our friendship. Ever since that day, whenever I hear the words 'the Father, the Son, and the Holy Spirit,' I remember that feeling of being surrounded by God's love as I was sitting next to my friend Janet in her hospital room. Those words mean so much more to me now."

How Do You Renew a Relationship That's Been Taken for Granted?

Whether you are currently feeling distant from a close friend, a spouse, your children, a difficult relative, a business associate, or God, it's never too late to stop taking these important relationships for granted. If you think about this fourth interpretation of the Third Commandment seriously, it can help you focus your life in a number of useful ways:

• Remembering on a daily basis not to take God's name in vain can help you open up to the possibility of creating a more heartful relationship with God or your spirituality, rather than settling for empty words or trite phrases. Are there some prayers or rituals that you've been performing mindlessly for years that you now would like to learn more about, to understand better so you can respond to them more heartfully? Are you willing to become more conscious and respectful in the way you speak the mysterious and holy name of God? Are you more interested in finding out what it will feel like to have a deeper relationship with the Divine Presence?

• Remembering not to take anything holy or special for granted can help you open up to the possibility of reenergizing your most cherished love relationships or friendships, rather than settling for the emotional distance or empty routines that most people fall into. Are there some special times you want to create for you and this other person? Are there some things you need to talk about and clear up from the past? Are you interested in finding out what it will feel like to have a renewed and more fulfilling relationship with this person you have known for so long?

• Remembering to treat God's name with tender care can also remind you that important relationships, whether they are with God or with a human loved one, require attention and persistence. If you simply fall back into a meaningless routine or take these heartful connections for granted, very soon you'll find you've diminished the specialness and the closeness.

Even though the words of the Third Commandment sound simple—"Don't take God's name in vain"—observing and practicing the four possible meanings can make a huge difference in the quality of your relationships. The third challenge is actually a four-part challenge: stop making false promises, learn to control our self-righteousness, curb our anger, and take time to reenergize our most important relationships.

I recently spoke with a couple at a workshop who told me they had been together for twenty-seven years and would soon be celebrating their anniversary. I figured they probably were going out to dinner or buying each other a card like most couples do. But then they told me, "We have a ritual we do each year around our anniversary. We set aside one day in which one of us plans a surprise getaway that the other person is likely to find wonderful. Each year we take turns as to who gets to be the surprise maker and who gets to be the receiver. Every year the surprises get more fun and creative."

If each of us treated our most important personal, work, and family relationships with the same type of creativity and care as this couple, you can imagine how much more satisfying our lives would be. No matter how long you've known a close friend, business associate, or family member who means a lot to you, make sure you don't treat this special human being thoughtlessly or carelessly, because the more you cherish and nurture the relationship, the more it will grow.

4

THE FOURTH CHALLENGE

*The Struggle to Unhook from Your Everyday
Pressures and Connect with Something
Profoundly Joyful*

Imagine for a moment that someone who cares about you
has sent you a gift certificate for a day that is to be devoted
entirely to the needs of your soul. On that day you don't
have to work. You can take a walk and have a relaxing conversation with friends or loved ones about the things that really
matter. You can meditate, pray, and read the books that speak
to your soul. You can nap and let your mind take a rest, or
dance and sing to let your spirit soar. For one day, you can stop
trying to prove yourself out in the world. You can look at your
life as a blessing and feel at peace with where you are right now.
Instead of feeling fragmented and pressured, you can spend the
day in a generous, positive, and contemplative mood.

Does this sound too good to be true? Does it sound wonderful
but unattainable to have a day devoted completely to the needs
of your soul?

You may be surprised to discover that this gift certificate
entitling you to spend a day responding to the special needs of
your innermost being is actually the Fourth Commandment
from the Book of Exodus, which says, "Remember the Sabbath
day to keep it holy." Over the centuries it has been interpreted
by scholars and teachers as an opportunity to let go of your
everyday pressures and connect with a joyful, sacred way of
being alive.

In writing about this Fourth Commandment, I have to begin

by confessing that I sometimes find it extremely difficult to unwind and let go after a hectic week. As much as I respect and enjoy the beauty of a day for one's soul and one's connection with God, I often find myself battling my own internal voices that say, "What about this piece of unfinished business?" or "What about that pressing need?," which can interrupt the peacefulness of the Sabbath.

What about you? Do you observe the Sabbath frequently, rarely, or never at all? It's not easy to let go each week of the incessant thoughts inside our heads. If letting go were a simple thing for human beings to accomplish, then we wouldn't need a biblical reminder to do so.

Learning how to make the Sabbath into a day for breaking free of the pressures of your life and finding a peaceful connection to your inner spirit does not happen the first few times you attempt it. Attaining the true joy and release of the Sabbath takes practice; it is an art. Some people take a few years and others an entire lifetime before they develop the ability fully to let go.

WHAT YOU CAN GAIN

If you have never experienced a joyful and meaningful Sabbath, this chapter will give you ideas on how other people do it and where to get started. You can decide for yourself how you'd like to try to improve the weekly rhythms and spiritual depth of your life.

If you grew up in an environment in which observing the Sabbath entailed following a joyless list of prohibitions, then, just as the First Challenge presents alternative views of God and spirituality, this chapter and challenge will ask you to reexamine what Sabbath really means and how to make it a healthy and positive part of your adult life, as well as making it something your children will enjoy and cherish.

WHAT EXACTLY DOES THE WORD SABBATH MEAN TO YOU?

According to most Hebrew scholars, the word *Sabbath,* or *Shabbat,* means a lot more than just resting. To nineteenth-century German Orthodox rabbi Samson Raphael Hirsch, the root letters of *Shabbat* have two meanings. The first is to cease from an activity in progress, which is what God did after creating the world. God then stepped back to say, "I'm pleased with what I've done so far. It is good." The second meaning of *Shabbat* means to put everything in its proper place, which can only be done if you step back from your material pursuits and look at your life from a different perspective.

The twentieth-century founder of the Reconstructionist movement in Judaism, Rabbi Mordecai Kaplan, offers a similar definition of Shabbat:

"An artist cannot be continually wielding his or her brush. The painter must stop at times from the painting to freshen his or her vision of the object, the meaning of which the artist wishes to express on canvas. The Shabbat represents those moments when we pause in our brushwork to renew our vision of the general plan. Having done so, we take ourselves to our painting with clarified vision and renewed energy."

The mystical Kabbalistic teachings about the Sabbath point out that the Hebrew letters in "the Sabbath" (H,Sh,V,T) are the same letters used in the word *teshuvah* (T,V,Sh,H). Since *teshuvah* means to turn oneself toward a more holy direction, then the Sabbath can be seen as an opportunity to break free of the unfulfilling directions we get pulled into during the week and turn ourselves toward a more spiritual way of living.

This notion that the Sabbath is more than a day of rest also appears in Islam, where the Sabbath is called Yom Aljum'ah, the Day of Assembly, and is observed on Friday. According to the Quran, the holiest book of Islam, the Sabbath is not just a day of rest but a call to midday worship. Even if a Muslim has been unable to pray during the week, he or she is expected to set aside time on Friday to connect with God.

In Christianity, most observant Catholics, Protestants, and Eastern Orthodox Christians celebrate the Sabbath as "the Lord's day" on Sunday, while some (including Seventh-Day Adventists) celebrate it on Saturday. Various Christian teachings have also explained why keeping the Sabbath goes deeper than just resting. For example, in the first few centuries after Jesus, the tradition grew to celebrate Sunday with a worship service to commemorate the creation of the world, which took place on the first day, and as a reminder of the resurrection of Jesus, which also took place on a Sunday.

When Martin Luther spoke passionately, in the sixteenth century, about the need to keep the Sabbath he said, "The Sabbath is a day of special communion between God and humanity, a day on which God speaks with us through His Word and we in turn speak with Him through prayer and faith."

In more recent years, one church publication explained, "People need a day to reflect, meditate, contemplate, and to turn their eyes inward, as it were, rather than outward. This has always been true, but surely it is truer now in this strenuous age of the world than ever before." Another Christian minister wrote, "Sunday does not belong to business. It does not belong to industry. It does not belong to government. It belongs to God."

Judaism and Christianity share a common vision of a Sabbath tradition, a day set apart from secular pursuits in the material world.

For traditional Jews, the Sabbath is a joyful envisioning of what life will be like when the brokenness of the world is repaired. As described by Rabbi Irving Greenberg, an Orthodox scholar who is president of the National Jewish Center for Learning and Leadership in New York City, "Shabbat is a taste of what life will be like when the Messiah comes, when the world has been perfected. According to the Genesis account, this world originally was and is still meant to be a paradise. But only when there is peace, with abundant resources and an untrammeled right to live, will the world be structured to sustain the infinite value of the human being. This is the heart of Judaism, the dream. . . .

"By an act of will on Shabbat, we step outside the here and now and for approximately twenty-five hours all things are seen through the eyes of love, as if all were perfect. Every seven days we reaffirm our connection to God, to be 'married to the Divine lover.' Is this an escape from reality? No, it's an act of faith to be committed to live a life that is growing and seeking perfection, to be so nurtured by *chesed* [loving kindness] and the taste of Shabbat as to go out and transform the world."

This Messianic optimism also appears in Christian views of the Sabbath. As early as the second century, one of the church scholars, named Justin Martyr, wrote that the Sabbath was less about rest and more about honoring the beginning of a second new creation, which the church said had started with the resurrection of Jesus. In the sixteenth century, the founder of Protestantism, Martin Luther, also wrote that the Sabbath is a day in which Christians "might keep a sure hope of eternal life, for all the things God wants done on the Sabbath are signs of another life after this life." Alternatively, you can view it as the opportunity to celebrate the beginning of the creation of a new week and the positive potential for re-creating your life.

THE DREAM AND THE REALITY

With all this hope for a day devoted to God and a vision of a better world, it is extremely ironic that for most people in the 1990s the Sabbath is a day of catching up on work, running errands, watching football, or playing golf. The Christian spiritual writer Edythe Draper quotes an unnamed minister who commented, "In my grandparents' day it was called the Holy Sabbath, in my parents day the Sabbath, and today we just call it the weekend."

Most Jews and Christians today have grown up believing that the Sabbath is an anachronism. Many nonobservant Jews today sense that keeping the Sabbath would be a painful step backward into the past. As Rabbi Zalman Schachter-Shalomi, the founder of the Jewish Renewal movement, explains, "The Sabbath is such an important gift that the world needs desperately. It's like the healing exhale each week after too much inhaling. But people are so worked up about the 'Nos' of Shabbat because no one has modeled for them the joyful 'Yeses' of Shabbat. If you make each Sabbath a fun and spiritually transforming day, especially for young children, then people will be saying, 'Hooray, it's Shabbos,' instead of 'Oy vay, I can't do such and such because it's Shabbos again.' "

Christian theologian Harvey Cox, an acclaimed author and professor at Harvard Divinity School, suggests:

"Few Jewish practices are more misunderstood by Christians than the Sabbath. One reason for this misunderstanding is that several of the stories of Jesus in the Gospels depict him as deliberately breaking Sabbath rules, especially by healing people. Because of the way these stories are often interpreted in sermons and church-school lessons, many Christians grow up with an image of the Jewish Sabbath as a compulsively legalistic straitjacket or an empty attempt to observe meaningless ritual rules. No doubt there were abuses of the spirit of the Sabbath in Jesus' time. But most Christian educational material fails utterly to point out why the Sabbath was instituted or to describe its ingenious blending of contemplative and ethical purposes."

Harvey Cox recommends, "To rediscover in our time the superb meaning of the Sabbath should make Jewish young people think twice about whether they want to follow in the footsteps of their 'enlightened' parents who have shied away from Sabbath observance as an embarrassment. And it should cause Christians to wonder how some of the seventh-day spell—so spoiled by misguided Puritan opposition to enjoying its freedom —can be found again."

HOW DO YOU PUT MORE JOY AND BEAUTY INTO YOUR SABBATHS?

For the past fifteen years, I've been asking people of various backgrounds to tell me how they unwind each week and whether they include spirituality in that process of letting go. The answers I've received are as varied as the individuals I've spoken with:

1. "LOOKING INTO THE FACES OF PEOPLE I CARE ABOUT"
Robyn is a woman in her thirties who grew up in a mostly nonreligious household, but over the past ten years she has become more interested in spirituality and religion. A middle-level manager for a large company during the week, Robyn admits, "When I think about how I was fifteen years ago, I never

would have imagined that I'd be as observant as I am today, especially when it comes to the Sabbath."

Robyn explains, "I happen to love having people over for Shabbat dinner, lighting the candles, saying the blessings, and looking into the faces of people I care about. Even though I'm not married and I don't know if or when that might happen, I feel so lucky to have co-workers, friends, and friends of friends invited over at least two or three Friday nights a month. It's funny that I make the same traditional matzoh-ball soup, roasted chicken, and vegetables, along with the braided challah [the traditional Shabbat loaf of bread] that I vaguely remember from the few times we visited my father's mother back in New Jersey. Sometimes it feels like a lot of work getting ready for Shabbat, but when we're there at the table singing the songs which I've typed up on song sheets and telling stories after the meal, I feel so connected—not just with these six or eight people but with thousands of years of tradition. I hope someday I have a daughter, or even a son, who likes to cook, so I can pass this on."

2. "I Need a Service Where the People Are Excited and Alive"

Carl is a man in his forties who grew up in a strict religious household, where going to Sunday services felt like "torture" to him. According to Carl, "The church where we went when I was a kid felt so scary and oppressive to me. Lots of cold, disapproving faces, lots of people saying 'Sit still' and 'Shhhh!' And a preacher who made it sound like God was going to punish me for every little thing I wanted to do. I remember sitting in that uncomfortable church pew and counting the minutes until I could go out and be a kid again."

Carl adds, "Now that we're parents, my wife and I were very careful about how we were going to do Sunday services with our kids. We looked around for quite a while before we settled on a church where the Sabbath is celebrated with a lot of singing and joy. After what I went through as a kid, I need a service where the people are excited and alive. And at lunch every Sunday we try to make sure our three children feel loved and appreciated, not shamed or afraid of God and the church, the way we were as kids. We each take turns at the table saying what blessings we feel good about from that week and what parts of ourselves we're still working on to become more of who we were meant to be. The kids seem to enjoy these Sundays, especially the way they get to sing and dance in church and feel they are a part of the celebration."

3. "I HOPE I CAN FIND IT DURING THE YEARS I STILL HAVE"

Evelyn is a woman in her fifties who grew up with two highly educated parents who believed that all people belong to the same human family; as a result, Evelyn's parents spoke harshly against all the major religions for claiming to have a special relationship with God.

Evelyn says, "My mother was from a politically active Jewish background and my father was a lapsed Catholic who was somewhat unresolved about his parents' strict Catholicism. So they thought they were doing me a favor by not exposing me to any formal religion."

As an adult, Evelyn has been searching for a base from which to explore her many questions and spiritual needs. She told me, "I have tried just about everything. I've studied Buddhism, Religious Science, the Bahai faith, various New Age groups, a little bit of Christianity, and a little bit of Judaism. What I keep coming back to is that I need a structure and a community in order to keep deepening my spirituality.

"It's like you need solid roots in order to have wings, and unfortunately my well-meaning parents taught me quite firmly never to surrender to one path or one community. Yet on those few times when I've really let myself get into a spiritual routine and a formal structure, like recently when I've been keeping the Sabbath a little more than I did previously, it feels so grounding and comforting. I'll probably always be a rebel and a searcher, but every so often, like on a Sabbath when I've tuned out the world and I spend some time taking walks in nature and connecting with God, I feel like I'm starting to find my spiritual home. I hope I can find it during the years I still have."

WHAT ARE THE ELEMENTS THAT WOULD DEEPEN YOUR SENSE OF FREEDOM EACH WEEK?

Many people feel overwhelmed and turned off by the many rules and guidelines for how to observe the Sabbath, but Conservative Jewish educator Dr. Ron Wolfson suggests, in his book on keeping the Sabbath in a modern context, that if Sabbath observance is new to you, you shouldn't let the "seeming enormity of it overwhelm the initial effort. It is not only possible but advisable to begin one step at a time. If you begin with a few of the basic rituals and become comfortable with the first steps, the other parts will fall into place."

Whether you identify yourself as Jewish, Christian, Muslim, or Buddhist or follow another practice, think about your own need to unwind each week and connect with something meaningful. In order to help you decide what to explore next, here are a few ideas that I've gathered together from people I've interviewed and from Sabbath rituals that friends, family, and I have practiced over the years. Perhaps they will help you begin to create your own way of connecting with the spiritual energies of the Sabbath:

Step #1: Decide what you need to stop doing each Sabbath in order to have a day of freedom from the strivings of the material world.

In order to make room for the beauty and healing qualities of the Sabbath to enter the deepest parts of your psyche at least once a week, you will need to let go of whatever gets in the way. Deciding on which actitivies and how much to let go depends on what type of religious practice you identify with or want to explore.

For example, if you are Christian and your denomination has specific activities that are discouraged or forbidden on the Sabbath (such as working, drinking, shopping, or being away from your family), you have two choices: You can rebel and say it's not for you, or you can experiment with whether or not there's a deeper sense of meaning and calmness available to you if you let go of these practices on the Sabbath. As described in the 1994 edition of the influential Christian text *The New*

Interpreter's Bible, "Contemporary practice of Sabbath concerns the periodic, disciplined, regular disengagement from systems of productivity whereby the world uses people up to exhaustion. Instead it's a day of special dignity."

If you are Jewish and you want to learn more about an Orthodox Jewish Shabbat, I recommend that you read the chapter called "The Dream and How to Live It: Shabbat" in Rabbi Irving Greenberg's book *The Jewish Way.* Greenberg not only lists the thirty-nine types of labor that are prohibited on Shabbat, but he also writes poetically on the spiritual reasons for letting go for twenty-five hours of anything that tries to tamper with God's world as it is.

If you have a respect for tradition but you want to be able to update it slightly to suit your modern lifestyle, then I recommend both the Conservative Jewish guidebook by Dr. Ron Wolfson mentioned earlier as well as the Reform Jewish guide to the Sabbath by Rabbi Mark Dov Shapiro. In these books you will discover how to develop, one step at a time, a meaningful Shabbat that honors your choices about what you decide to stop doing on the Sabbath and what you personally feel isn't getting in the way.

Finally, a brief but extremely useful set of guidelines on how to create a meaningful Shabbat was suggested by Rabbi Arthur Green, the former president of the Reconstructionist Rabbinical College. Rabbi Green offers only four *Don't*s:

A. Don't do anything you *have to do* for your work life. This includes obligatory reading, fulfilling unwanted social obligations, and preparing for work, as well as doing your job itself.
B. Don't spend money. The atmosphere of Shabbat is best protected by complete separation from the commercial culture.
C. Don't travel. This refers especially to long-distance travel involving airports, hotel check-ins, and similar depersonalizing commercial situations. Stay free of encounters in which people are likely to tell you, "Have a nice day!"
D. Don't use commercial or canned video entertainment. This refers especially to television, films, and computer

games. Stay in situations where you are face-to-face with those around you, rather than together facing the all-powerful screen.

To illustrate the importance of deciding carefully what you will let go of in order to have a spiritual and peaceful Sabbath each week, here are two brief examples from friends of mine:

"We Had No Idea How Much
We Were Trapped by Those Two Things"

Danny and Rachel were both raised in nonreligious homes. When they got married they decided they wanted to explore their spirituality, which included learning more about how to experience Shabbat each week. At first they started slowly, by lighting candles, saying a few prayers, having friends over, and sometimes attending services. But as their enjoyment of the Sabbath grew, they decided to let go of a few things that seemed to be getting in the way.

Rachel told me, "Danny and I noticed that if we were napping, reading, talking to each other, or even making love on Shabbat—which incidentally is a mitzvah [a good deed or commandment] recommended by the ancient rabbis—we were constantly interrupted by the phone ringing. So we bought an answering machine that had a monitoring device that allowed us to screen calls. But after a few weeks, even that felt like an interruption of the sacredness of the Sabbath. So we decided to turn off the incoming volume on the answering machine and just not answer the phone for twenty-five hours on Shabbat.

"We also decided not to watch TV on the Sabbath just to see if we were capable of going one day a week without the tube defining our lives."

Danny concludes, "We found that just those two decisions have made a huge difference in how fun and freeing our Shabbats have been. We had no idea how much we were trapped by those two things—the phone and the TV. But letting go of both of them one day a week has opened a huge space for spiritual energies to enter our lives."

"It's the Closeness I Never Had"

George is a researcher and technical writer for a large corporation who usually finds there are not enough hours in the week for catching up on all of his work. George grew up in a spiritual but nonreligious Christian household, and he stayed away from organized religion for many years. It wasn't until he was married and his kids were of Sunday-school age that he and his wife, Ellen, decided to join a church and enroll their kids in Sunday school.

George says, "That was when my own indifference to religion got challenged by the minister. Ellen and I really liked this minister, and so when he began talking to us about the importance of giving a day to God each week I had trouble dismissing him the way I'd always dismissed religious talk like that. Even though a part of me was saying, 'Can I really afford to give up a day from my work?' I noticed I actually felt much healthier on those weeks when I'd attended Sunday services. I got inspired by his sermons and I usually came home feeling a lot clearer about who I am and what really matters in life. It didn't feel like too much of a sacrifice to give up a few Sunday mornings a month to enhance my spiritual life."

But a few months later, George's older daughter, Krista, who was then six years old, began crying one Sunday afternoon. Ellen asked Krista, "What's wrong?" Krista replied, "In church this morning they said that Sunday was a day for families to be together and share their love for each other. But I guess Daddy doesn't love me, because every Sunday afternoon he spends all his time working on the computer."

George's first reaction was, "Oh no, now what have I gotten myself into?"

But after George and Ellen talked it over, they decided they were going to have to make a choice. They could ignore or downplay Krista's concern. They could even get mad at the minister and quit the church for asking them to change their lifestyle too much. Or George could let go of working on his computer and surfing the Internet for hours each Sunday afternoon and evening, which would free up more time for being with his children.

George later told me, "I never thought I'd be the kind of person who was so religious he couldn't work or do frivolous things on the Sabbath, like going on the Internet and talking for hours to people from the far corners of the world. But I gotta tell you, it's really an unexpected pleasure to spend each Sunday with my family, going to services, taking walks, and having good conversations.

"It's the closeness I never had with my parents when I was a child. I realize it means I'll have to be a little more efficient on the other days, and I may miss out on some great debates on the Internet. But I decided my kids are more important than my beloved computer."

Step #2: Select a few favorite activities that will reawaken your sense of Sabbath joy each week.

Even though most people focus more on the Sabbath prohibitions against work and other activities, in fact the things you *can do* on the Sabbath are far more important and plentiful.

To make your Sabbaths deeply spiritual and enjoyable, the following are traditionally recommended:

• Lighting candles. Many people, both adults and children, describe the warmth of lit candles in their home as their fondest memories of the Sabbath. If done with feeling, there is something beautiful and spiritual about watching a loved one light the Sabbath candles and sing the blessing. Or if you are the person who gets to do it in your home, you can make it an opportunity to send warm healing light to each of the people gathered around you. Many rabbis teach that the light of the candles symbolizes and reawakens the divine inner light we carry inside our hearts. Regardless of how religious you consider yourself, if you do nothing else on the Sabbath but light candles, you will be amazed at how it can stir up spiritual feelings inside you.

• Napping. A brief nap is traditional on the Sabbath, both for its healing benefits and for the spiritual significance of having no work to do except to connect with the dreams of our souls. This sense of letting go in order to make room for holy energies is a central idea in Jewish, Sufi Muslim, Christian, Buddhist, Hindu, and Native American spirituality. When we sleep and dream, our souls have greater freedom to connect with the Divine.

• Making love. As mentioned earlier, it is considered a special mitzvah (a commandment or good deed) for married partners to appreciate their spiritual commitment to each other on the Sabbath by making love or at least spending some private time with each other. This idea of making sexuality into a sacred moment of connection with the Divine Oneness is also found in the writings of many other spiritual traditions. Lovemaking that is relaxed, unrushed, and devoted to a higher purpose can be the most cherished spiritual moments for a busy couple who have lost touch with the sacredness of their love for each other.

• Walking. Many scholars and teachers suggest walking slowly and calmly on the Sabbath, especially if on the other six days of the week rushing is your norm. In his recent book *Renewing Your Soul: A Guided Retreat for the Sabbath and Other Days of Rest,* Rabbi David Cooper of Jamestown, Colorado, describes in detail two Sabbath walking rituals, Walking Meditation and Lucid Strolling, that combine Zen Buddhist techniques with Jewish Kabbalistic practices to help you reach a deeper level of inner peace during your Sabbath strolls. Learning to walk with a sense of inner calm is not easy for most people, but if your Sabbath walks help you find a quiet center inside, then your life will feel much richer as a result.

• A special meal. It's traditional to prepare your favorite foods, to use special dishes, and to invite friends, neighbors, and family to join you for a Sabbath meal. Just as many Jews recall the warmth and good times of a grandparent's family Shabbat meals, so do many Christians describe how much they liked the togetherness of a relaxed Sunday meal after church as one of the highlights of their sense of extended family. For many busy people and two-career couples, this weekly ritual can be the one meal where the entire family gets to sit down and eat together without rushing off to another commitment.

• Singing. Whether you have a good voice or not, the joy of singing with children, friends, and relatives can give you a sense of warmth and closeness. For many people, the lively songs and spiritual melodies help them break out of the stressful pace of the work week and open up to the joy of the Sabbath.

- Dancing. It could be Israeli dancing, Eastern European klezmer music, Irish or Scottish folk music, African or Latin American drum rhythms, whirling and mystical Sufi Muslim dances, or some other folk or ethnic dancing. Getting in the habit of dancing on the Sabbath not only is fun but also helps your children appreciate their roots.

- Blessings for family members. It's traditional to say prayers of gratitude and encouragement for one's spouse and children on the Sabbath. Regardless of your spiritual background, you probably can see that remembering at least once a week to thank God for your loved ones is a good way to avoid taking them for granted.

- Spiritual study. If you go a little deeper each week in your spiritual quest for knowledge, imagine how much you will know at the end of 52 Sabbaths or 104 Sabbaths.

- Giving to charity. For centuries, no matter how poor or struggling a family was, and even during times of persecution, a little box for collecting charity was kept inside the home and filled with coins by parents and children prior to sundown on the eve of the Sabbath. If you and your family can develop a habit of giving money and visiting the aged or ill as part of your Sabbath, it can have several benefits: giving your family a sense of sharing even during lean times, modeling for children the habit of giving generously to strangers and loved ones in need, and reminding us of how much we can be thankful for on this day that celebrates freedom from the pressure to have or do more.

- Special conversations. Most Sabbath guides strongly urge that you not talk about business or everyday money concerns on this sacred day but rather focus on the blessings for which you are grateful and the personal growth you each have achieved in recent weeks.

This list is only a brief sample of the many ways to make the Sabbath a richer experience, both for adults and for children. Throughout history, many people have found their most joyful and spiritually uplifting moments during the "time out of regular time" that is the Sabbath. I'd like to pass along two brief stories of how the world feels different when you let yourself have a Sabbath each week:

The first story comes from the Talmud and deals with the special foods and meals that are traditional on the Sabbath. In this often-told story, Rabbi Judah makes a Sabbath feast for the Roman emperor Antoninus. Though the food was prepared earlier and is served cold (because of the traditional Shabbat restrictions against working at making a fire), it is nevertheless quite delicious.

Some time later, the emperor is the host at a huge banquet feast where Rabbi Judah is a guest. Lavish and spectacular hot dishes are served. At the conclusion of the feast, Antoninus says to Rabbi Judah, "The meal you served was better." Judah responds, "That's because this banquet feast lacked a particular spice."

The emperor is concerned. "Is my treasury missing something, a spice, a flavoring, a certain type of preparation? Should I fire my cooks? Tell me what it is, and I will purchase whatever it takes."

Judah replies, "The missing spice is the Sabbath, and it cannot be bought."

The second Sabbath account is from a Christian woman named Charlotte Forten, an African-American teacher of newly freed slaves in the 1850s whose journal was discovered and later published in the 1960s.

Like many people, Charlotte Forten experiences the essence of the Sabbath when she's out strolling slowly in nature. In her journal she wrote, "I love to walk on the Sabbath, for all is so peaceful. The noise and the labor of everyday life has ceased, and in perfect silence we can commune with nature and with Nature's God."

Step #3: Use the blessings and prayers of the Sabbath as a way to open up your heart.

Many people think of going to Sabbath services in a church, synagogue, temple, or mosque as a burdensome obligation or a boring routine. From the people I've interviewed and counseled over the years, it seems to be the one Sabbath activity that provokes the most ambivalent or negative feelings. One client told me a few years ago, "I like the idea of having a day each week to be at home and unhook from my work pressures. But sitting through a religious service and listening to a sermon usually makes me feel bored, trapped, or frustrated."

Does that sound like you or someone you know? Is there something about the Sabbath services you've attended that leaves you feeling empty or dissatisfied?

As a psychologist I am extremely interested in why some people report feeling deeply moved and spiritually nourished from weekly Sabbath services, yet others come away feeling alienated or frustrated. Specifically, I am interested in why some people describe Sabbath prayers, hymns, and blessings as a profoundly inspiring activity while others feel very little connection to God or to their spirituality when they recite the words written down in the Sabbath prayer books.

While there are many possible explanations for why some people enjoy a religious service and others don't, I want to mention one specific thing you can do in your own spiritual life to dramatically improve the way you experience the words of prayer spoken in your particular denomination's religious services.

This technique for making prayers, hymns, and blessings more meaningful and inspiring was given to me several years ago during the discussion following a Sabbath service at a weekend retreat I attended.

It was not your usual religious service. The rabbi wore blue jeans and sneakers. The mood felt informal, and the discussion after the service became quite honest and revealing, especially when the rabbi asked, "So what's the deal with prayer? Why do we pray?"

Despite the informal setting, most of the people who spoke first offered only safe and acceptable answers. A few seemed to want to impress the rabbi with their knowledge of certain prayers. Others asked the rabbi to clarify one thing or another. No one seemed to want to rock the boat, until one woman in the back of the room raised her hand and spoke deeply from her heart.

This woman commented, "I truly don't know why we say the prayers we do. They feel strange and rather subservient to me. Almost like we're begging God or trying to praise God with all these lofty phrases: 'O merciful One. O beneficent One. O majestic One.' It's like we're these terrified little kids trying to get our abusive father not to smack us. I don't understand what kind of egotistical God we think we're praying to. Does God really need all that praise? And does God really enjoy all the begging and pleading we do?"

For most people at that retreat weekend, the mood had suddenly changed. Many people seemed upset at what they considered to be her hostile and irreverent tone.

But the rabbi smiled and said, "That's an excellent question. Let's look at it carefully. Because what you're saying is what a lot of people have felt over the years when they've picked up a prayer book and the words seem to be praising a distant and scary God. Yet for me, saying polite things to an egotistical or angry God is not at all what I experience prayer to be."

The rabbi continued, "If we study together the origin of most prayers, hymns, and blessings, we'll find they were written not out of fear but out of deep, passionate love and gratitude for the miracle of being alive. Imagine how open David's heart must have been when he wrote those passionate psalms, those love poems to God. He was pouring out a spontaneous burst of love and excitement for being alive in God's world. David wasn't begging God, stroking God, or trying to impress God. These psalms and prayers are the intimate words of thanks that you say to someone who really loves you and who deeply understands you."

The rabbi went on, "The first time David or some other poet poured out his or her soul into a prayer it was a pure spontaneous outburst of love and appreciation. But then it gets written down and repeated with a lot less feeling. Then it gets formalized and recited thousands of times with absolutely no emotion, and pretty soon it sounds like the whiny and servile words that you described so perfectly in your question. Pretty soon it's no longer a passionate love poem to a caring God, filled with joy and gratitude for the miracle of being alive. It becomes a boring recitation. Unless you are willing to do something about it."

He suggested, "If you want to get back to the love and the excitement for life that is deep inside most of these prayers, then you have to make them your own. You have to make them come alive for you, not the way you would talk to an abusive parent but the heart-to-heart way you would thank the most wonderful friend and partner."

A Different Way of Looking at Prayer

As I was sitting in that room listening to this discussion of how to pray, it occurred to me that I had always wondered why in Judaism, Christianity, and Islam most of the prayers are so filled with extensive words of praise. I, too, had wondered whether human beings were saying these words out of love or out of fear.

To help you have a more positive experience the next time you are participating in a Sabbath worship service, and to make it more meaningful and inspiring, I want to pass along the exercise this rabbi suggested during that retreat weekend. It's an exercise you can use whether you are agnostic, Buddhist, Christian, Jewish, Muslim, or anything else in the family of spiritual traditions. The exercise is as follows:

• At home or in a congregation where Sabbath prayers are recited, read at least one prayer or psalm as if you are the person who wrote it. Imagine that you are trying to put into words how grateful and appreciative you feel about whatever blessings you have experienced in your lifetime.

• Say the prayer or psalm not to impress God or soothe God, but rather so that *your heart will open* to a feeling of deep gratitude and connection to the Source of goodness. This feeling of gratitude is very different from how we feel most of the other days of the week.

• Let the words of the prayer or psalm open you up to a sense of profound receptivity. According to this rabbi and many other scholars from various spiritual traditions, the purpose of prayer is not to open God's heart (which is already open to us), but to open up our own hearts, which are closed most of the week.

For the rest of that retreat weekend and quite often at the Sabbath services I've attended since that day, I have tried out this exercise and found it to be very useful. Instead of thinking the prayers are shallow compliments to a scary God, I imagine them to be the passionate words of love from someone whose heart at that moment is filled with gratitude for the miracle of being alive. If you approach each Sabbath prayer with that much feeling and openness, you will be surprised at how much more joyful and meaningful your worship services can be.

I have also found that many people who have never felt comfortable in a formal prayer service experience a much deeper sense of spiritual connection when they take at least one prayer or psalm to heart and imagine themselves to be the poet speaking that prayer for the first time in a burst of gratitude.

For example, I once counseled a man named Roger who was in therapy to deal with the painful illness and death of his long-time lover Jean. Raised in a religious family but never very religiously inclined himself, Roger told me he felt a certain obligation to attend Sabbath services and say prayers for Jean's soul, yet he also felt a hesitation because, as he described it, "I've never been very connected to organized religion or prayer. It's always seemed too structured and rigid, without any spontaneity or real feeling."

I explained to Roger the approach to prayer described earlier and I asked him if he would be willing to experiment with it the next few times he attended a Sabbath service to pray for Jean. I asked him to find at least one prayer or psalm that he could feel in his heart and say with a deep sense of meaning.

When Roger came to see me a few weeks later, he told me an interesting story that is similar to what I've heard from other clients as well. He explained:

"I wasn't sure at first when I walked into the regular Sabbath service whether I was going to be able to do what you'd suggested. I've never felt very open or relaxed in a formal religious service, and I've never really found anything in the prayer book that spoke to me in a deeply personal way.

"But after a while of sitting there, I began looking at the prayers differently this time. Maybe they actually were passionate poems of appreciation and gratitude. Maybe they could help me talk to God about how much I appreciated Jean and how much pain I'm in right now.

"Then I came across a prayer I'd never liked before and that always felt somewhat subservient and weak. It's a prayer that says, 'May the words of my mouth and the meditations of my heart be acceptable in Thy sight, O God, my rock and my redeemer.'" (This passage from Psalm 19, verse 15, is found in most Jewish and many Christian Sabbath services.)

Roger continued, "I took a moment, and for the first time in my life I said the words as though they were my own spontaneous poem to God. Thinking of Jean's life and how much beauty and goodness was in that life, I offered up a sincere desire that God might hear and appreciate how grateful I am for my having known Jean and our having spent so many years together.

"Instead of feeling like the prayer was saying in a weak way, 'May my inferior words be somehow acceptable to you, O great God,' I felt for the first time a deep sense of friendship and partnership with God, who probably loved Jean as much or more than I did. When I said to God, 'I hope my words about Jean are acceptable to you, my rock and redeemer,' it was from a place of knowing that God and I are grieving Jean's loss together, and that God is there for me to lean on like a rock and to help me redeem or make sense of this painful loss. I had tears in my eyes as I felt a tremendous closeness with a God who cares, instead of the distant and inaccessible God I had always shied away from."

Step #4: See how much of the Sabbath feeling you can take with you into the week.

There's one more step that can add to the healing and beauty from your Sabbaths. It's the step of carrying some of the spiritual insights and good feelings of the Sabbath into the other six days of the week.

Making the transition from the peaceful Sabbath to the stressful workweek is not an easy thing to do. Many years ago I met an elderly man who as a young child at the turn of the century had lived through Russian pogroms (brutal attacks by Russian Cossack guards on Jewish villages) and was later captured during World War II by the Nazis. He told me, "In Eastern Europe, when the sun would go down and the Sabbath was over, there was such a sense of loss. During the week we were peasants, outcasts, scorned people. But on Shabbat we were God's lovers in paradise. The only thing which made the weeks bearable was the taste of Shabbat that still lingered in our souls and that we knew would be ours again in just a few days."

I think of this man often, especially when I look at the sun setting at the end of a beautiful and relaxing Sabbath. There is something amazing about a day out of regular time, a day for connecting with loved ones and dreaming about a future in which no one is hungry and no one is mistreated.

To carry the peaceful and hopeful feelings of the Sabbath into your own workweek is the ultimate challenge for making the Sabbath a rich part of your weekly rhythms. As the poet Henry Wadsworth Longfellow wrote, "Take the Sabbath with you through the week, and sweeten with it all the other days."

For many people, the relaxed peacefulness of the Sabbath gives them renewed interest in developing a regular prayer or meditation practice during the weekdays. If the thought of having a more centered and spiritual daily life appeals to you, you may want to find a meditation teacher or a prayer group in your particular tradition. For specific books on how to meditate or understand prayer in the Jewish, Christian, Muslim, Buddhist, Hindu, and Native American traditions, please see the Sources section at the back of this book.

Finally, in Judaism there is a specific ritual to help take the beauty of the Sabbath with you into the other six days. At the end of the Sabbath, when the sky is dark enough to see the stars, you light a special braided candle, say a blessing over wine and spices, and recite the Havdalah prayers. (*Havdalah* is a Hebrew word that means to notice the separations or to make distinctions, such as between Shabbat and the six days of the week.)

There is one particular moment in the Havdalah service, which you can do at home or in a group setting, that helps the beauty of the Sabbath flow into the week. First you say a blessing to thank God for the spices of life. Then you shake a small decorative spice box and take in a deep whiff of the fragrance, which might be cloves, cinnamon, or some other spice. As the sweetness of the Sabbath fills your senses one last time, you make a silent vow to carry the vision of Shabbat into the other six days of the week.

Revived and renewed by the spiritual energies of the Sabbath, each person then has the challenge of how to translate the hope for a better world into specific ways of relating to people in our everyday lives. This charge is described by the award-winning novelist Alice Walker, best known for *The Color Purple:* "Anybody can observe the Sabbath, but making it holy surely takes the rest of the week."

That's why many people believe the Fourth Commandment from the Book of Exodus challenges us not only to find a way to unhook each week from the treadmill of our lives but also to connect with a deeper spiritual vision of how we want this world to be in the future. Then, during the weekdays that follow, we get a chance to take small steps toward that vision of a world that is a much healthier and freer place for everyone to live. I hope this chapter has made you curious both about the beauty of a restful Sabbath and also about the possibility of stepping back each week to see how to make our lives and our world more peaceful and more humane.

5

THE FIFTH CHALLENGE

How Do You Honor a Parent When There's Tension Between You?

Sometimes in my psychotherapy practice, two clients show up on the same day with opposite versions of the same problem. For example, a few months ago I had a first session with a woman who was grieving over the loss of her father and felt conflicted about how she had given a lot of time and energy, maybe too much, to her distant and noncommunicative father. During his final months, she had felt drained and frustrated. She wondered out loud, "Why did I think I had to spend every waking hour taking care of my dad and not letting anyone else help out? Was there some other way I could have honored my dad without neglecting my kids, my spouse, my work, and my own needs so much?"

Later that day I had a first session with a man who similarly was grieving over the loss of his father, except this man felt conflicted about the fact he had given too little to his rigid and controlling dad. When his father died, this man felt incomplete and frustrated. He wondered out loud, "Was this the right choice, to keep my distance and protect myself from my father's harsh judgmental opinions? Was there some other way I could have connected with my dad while there was still time?"

The Fifth Commandment says, "Honor thy father and thy mother." But the question of how to honor a parent, especially a parent with whom you have had disagreements or painful interactions, is no simple matter. How to juggle your aging parent's needs with your own needs is a complex problem for most people. How to do right by your parents without neglecting responsibilities that are equally pressing—toward your other family members, work, and your own life—is something that baffles even the most organized, competent individuals.

YOU ARE NOT ALONE

If you sometimes say to yourself, "I just don't know how I'm going to give my parents what they want and at the same time have a life of my own," don't feel guilty. You are in good company trying to sort out one of the most complex challenges of life. You'd be surprised just how many people struggle with a similar problem.

For example, Gordon is a well-liked and dynamic member of the clergy who came to my office for counseling one afternoon. He told me, "All my life I've advised other people to honor their parents like it says in the Bible. But what I've never admitted to anyone else—and it feels like an embarrassing secret—is that I don't have a very good relationship with my own mother. I try to do the best I can to please her and care for her needs as she grows older, but no matter what I do she finds something to complain about, and it never seems to be enough for her. I sometimes wonder if I'll ever be less uptight around my mother or if I'll always come up short regarding the Fifth Commandment."

Many people tell a version of this same story. In the fourteen years since Harold Bloomfield and I wrote *Making Peace with Your Parents,* thousands of women and men have confided to me that they have a strained relationship with either their mother or their father or both. Affluent people as well as those with low incomes, from all races and ethnicities, religious and nonreligious, the most rational individuals, even the most kind and thoughtful—all carry the pain of a difficult relationship with their parents.

When the Fifth Commandment says, "Honor thy father and thy mother," how exactly do you do that when:

- Your parents' expectations of how you should honor them are so out of line that you feel you can't possibly live up to their wishes?

- Your mother or father is a difficult person with whom it is frustrating to talk or hard to get along?
- One (or both) of your parents continually criticizes your appearance, your choice of career, your romantic partner, how you raise your children, how you practice religion, or how often you call or see each other?
- Your parents begin to decline in health and they start to require more from you than you know how to provide? Will you be able to care for your parents well enough to say afterward, "Yes, I honored them as best I could"?

"A CONFUSED MIXTURE OF EMOTIONS"

Honoring your parents is difficult even if you were raised by extremely decent and caring people. The very nature of the parent-child relationship is filled with highly charged emotions. These tensions, which add to the basic challenge of the Fifth Commandment, are not just the product of our progressive modern era. Almost eighteen hundred years ago one of the Talmud's most respected rabbis, Simeon ben Yohai, suggested that the most difficult of all the 613 commandments in traditional Judaism is "Honor thy father and thy mother."

Many Christian scholars agree that honoring your parents is neither easy nor automatic. In his book *The Ten Commandments and Human Rights,* Vanderbilt Divinity School's Professor Walter Harrelson explains, "The relations of parents to children and children to parents is an enormously complex relationship, perhaps the most complex of all human relationships, including that between husband and wife. So much depends on this relation, and in so many ways, that the issues inherent in the Fifth Commandment are particularly sensitive and difficult to sort out and state rightly."

Some experts have pointed out that even the Bible takes into account how hard it is to get along with one's parents. In his 1994 book *Jewish Wisdom,* scholar and writer Rabbi Joseph Telushkin discusses how "the often confused mixture of emotions that children feel for parents perhaps accounts for the peculiar fact that while the Bible legislates love of neighbor (Leviticus 19:18), love of the stranger (Leviticus 19:34), and love of God (Deuteronomy 6:5), it does not do so for parents.

In so vital and intense a relationship, love is too volatile an emotion to be commanded; therefore, the Bible demands a standard of honor and respect that can remain in force even in times of estrangement."

THE BURDEN AND THE OPPORTUNITY

Even the specific word used in the Hebrew text of the Fifth Commandment illustrates the complexity of honoring your parents. If you look at the original scroll of Exodus 20:12, you'll find the first word of the commandment is *cahbeid,* which has a two-sided meaning. On the one hand, *cahbeid* means heaviness, weightiness, difficulty, or burden. On the other hand, *cahbeid* also means to honor and give importance or weight to someone.

So clearly the Bible doesn't pretend that honoring your parents is always easy or light. The two-sided word *cahbeid* can mean honoring your parents is a heavy burden or, on the other hand, it can be an opportunity to give weight or importance, to bring honor and dignity to two people who need your support.

Each of us has some control over which sense of *cahbeid* actually occurs between us and our parents. Whether the process of honoring your parents tends to be an irritating burden or a heartful opportunity *depends on how you handle three crucial factors.* In counseling many people on this issue I have found that there are three steps you can take to feel less weighed down by the challenge of honoring your parents and more gratified by this opportunity to come through for the two people who, along with the eternal breath of life, brought you into this world. These three steps are:

Step #1: Deciding whether or not to forgive
One reason so many people feel weighed down and burdened by the idea of honoring their parents is that they have unresolved resentments toward their mother or father. Even if your own resentments are justified, you still can choose to forgive these hurts in order to allow yourself to open up to the possibility of better feelings toward your parents. In the words of the nine-

teenth-century philosopher Edwin Hubbell Chapin, "Never does the human soul appear so strong and noble as when it forgoes revenge and dares to forgive an injury."

Yet many good people are reluctant to forgive their parents. It is deeply painful to be betrayed, neglected, or belittled by your own mother or father. As an old Yiddish proverb says, "Even a little hurt from one of your kin is worse than a big hurt from a stranger." The hurt can become a primary experience through which you view other people, but even so, it's much easier to forgive almost anyone in the world except your mother and father. Their job was to be sensitive to your needs and feelings, yet their actions or inactions may have caused you tremendous pain.

In addition, many people hold back from forgiving because they incorrectly assume that forgiveness means they have to forget, whitewash, or minimize the painful things that happened to them because of their parents. As you read the following critique of the "forgive and forget" approach, notice whether you, too, have mistakenly believed that to forgive your parents means to erase, deny, or downplay the pain they caused you.

The Problems with "Forgive and Forget"

As far back as the first century, when the scholar Philo said "I forgive and forget," to the current era, when novelist F. Scott Fitzgerald wrote that "forgotten is forgiven," numerous preachers, teachers, and writers have insisted that we have to block out, dismiss, and deny what happened in order to forgive and get on with our lives.

Just a few years ago, I attended a workshop in which a well-known pop psych guru asked all the participants to "close your eyes, take a deep breath, and now completely let go of any resentments you carry in your heart toward your parents. You must forgive and forget whatever they did which you are still holding against them. Wipe it clean from your memory. Now open your eyes and share with us how you feel."

I didn't know whether to laugh or cry at the absurdity of his request. How could he believe he was doing anything except glossing over the genuine pain that so many people feel? Did he really think it was possible to close your eyes and so quickly wipe your memory clean, like a child's Etch-A-Sketch?

"Forgive and forget" is the opposite of what actually takes place in the mind: if you forget the wrongs done to you then you will have no memory left of what you're trying to forgive. Or as the twentieth-century Protestant theologian Paul Tillich explained so clearly, "Forgiveness presupposes remembering."

The nineteenth-century pastor Henry Ward Beecher (whose sister Harriet Beecher Stowe wrote *Uncle Tom's Cabin*) argued that "those who say 'I can forgive but I cannot forget' are only another way of saying 'I will not forgive!' "

"Forgive and forget" sounds kindhearted and simple, but in numerous instances, it is naive and potentially dangerous. For example:

A client named Suzanne, whose father molested her as a child, was told by another counselor that she must "forgive and forget" what her father did to her in order to be a healthy adult. This troubled Suzanne a great deal. As she told me, "It would be foolish to whitewash or forget what he did, especially when as an adult I want my own daughter to know her grandparents but not to be left alone with her grandfather, who is still a perpetrator who has never really apologized or made amends for what he did to me as a child."

After a careful process of soul-searching, Suzanne decided in therapy to begin to look for a way to forgive her father in the light of the fact that he, too, had been abused as a child and because he was in most other ways an excellent father. But I advised Suzanne not to forget what he had done and was capable of doing again. So we designed together a few ground rules that were necessary for Suzanne to develop a healthier relationship with her father. These ground rules included: Suzanne should not let her father be alone with his granddaughter; Suzanne had permission to cut short any phone call or visit in which her father talked to her in a suggestive or manipulative way; and Suzanne had the right not to hug or kiss her father whenever she felt reluctant to do so. With these ground rules, Suzanne could then have a safe and healthy connection with her father. Her forgiveness had to include remembering so that she could protect her daughter and herself now and in the future.

"Forgive and forget" can sometimes be dangerous. Brian's

mother had a drinking problem that often caused her to lash out with cruel and belittling remarks. Brian discovered a principle in therapy: "I can forgive my mother for her addiction to alcohol, but I won't forget what she's capable of doing to hurt my younger sisters and me when she's had one too many. Now we stand up to her as a family and we firmly but lovingly tell her when she's crossed the line. It's much healthier now that we're no longer pretending to forget or hide from the problem that we all know is there. I can enjoy my family get-togethers much more now that we're being honest and speaking up for ourselves."

An old Japanese proverb says, "Forgiving the unrepentant is like drawing pictures on water." The forgiveness is quickly dissipated by the continued mistreatment from the other person. A more realistic and sensible kind of forgiveness besides "forgive and forget" seems to be necessary with certain types of people.

What You Can Do When You're Ready to Start the Healing Process

If blocking out or forgetting is *not* the way to heal from past hurts with your parents, what exactly is forgiveness, and how do you do it more sensibly?

If you look in the dictionary under "forgive," you will see three actions of the heart that can change how you relate to another person and how you heal the hurt you've carried inside. These three definitions are: to pardon or release from punishment for a fault or offense; to give up anger, resentment, or the need for revenge; and to show mercy or compassion. These definitions all acknowledge an offender and an offense, but the process of forgiveness allows you to turn your heart toward healing, release, and compassion instead of using your energy for revenge or punishment. In other words, forgiveness allows you to build something positive in the present while still making sure not to repeat what happened in the past.

The two-part approach to forgiveness that follows can help you heal your bitter thoughts about your parents, and it can assist you in finding a deeper soul connection to them. Even if the wrongs they committed are terrible, you can still reach a healthy sense of forgiveness in which your heart is open again to whatever good they did. They have been an important part of your life. At the same time, this approach will also protect you from further hurt or harm.

THE FORGIVENESS PROCESS

In the first part, sit down and write a letter (or talk into a tape recorder) and say exactly what you resent or dislike about the way your parent treated you. Describe exactly what occurred from your point of view, and don't be shy about detailing precisely how you felt when your parent did something (or failed to do something) that left a painful scar on your psyche. Take your time, be honest, and most of all recognize that you are doing this not to get back at your parents but to let go of the bitterness you've been keeping inside for too long. Be gentle with yourself, and make sure you give yourself time to relax and recover after doing this first part of the exercise.

Don't send the letter or tape to your parents. Read it privately to a friend, counselor, minister, priest, or rabbi who can listen supportively to your pain. Then tear it up and throw it away where it won't be found by anyone.

Some therapists, including Dr. Susan Forward, the author of the 1989 best-seller *Toxic Parents,* would advise you to confront your parents in person or to send this letter or tape. Dr. Forward argues in her book, "Confrontation works, it begins to change the balance of power between you and your parents, and what you don't hand back you pass on or take out on your partner or your children."

While for some people Dr. Forward's approach can be successful, it can also worsen the conflicts and pain for many, many families. That's why I recommend you first heal internally and discuss the letter or tape with a supportive friend or counselor. *Don't* turn this healing process into renewed warfare or into a foolhardy attempt to get your most difficult parent to change their nature and say, "Oh yes, dear, you're absolutely right. I apologize." In too many families, the adult child dumps a load of resentment on the parents and then feels worse when the parents still don't understand the pain they caused and respond defensively or angrily.

Another reason not to send or show the letter or tape to your parent is that it frees you to pour out the absolute uncensored truth. Most people get all bottled up second-guessing their feelings and editing their own words when they think they might become known. Writing or speaking the truth about your parents solely for your own internal healing and growth gives you the power and freedom to be 100 percent truthful. Tremendous release and healing can result from this first part of the process.

Discovering the Person You Never Knew

For the second part of the healing process of forgiveness, look at an old photograph of your parent from before you were born (or imagine your parent as a young child or teenager if you are unable to locate an old photo). You might want to use a photo of your parent as a young child, or an old school or army photo, or any old family photo you have in a box or can borrow from an aunt, uncle, or family friend.

With this image of your parent as a young person in your mind, start a conversation with the young soul of your mother or father. Talk to the vulnerable, curious, loving person they were long before you were born. Ask this gentle soul what her hopes and fears are. Ask this fragile human being what it was like growing up when he did, with the parents (your grandparents) he had, and with the influences and pressures that made your parent into the adult you saw years later when you entered the world. If you don't have much information about your parents' early years, you may need to ask aunts, uncles, friends, or other relatives for their best sense of what made your mom or dad act in certain ways.

As you talk to the photo or imagined likeness of your parent as a young child, begin to sense a warm heart connection to this person's innermost being and begin to appreciate this tender soul's unique life path. Even if you have spent years in conflict with your parents' adult personalities and habits, you can still go deeper to the soul level and see their vulnerable essence, the wounded spirit that possibly got covered up all these years with layers of defenses and traits you were unable to change. Even if you don't consider yourself a spiritual person, see if you can find your way to a deeper sense of relating to your parent not as a powerful adult but as a fragile and lovable child.

"Everyone Tells Me I Need to Forgive My Dad, but I Don't Know How"

The two-part process of forgiveness has helped many people transform their internal feelings and improve their relationships with even the most difficult father or mother. Caroline, a divorced mother in her forties with two sons, came to see me for therapy because she had come to a realization:

"I have spent my whole life intimidated by my father and I'm noticing how much it's held me back in my relationships with men, in my career, and in raising two teenage sons. My father's booming voice and condescending remarks usually make me cringe. Now that I'm a grown woman I'm tired of cringing."

As part of Caroline's therapy, we worked on the bitterness and fear she carried inside as a result of her long-standing conflicts with her father. These painful emotions had caused Caroline to become severely depressed on three occasions in her life; she also tended to become anxious and tongue-tied whenever an intimidating person (a demanding boss, an irate customer, an opinionated boyfriend, or her two stubborn sons) subconsciously reminded her of her father.

When I mentioned the possibility of forgiveness as a step in her own healing, Caroline was hesitant. She explained, "Everyone keeps telling me I need to forgive my dad, but I don't know how I'm going to do it. He's so impossible. I'm afraid if I let go of my anger at him I'll just become weaker and more vulnerable to his bullying."

Like many good people who are reluctant to forgive, Caroline had a legitimate concern. She didn't want to become even more susceptible to her father's intimidation, and so she worried that letting go of her anger might be a step in the wrong direction.

Over a period of weeks, however, Caroline tried out the steps listed above and discovered that these forgiveness techniques are a positive way of reclaiming strength. Releasing the fear and resentment you've stored inside can help you break free of years of feeling victimized by your parents and give you the possibility of a healthier relationship with your mother and father.

Caroline wrote a profoundly truthful letter to her father, which she read out loud to one of her closest friends and to me. It described the details of her oftentimes frightening childhood and several recent incidents in which her father used his booming voice and stubborn will to diminish Caroline's independence and confidence. She was shaking and crying as she read the letter to me, but over the next few weeks she became stronger and better able to deal with angry or intimidating men in her life.

Caroline borrowed an old photograph of her father as a child from her dad's sister and had a conversation with it. "I looked at this old black-and-white photo of my dad's face when he was just a little ten-year-old. It was during the Great Depression, and I think that was the year his own father died and my dad had to become a responsible adult long before he was ready."

Caroline told me, "It felt so liberating to be able to see the child in him and connect with my dad in his pure essence as a scared little boy-man. I realized that his booming voice and his intimidating style are just a mask to cover up the terrified and anxious little ten-year-old he still is in his heart. Once I saw this, I could forgive this man for being so difficult at times, and I could love him again. It felt so good to be at peace with my father and to be open to getting to know him as a vulnerable human being."

WHAT IF YOU'RE STILL UNABLE TO FORGIVE?

Some people are reluctant to do exercises like those described above, yet forgiveness can still come from other methods. As one alternative, if you want to be inspired to forgive your mother or father for even the worst transgressions against you, I recommend you read an intriguing novel written in 1987 by Michael Dorris called *A Yellow Raft in Blue Water*.

In the first section of the book, the reader is immersed in fifteen-year-old Rayona's point of view as she describes her unloving and troubled mother, Christine. Christine abandoned and mistreated Rayona, so, reading from Rayona's viewpoint, it's hard to feel any compassion or forgiveness toward Christine.

Until, that is, we enter the second section of the book, Christine's story, and we are suddenly and completely immersed in Christine's point of view as she describes her painful life. We appreciate the depth of what she means when she says, "You had to have lived my life to understand it."

Finally, in the third section of the book we get the story from the point of view of Aunt Ida, a woman who seemed negligent and unloving toward Rayona and Christine when they needed her desperately. But when we discover Aunt Ida's point of view in the final section of the book, her loneliness and her reasons for being so remote and cold make her a fascinating character as well.

If someone were to write a three-part novel that included your life entirely from your point of view, your parents' lives from their point of view, and finally their parents' stories as well, what would you learn about the hurts and shortcomings each of you struggled with? Instead of seeing your relationship with your parents in terms of "good guys" and "bad guys," you would begin to see that each of us has a twisting and complex path that deserves compassion. We all have wounds we were unable to heal and as a result we did or said some hurtful things to people we love. This is *not* to excuse or whitewash the harmful things that your parents may have done to you, but rather to open up the possibility of a new way of seeing the many layers of truth regarding your parents. As Gandhi suggested, "The challenge is to hate the sin but love the sinner."

Step #2: *Learning to create healthy and respectful limits*
As shown in Step 1, forgiveness can be extremely useful for release and recovery from past hurts, but what do you do about current and future tensions with your parents? If you simply go back to "business as usual" with your mother and father, you will probably end up feeling burdened or resentful again. On the other hand, if you would like to honor your parents in a healthy way, you can set healthy, respectful limits or boundaries for more satisfying interactions. Boundaries and limits refer to how close you let people get to you emotionally and how well you protect yourself when someone is too close or too invasive.

Limits and boundaries have a tremendous amount to do with whether you will feel constantly at war with your parents or whether you will find the strength and clarity to connect with them and come through for them as they grow older. Think for a moment of the kinds of limits or boundaries you've set in the past. See which of the following sound like you and your parents. Do you have:

- Boundaries that are too weak? Most adults never discover an effective way to say no to their parents or to set healthy limits. For example, if one or both of your parents calls on the phone five times a day to tell you how to run your life, it might be a good idea to set a limit on their calls. You may feel you're unable to set a limit of one call a day or three calls a week with this parent, however, because he or she tends to sulk, complain, or explode in an angry tirade whenever you have tried to do so. So you may have given in to having a weak boundary.

- Boundaries that are too rigid and inflexible? Many people resort to the opposite extreme. They put up so many psychological layers of protection against their parents, and quite often toward other people as well, that they are locked into isolation or a fear of intimacy with almost everyone who tries to get close to them. If this sounds like you or someone you know, don't be harsh in your judgment—we all have to put up walls in our lives to protect ourselves. If the boundary between you and your parents is so rigid and inflexible that you can't let in any love from them or connect with them in any way whatsoever, then you need to reexamine and reset your restrictions so that you can let your parents get near your heart.

- Boundaries that are strong enough and flexible enough? The ideal solution is to set limits that protect you from getting walked over by your mother and father yet are flexible enough so that you can enjoy your parents' good qualities, honor them, and connect with them to whatever extent feels right for your particular family situation. This means learning how to set a strong limit that ensures your parent is *not* going to continue to call you five times a day to tell you how to run your life but at the same time allows you and your parent to connect lovingly, establish some enjoyable ways of being together, and come through for each other in times of need.

THE THREE BEST COMEBACK LINES

You might be wondering how exactly you are going to do this "healthy boundary" stuff, especially if your parent is stubborn or tends to complain or lash out in anger whenever you attempt to say no or set a limit. If that happens, you will have at least these "three best comeback lines" for setting a healthy and respectful limit. Decide which of the following three approaches feels most useful and effective for your parent:

The first comeback line is only for those who feel comfortable being assertive and have a parent strong enough to deal with a firm limit. It is respectful but draws a firm boundary. When your parent attacks you verbally or belittles you, you can say:

> "Stop! I don't appreciate being talked to this way. Let's start again."

This comeback line doesn't blame, explain, or argue. It doesn't call names or use provocative trigger words such as "You *never* listen" or "You *always* criticize" to escalate the conflict. You simply say what your limit is and that you want to start again in a different manner.

In some families, this line does the job beautifully. Your parent realizes that you are no longer a pushover and that he or she has pushed too far. In addition, the invitation at the end—"Let's start again"—says you still respect and care about him or her and you are ready to try something more positive.

In many families, however, this comeback line would be a major "scandal," and it would take weeks or months for your parent to stop acting hurt and for you to stop feeling guilty for setting such a clear and firm limit. If that sounds like what would happen in your situation, then consider a less rough but equally clear way of telling a parent who is pushing you too hard, insulting you, or hurting someone you love:

> "Mom (or Dad), I know you don't want to hurt me, but when you say———, it hurts. So let's start again."

This comeback line is a little gentler and warmer. Instead of saying, "Stop," it starts with a compassionate reminder that tells your parent you realize he or she is good at heart and doesn't mean to be hurtful or difficult. Then it points out what was hurtful and ends with the warm invitation "Let's start again." As with the other comeback lines, all name-calling and trigger words are avoided so that the conflict doesn't escalate.

As one client told me, "Saying to my mom 'I know you don't want to hurt me' seems to calm her and reassures her I'm respecting her good intentions. That's helped us to stop arguing as much, and it's made me feel good about being able to do *something* to get her to stop saying the hurtful things that used to drive me crazy."

In some families, even this gentler comeback line is too rough. If the simple words "it hurts" would start a major defensive argument, then this third comeback line is the gentlest and most calming. If your parent starts to get on your nerves or refuses to consider your needs or feelings, then simply say:

"Mom (or Dad), I care about you and I want to do what works for both of us. So let's talk about this calmly and come up with something we both feel good about."

Notice there are several reassuring elements to this way of setting a respectful boundary. First, you are reminding your mom or dad that you care about him or her. That usually leads to a much better conversation than if you start out with typical child-to-parent lines like "You make me want to scream" or "You don't understand me at all." Second, you are taking on the role of a gentle but firm facilitator, traffic director, or talk-show host who can reassure your parent that both of you will have a turn to speak and both of your viewpoints will be taken seriously as you work together toward a solution you both feel good about.

Even the most agitated or demanding parent will feel somewhat calmed by this kind of respectful but firm approach. You are modeling for your parent a type of healthy cooperation and mutual respect that may have been missing from your relationship with each other for most of your life.

To illustrate how the third comeback line is effective most of the time with even an extremely difficult parent, consider what happened for Caroline, the woman mentioned earlier whose intimidating father used to make her cringe. In Caroline's words:

My father called me early on a Sunday morning. I think it was close to 7:30 and I'd been out late the night before. First he starts in on what a "lazy" person I am, which is far from the truth. Then he insists I need to make a command appearance at a dinner he's throwing that night for some out-of-town relatives. I knew I couldn't go because my youngest son needed me to help him study for an important test that was coming up the next day.

When I mentioned that to my dad, he blew up and started saying what a selfish daughter I am and how I *never* do anything for anyone but myself, which is also far from the truth. I wanted to tell him where he could stick it, but I kept my cool because we'd been making such good progress with each other these last few months.

So I took a deep breath in and out. And in my most calm and unflappable tone of voice I said, "Dad, I care about you and I want to do what works for both of us. So let's talk about this calmly and come up with something we both feel good about. There's got to be some way I can still help my son study for his test and also let the out-of-town guests know they're important, too."

At first my dad got a bit defensive and said, "Calmly? I can talk about this calmly. You're the one who gets all worked up all the time."

Well, I didn't bite the bait on that one. I simply repeated the comeback line with a slight variation, saying, "Dad, I care about you and I know we can come up with something we both feel good about."

And for the next ten minutes we did have a decent, adult-to-adult conversation, at the end of which we came up with an excellent compromise. I was going to stay here for my son, but at exactly eight that night I was going to call my dad's place and talk for a few minutes with the out-of-town guests. My dad would be able to feel proud that his daughter has some manners and I'd be able to honor his needs without neglecting my son and my own needs.

But most of all, it felt great to see myself in the role of the calming, reassuring facilitator who can get my dad to work cooperatively with me. I finally found the words that helped me feel like an adult and not like a rebellious child.

Despite the success that Caroline and many other clients have had in using these firm but respectful comeback lines, they may not work in every situation. You may need to keep refining and trying out different approaches that give you a chance to feel calm and in control no matter how agitated or demanding your parent becomes. When you finally discover you can have an adult-to-adult, equal-to-equal conversation with your most difficult parent, it will feel like a tremendous breakthrough in your own healing.

Step #3: Uncovering the best ways to help your parents as they grow older or decline in health

One of the major reasons for the Fifth Commandment, according to most commentators on the Bible, is that the ultimate test of honoring your father and mother comes when they feel isolated, become ill, or rely increasingly on you for financial, emotional, or caregiving support.

Your first reaction to your parents leaning on you, or needing you more than before, might be a sense of loss or confusion. You might even feel some anger that suddenly your parents are expecting things from you that you're not sure you know how to give.

One therapy client told me, "When my mom died and my dad began leaning on me for support, it was awkward at first. How did we suddenly change from my being the child he wanted to protect to him being almost childlike in his own neediness?"

In the seventeenth century a Torah scholar named Gur Aryeh ha-Levi suggested, "It is natural for old people to be despised by the general population when they can no longer function as they once did. The commandment 'Honor your father and your mother' was given specifically for this situation."

Even if you've done a great deal of inner work to forgive your parents and you've learned to set respectful boundaries with them, this next phase of parent-child connection will still present new challenges for you to learn about and handle.

The Key Factors for Being a
Healthy and Effective Caregiver

If you want to respond successfully to your parents' increasing reliance on you without becoming overwhelmed, impatient, or burned out by the challenge, how exactly will you do this? Over the past twenty years an enormous amount of excellent scientific research has been done to identify the stress factors and best coping strategies for taking care of aging or ailing parents.

Working from these research studies and from what I've observed while counseling families and being a caregiver several times in my own life, I've found three key factors that can help you do a better job for an ailing parent while at the same time taking good care of your other responsibilities and your own health.

See which of the following you already know how to do well with your parents and which you will need to develop in order to rise to the challenge that sooner or later most adults will face:

Key #1: Overcoming the fear of asking for help and making sure you get as much information and guidance as your parent's situation requires

Whenever a parent becomes ill or faces emotional or financial problems related to aging, you will need to become educated quickly about how to help your parents respond to these perplexing issues. Discovering where to get expert advice and assistance is crucial.

I recommend calling at least one information source from each of the following categories:

- Experts on aging issues and resources. If you call (800) 555-1212 you can get the phone number for your state's Area Agency on Aging and for the American Association of Retired Persons. Both have a wealth of free and low-cost information on any issue affecting aging parents.
- Local agencies who want to assist adult children do a better job of caring for their parents. If you call your local chapter of Jewish Family Service, Catholic Social Services, or other family service agencies, you will find someone who is trained to answer almost any question you might have or who can refer you to someone who can. Or you can call the national office of the Children of Aging Parents (call [215] 555-1212 for their current number) and find out if there is a local chapter of their helpful organization near you.
- National organizations and information clearinghouses for whatever illness your parent is facing. You can receive an extremely useful set of pamphlets and referrals if you call (800) 555-1212 and ask for the hot-line number of the organization that helps with your parent's situation (i.e., the Alzheimer's As-

sociation, the American Cancer Society, the American Heart Association, the Better Hearing Institute, the National Alliance for the Mentally Ill, and so on).

Connecting with expert advice and assistance is an essential step that many children of aging parents *fail to do* for three common reasons:

1. They have been told by their families it's wrong to let outsiders know about any problems in the family.
2. They mistakenly believe that social workers and health agencies are only for people who have no money.
3. They mistakenly believe that being a good son or daughter requires you to do 100 percent of the caregiving and not to ask anyone for help or advice.

Refusing to ask for help because of these or other faulty beliefs can not only cause you to feel burned out and overwhelmed but can also be extremely harmful to the level of care and support your parent receives. When I was researching my 1990 book *When a Loved One Is Ill: How to Take Better Care of Your Loved One, Your Family AND Yourself,* I interviewed dozens of experts in the field and asked them, "What is the one mistake most adult children make when a parent is ill?" Nearly every expert gave the same response: the biggest mistake you can make is to try to do it all by yourself and to refuse to get the help and expert guidance that is so readily available in our society.

Key #2: *Instead of seeing yourself as victimized by your parent's increasing needs, begin viewing yourself as a "caregiving manager" who's making sure you delegate most of the tasks to someone you trust*

Whether you live near or far from your parents, you can help manage their daily care by asking one or more social-service agencies to help you find the right resources and people for many different caregiving tasks. For example, if you ask around you can probably arrange for: low-cost meal delivery, transportation, medical second opinions, home health care, daily check-in phone calls or visits from a volunteer, adult day-care facilities for a parent with Alzheimer's or dementia, nursing-home monitoring for quality of care, and many other valuable services that will allow you to juggle the other responsibilities in your life.

Even though "managing" your parent's care involves finding good people and delegating certain tasks to them, you can still reserve for yourself the things you want to do personally for your parent in your own style. For instance, do you want to cook a special meal at least once a week for your ailing parent? Do you want to make sure you are the one to drive him or her to a specific appointment in which key test results or important options will be discussed? Do you want to set aside time for quality moments of connection with your parent when there is the greatest likelihood of closeness? Do you want to help ar-range for your ailing parent to have heartful connections with old friends, grandchildren, and others who can boost his or her spirits?

Sometimes the most loving way to honor your parent during a debilitating illness is to recognize your own limits and make sure you find the best home health care, quality nursing facility, or hospice care that can help your parent live with dignity and as little pain as possible. Unfortunately, many people feel so guilty about letting a parent be cared for by someone else that they fail to seek out the best affordable option.

Yet even the most traditional religious commentators on the Fifth Commandment urge you to know your own limits and be willing to seek out the best affordable assistance for what you can't do by yourself. More than eight hundred years ago the great scholar Moses Maimonides wrote, "If the condition of the parent has grown worse and the child is no longer able to endure the strain, the child may leave his father or mother and delegate others to give the parent proper care."

Making these kinds of decisions is never easy. But I urge you to take into account what is best for all the people involved: your parent, your other family members, and yourself. If you talk these decisions over with a geriatric social worker, with your rabbi, priest, or minister, and with your parent if at all possible, I trust you will make a good enough decision. And when it comes to caregiving dilemmas like these, we often have to settle for "good enough" or "the best that was affordable," which at times feels less than what we ideally wish we could offer our parents.

Key #3: *Overcoming your guilt feelings and finding a way to stay healthy yourself so you can come through for your parent*

Too many adult children with ailing parents feel guilty for thinking about their own health and well-being when a parent is in worse shape. But I assure you it's not selfish to take time to replenish your energy; in fact, it's essential that you take good care of yourself in order to recharge your batteries and regain the patience, clarity of mind, and calmness it will take to do a good job caring for your ailing parent and managing her or his health care.

There's an extremely useful piece of wisdom that most everyone has heard. If you've flown on a commercial jetliner and listened to the flight attendant's standard safety speech, you may not have realized how useful this instruction can be when applied to the challenge of caring for an ailing parent. You probably recall that when you're about to take off, the flight attendant says, "In the event of an emergency, put the oxygen mask over your own face before helping the person next to you."

That would never be your first reaction. In an emergency it's natural to rush in and help an ailing child, parent, or friend. But if you don't put the oxygen mask over your face first, you will quickly burn out and you won't be able to breathe, make important decisions, or stay healthy and calm enough to come through for the person who desperately needs you.

Please be clear that I'm *not* saying to ignore your ailing parent or to run away from the challenge, but I am saying that instead of feeling guilty for taking good care of yourself, be aware that when you set aside a few moments each day to meditate, pray, exercise, or do things you enjoy, you can then offer your parent more healing energy. The next time you feel that twinge of guilt for thinking about your own needs, make sure you remember the wisdom of the flight attendant: "Slow down, breathe in some oxygen, and stay healthy and mindful so you can make good decisions and be gentle with your mom or dad who needs you."

"A CHANCE TO BE CLOSE"

The steps described in this chapter can change your relationship with your most challenging parent from a burden to an opportunity for closeness and heartful connection.

You might remember that at the beginning of this chapter I introduced Gordon, a well-liked and dynamic member of the clergy, and his widowed mother, who was constantly telling him he wasn't doing enough for her. An only child ever since his older brother was killed in Vietnam, Gordon knew that the time was rapidly approaching when taking greater responsibility for his elderly mother would fall on his shoulders. He told me during one of his first therapy sessions, "I worry that I won't know how to be there for my mom. We've never gotten along that well when she was relatively healthy. I wonder how stressful it will be if she becomes seriously ill."

After a few months in therapy, however, Gordon was feeling hopeful. His counseling was going well, and he had successfully used the forgiveness and boundary-drawing steps to gain a new perspective on how to deal effectively with his demanding mother. He described the situation to me on the day he stopped therapy:

"Mom is still negative and critical every so often, but now that I've been able to work through most of my resentments and set better limits with her, it's a lot easier to dodge her negativity and enjoy the warm and playful side of her, too. Despite her occasional barbed remarks, we've had more closeness and good times these past few months than we've had in years."

I didn't hear from Gordon for almost a year, but then I received a call from him and he sounded quite upset. Gordon's mother had suffered a severe stroke, and suddenly the challenge of honoring her had changed so that Gordon was now in charge of her daily care.

When Gordon came in again for counseling we discussed the three key steps listed above. Like most people, Gordon was reluctant at first to ask any social-service agencies for help or to admit his own limitations. Gordon said, "It feels like I'm shirking my responsibilities if I start asking other people to come in and take care of my mom. After all, she is my own flesh and blood, so no one else can be there for her like I can."

After several weeks, however, Gordon was beginning to burn out and become short-tempered with his mother. He explained, "I try to get her to do her rehabilitation exercises and eat the right foods, and all she does is resist me. Sometimes I feel like shaking her and saying, 'Mom, don't you want to get better? Why are you fighting me!' "

This happens quite often when any of us tries to do it all for an ailing parent. Burnout, impatience, and a battle for control are bound to occur.

During his next session, Gordon began to explore the ways he could hold on to certain caregiving tasks he wanted to do himself, like cooking special dinners for his mom and taking her out in her wheelchair for relaxing walks and talks on the weekend. But he also knew he was ready to start delegating some of the exhausting tasks he couldn't do himself without burning out.

Over the next few weeks, Gordon brainstormed with his mother's doctors, a local social-services agency, and a very helpful hot-line counselor at the American Heart Association to come up with creative strategies for taking better care of his mother. By asking around, they were able to arrange for a daily program of low-cost home health care, meal deliveries, transportation to doctors' appointments, an excellent rehabilitation program, and some enjoyable social activities for his mom.

Instead of remaining overwhelmed and isolated, Gordon discovered that he could do a lot for his mother. "With so many experienced people helping out with advice, resources, and programs that I didn't know about before," he said, "I've been able to come through for my mom and make her life a little easier and more hopeful. There are still days when she has a setback and we both feel discouraged. And she still criticizes me at times, but I know in my heart I've been able to honor her far better than I ever imagined."

Gordon also told me later, "One unexpected outcome of my mother's stroke and the added responsibilities of managing her care is that it's given us some chances to relax and be close to one another like never before. Last week I bought an audiotape of one of her favorite musicals, *The King and I,* and we sat and listened to it together. It was like a mystical connection, sitting there in her room with light trickling in from the sun going down outside her window and the music relaxing her and bringing a smile to her face. All the struggles and pain in our relationship melted away for a moment and I truly felt a sense of oneness with her. I'll never forget it."

Honoring your mother and father isn't supposed to be easy, but you *can* find a way to heal internally, set better limits, and honor even the most difficult parent. No matter how strained your relationship with your parents might be, there is always the possibility of some improvement and some moments of closeness that you will cherish the rest of your life.

6

THE SIXTH CHALLENGE

What You Can Do to Prevent the Crushing of a Person's Spirit

The Sixth Commandment from the Book of Exodus says, "You shall not murder," and for many centuries it has helped remind people that even though we are capable of destructive rages we can also respond rationally to any insult or issue or action against us. The Sixth Challenge, "Don't let your own anger or your despair cause you to shatter a human life," also applies to suicide. It is viewed by many scholars as one of the greatest spiritual contributions to civilization. According to a respected Christian commentary on the Scriptures, entitled *The Interpreter's Bible,* "If one were to appraise the success of the Ten Commandments, perhaps the Sixth Commandment has been the most successful of all. It has reminded us that a person's life is one's most precious earthly possession and one's right to enjoy life must be protected from idle irresponsibility which would deprive a person of it for 'thirty pieces of silver.' The respect for human life has definitely grown because of the Sixth Commandment. It is harder to pass off murder under a respectable name than any other of the forbidden acts of the Ten Commandments."

Despite this clear warning not to destroy a life, many people over the years have tried to find a way around it. Yet even when someone claims there is an overriding religious, political, or psychological reason to murder someone, most if not all scholars of the Ten Commandments point out that this person is wrong. For example, when Yigal Amir, the confessed assassin of

Israeli prime minister Yitzhak Rabin, insisted he had found a higher religious justification for killing his nation's leader, nearly every rabbi and religious scholar in the world said Amir was terribly incorrect and that Amir's arrogance constituted a clear example of why we need to stay humble and pay attention to the Sixth Commandment, the injunction against murder.

As the second-century teacher and interpreter Rabbi Yishmael pointed out, "If you believe the First Commandment that there is a God who is revealed in creation and in the human spirit, then the Sixth Commandment goes right along with it—don't destroy the Divine spirit that is in every human being."

THE DEEPER MEANING OF THE WORDS

In addition, the Sixth Commandment can be interpreted as calling on us to do all that we can to prevent murder or suicide from occurring. The Hebrew phrase found in Exodus 20:13 has a number of deeper meanings, too. According to one of the most definitive guides to biblical Hebrew, *The Hebrew and English Lexicon of the Old Testament,* by Brown, Driver, and Briggs, the warning *"Lo tirtza-akh"* has as its root the word *rahtz-akh,* which can be translated as:

1. Don't murder or slay another person or yourself.
2. Don't break, bruise, or crush, which can mean not to break the will of someone or crush his or her spirit. This would apply especially to a child, a spouse, a person who is having financial problems, or a person who can't defend himself or herself.
3. Don't batter or shatter, which can mean not to assault someone physically or verbally and not to humiliate someone.

The Talmud contains several warnings that humiliating someone or using sneering words is the equivalent of murder. In fact, in Hebrew the word for shaming someone, *mahlbeen,* literally means to "make white" or cause the blood to leave someone's face because the person is disgraced. That's why in the Talmud it says, "The person who makes someone else ashamed in the presence of others is as if this person has shed blood," and why in traditional Judaism causing someone shame is considered tantamount to murder.

APPLYING THESE PRINCIPLES TO YOUR DAILY LIFE

When we try to observe these more subtle meanings of the Sixth Commandment, not to shatter, batter, or bruise the spirit of people with whom we deal every day, it becomes far more of a daily challenge. Even if you could never imagine yourself murdering someone else or taking your own life, you probably *can* imagine being in a situation in which you are tempted to berate, emotionally crush, or say something disrespectful to someone who's gotten on your nerves. You may have had moments when you accidentally or inadvertently treated someone badly and it wounded his or her spirit for quite a while. Or you may have found that your own harsh self-criticism or sense of perfectionism has deadened your own spirit at times.

As Rabbi Harold Schulweis explains, "While the Sixth Commandment, 'You shall not murder,' refers to the killing of another, on a deeper level it means you are not to murder yourself. How does one murder oneself? There are ways we choose death, die a thousand deaths, eat at ourselves through the tortures of self-recrimination and guilt."

I've called this Sixth Challenge "Prevent the crushing of a person's spirit," because I've found it addresses the core issue raised by the Sixth Commandment—how to make sure we don't shatter the Divine essence that is within each human being, including ourselves. When you think of the Sixth Commandment "*Lo tirtza-akh*" as "Do not let yourself harm or injure someone's spirit," you have the opportunity to start treating other people and yourself much better. It puts us on notice that we live together as one human family and that we need to watch out for one another. It gives us motivation to look for ways to prevent the taking of human life and to halt the bruising, crushing, and battering that occurs in a large number of families, work settings, and social situations.

If you look around and ask yourself, "Is there some way I

can do something about the harshness of life or to protect human spirits that are at risk of being harmed?" you might find that the Sixth Commandment sparks useful ideas for your daily life. From this perspective of prevention and healing, you can take three specific steps to reduce the likelihood of harm or cruelty happening to someone in your corner of the world.

While I cannot guarantee that the majority of killings and cruelties will be stopped by these suggestions, I can promise you that if you *save or improve even one life* it will be worth it. As it says in one of the books of the Talmud, "The person who saves even one life saves an entire world."

Action Step #1: Find a way to resolve and heal the painful hurts you might be carrying inside from your past that can have lingering side effects

Regarding the first step: There are many hurtful experiences in life that can crush or wound a person's spirit unless he or she finds a way to resolve the trauma and its lingering feelings. These include the mistreatment one received as a child; witnessing one's parents' physical or emotional abuse of each other; cruel teasing from classmates or peers; a physically violent lover or spouse; painful verbal abuse from parents, siblings, lovers, or bosses; as well as other traumas such as sexual violence, muggings, and other types of violent crime.

You would be surprised to find out just how many people carry one or more of these wounds deep inside. While they outwardly appear to have these traumas resolved, in fact they may feel quite close to the edge emotionally because of the painful things they have experienced but never fully processed. Without intending to, a person who has been on the receiving end of emotional or physical violence can inadvertently be pushed by later circumstances to do hurtful or self-destructive things he or she deeply regrets but feels unable to control. Years or even decades after the upsetting incidents, the painful emotions inside of us still look for a way to be processed and released.

According to numerous psychological research studies, when a painful trauma from the past is not adequately processed in your psyche, it can lead to one or more of the following:

- An ongoing problem with food, drugs, or alcohol that serves the purpose of numbing the lingering pain you carry inside.
- A sense of holding back or being unable to relax in certain situations that remind you of the painful incident from the past.
- A deadening of your spirit, such that you sometimes can't feel joy, experience intimacy, or cry appropriate tears because of this psychological numbing inside you.
- Skin problems, stomach irritations, and other stress-related symptoms that may be due to the traumatic incidents from your past.
- A tendency to want to punish or put up a wall toward your children, your romantic partner, or your co-workers if they push you or act disrespectfully toward you in a manner that retriggers your hidden pain.

If you want to make sure not to crush someone's spirit, including your own, an important first step is to find help in resolving the painful memories that are still stirring inside your psyche. Even if you have promised yourself, "I will never do to anyone else what was done to me," research suggests there continues to be a moderate to high likelihood that you might have a short fuse, a lingering sense of agitation, or a tendency to be harsh on yourself or on people you love because of the traumatic incidents from your past. Even if you have no intention of taking your pain out on your children, your spouse, or your friends, your unresolved hurts may slip out and cause you to do things that are harmful to others or to your own well-being.

For example, Trina is a thirty-six-year-old divorced mother with two strong-willed children—an eight-year-old boy and a three-year-old girl. When Trina first came for counseling, she told me, "I need help to make sure I don't treat my kids the way I was treated by my parents. As a child I was only hit occasionally by my father, but I have a mother who still to this day can say the most invalidating and cruel things. I swore I'd never hit my kids or talk to them that way, but there are times when I feel this urge welling up inside me to smack the living daylights out of these two stubborn kids."

Like many good parents, Trina felt caught in a dilemma. If she was too lenient and unwilling to set up clear discipline and strong limits for her children, she would fail them as a parent. On the other hand, if she resorted to the same types of harsh discipline that had nearly crushed her own spirit as a child, she knew she would also fail them.

Over the next few months, Trina took several steps that helped her begin to act comfortably and responsibly with her children. She began by going to a few meetings of a group called Parents Anonymous, where she spoke with a wide variety of parents who were struggling with similar issues of not wanting to mistreat their strong-willed or difficult children. Then she took a parenting class at a nearby adult-education center, in which she learned specific ways to set limits lovingly and firmly without crushing a child's natural curiosity and willfulness. Meanwhile, in her individual counseling sessions, Trina explored the fears and sadness she had stored inside for many years as a result of growing up in an emotionally volatile family.

On her last day of counseling, Trina told me, "For years I had been trying to pretend I had put all that stuff from the past behind me. But when I saw myself getting close to losing it with my kids, I knew those issues were still festering inside me. Right now I feel a lot more in control, and I have things I can do to make sure my kids don't push me over the edge, into doing anything I'll later regret. My children are still a handful, but I feel a lot more alive and in charge now that I've taken these classes and worked on certain painful feelings from long ago. I guess I have to thank my kids for giving me a reason to resolve so many things that I was trying to keep hidden inside."

Whether you need to heal your spirit because of earlier experiences of childhood emotional abuse or any other type of trauma, there are numerous support groups, classes, helpful books, qualified counselors, and information clearinghouses listed in the Sources section at the back of this book. No matter what you have experienced in the past, you *can* heal from the painful events in your life that may have wounded your spirit or diminished your aliveness.

Action Step #2: Look carefully to see if there is someone in your personal life right now whose spirit sometimes gets crushed inadvertently by something that you do or say

Most people don't intend to hurt or crush others, but sometimes the words we say or the things we do, or fail to do, can inflict a lasting scar on the spirit of someone we care about deeply. Listed below are several common ways in which we wound others inadvertently. As you look at this list, be honest with yourself. If you tend to do one or more of these things, it doesn't make you a bad person, but you might want to change some bad behaviors so that you don't end up injuring the spirit of someone you care about:

- As a parent, do you sometimes try so hard to protect your child that you may be inadvertently crushing his or her independence, motivation, or ability to make self-reliant decisions?
- As a spouse or lover, do you sometimes feel competitive with your partner and say or do things that undermine your loved one's self-confidence?
- As a family member, do you find yourself so busy with your job or other activities that you often appear burdened, resentful, or impatient when a family member needs you to listen or pay attention to his or her legitimate needs?
- As a boss or supervisor, do you sometimes overmanage, exert too much control, or inadvertently squash the creativity and good ideas of the people who work with you?
- As a caregiver to an ailing or disabled loved one, do you sometimes rush in and do things for this person that he or she would prefer to do independently, thereby unintentionally dampening this person's spirit?
- When someone comes to you with an idea or the beginning of a project that needs support and guidance, do you sometimes harm this person's enthusiasm with your skeptical questions or anxious fears and concerns?
- When someone comes to you for emotional support, do you sometimes cut this person off by trying to fix the problem with unsolicited advice instead of being a good listener?

The Difference Between Empowering Someone and Frustrating Them

If you sincerely want to help and not crush the spirit of your children, your spouse, your co-workers, your family members, or your friends, you may need to watch out for the most common mistake that can inadvertently injure or frustrate the people you care about. That mistake occurs when you or I rush in with advice or an attempt to fix someone's problem when in fact what that person wanted from us was just to listen to them and support their solving the problem in their own way.

We all know there are times when a loved one needs us to slow down and just listen, but the revved-up motor inside us keeps going. At those moments, it's hard not to rush in and try to fix the problem with advice or criticism, which quite often can leave the other person feeling interrupted, patronized, or not fully understood.

To give you an idea of what I mean by the difference between empowering someone and frustrating them, here is a poem that has helped many people become better listeners for their friends, colleagues, and loved ones. It has some specific suggestions that all of us need to be reminded of occasionally so that we don't inadvertently crush or wound someone who needs us just to listen and be fully present with them while they find their own way out of a predicament. You may want to read this poem twice, first while imagining yourself to be the one who's saying the poem to someone who cut you off with advice, and then to imagine the poem is being said to you by a particular person in your life whom *you* sometimes frustrate with unsolicited advice.

PLEASE LISTEN

When I ask you to listen to me
and you start giving advice,
you have not done what I asked
nor heard what I need.

When I ask you to listen to me
and you begin to tell me why I shouldn't feel that way,
you are trampling on my feelings.

When I ask you to listen to me
and you feel you have to do something to solve my
    problems,
you have failed me—strange as that may seem.

Listen, please!
All I asked was that you listen.
Not talk nor "do"—just hear me.
Advice is cheap.
Fifty cents gets both "Dear Abby" and
astrological forecasts in the same newspaper.

That I can do for myself. I'm not helpless.
Maybe discouraged and faltering—but not helpless.
When you do something for me
that I can and need to do for myself,
you contribute to me seeming fearful and weak.

But when you accept as a simple fact that I do feel what
    I feel,
no matter how seemingly irrational,
then I can quit trying to convince you
and can get about to understanding what's behind
what I am saying and doing—to what I am feeling.

When that's clear, chances are so will the answers be,
and I won't need any advice.
(Or then, I'll be able to hear it!)

Perhaps that's why, for some people, prayer works,
because God is mute,
and doesn't give advice or try to fix
what we must take care of ourselves.

So, please listen and just hear me.
And if you want to talk, let's plan for your turn,
and I promise I'll listen to you.
                          —Anonymous

    This tendency that most people have for giving advice instead of listening carefully to the people we care about can be quite subtle at times. Yet as described by linguistics expert and best-selling author Dr. Deborah Tannen, who wrote the acclaimed book *You Just Don't Understand,* these subtle misses between people can severely frustrate or diminish the self-worth of the very person you are trying to help.

As Tannen explains, "Someone telling you about a problem is a bid for an expression of understanding ('I know how you feel') or a similar complaint ('I felt the same way when something similar happened to me'). In other words, the conversation is intended to reinforce rapport by sending the metamessage 'We're the same; you're not alone.' People get frustrated when they not only don't get this reinforcement but, quite the opposite, feel distanced by the advice, which seems to send the metamessage 'We're not the same. You have the problems; I have the solutions.' "

If someone at work or in your personal life has ever said to you, "It's frustrating when you try to fix my problems instead of hearing me out," you may need to examine how you interact with your co-workers, family, or friends.

Breaking the Habit

Brad's case illustrates how difficult—and how important—it is to listen patiently in a conversation. Brad is a marketing manager for a high-tech information-systems company who came into counseling because his fiancée, Julie, was considering calling off the wedding and had told Brad, "Look, you're a great guy and I still love you. But sometimes you just don't listen. You say you care about me, but then you cut me off and try to fix my problems with patronizing advice and picky comments that feel like you don't understand me at all." For the past six months at work Brad had been losing some major accounts to his competitor. When we began to explore in counseling why these accounts were leaving, Brad admitted, "Some of them never say why, but a few told me straight out that they feel I'm pushing too hard the items I want to sell and not really listening or caring about what they need. One former customer said my competitor is much better at helping them find their own unique way of solving complex problems and that they feel much better about the way he listens and draws out what they're going through before jumping in with specific things to consider."

I assured Brad that he was not alone in trying to help people by giving advice and making suggestions to fix problems. Yet something about the way he jumped in with comments and solutions without being fully present or helping the other person to feel understood was costing him a great deal both in his personal life and his job.

Over the next few months, Brad worked to become a better listener. He learned some specific skills that can make a difference in personal and work relationships:

- Practice calming yourself down and being fully present when someone is trying to tell you their feelings or frustrations about something.
- Stop yourself from rushing in with advice, criticism, or attempts to fix the problem, which can injure or alienate the person you are trying to help.
- Ask questions to make sure you fully understand what the other person is saying before you attempt to offer any comments or suggestions.
- Make sure to draw out from the other person what he or she needs *rather than trying to impose what you think he or she needs.*
- Work together as teammates or equal partners rather than as teacher-student or expert-novice.

When Brad began to use these listening and partnering skills with his fiancée and his most important customers, he noticed a significant change in the way things turned out. Brad explains, "I used to get frustrated a lot because I was offering what I thought was great advice but no one was responding without a fight. Now I'm not trying so hard to sell my point of view, but I'm taking the time to listen and work *with* the other person. It makes a huge difference. Not only do I get more information about what the other person wants, but the struggle for who's in control and who's going to win the conversation seems to disappear now that we're working together as equals."

Several months after Brad completed therapy, I attended Brad and Julie's wedding and heard from Brad that he's doing much better at work. At the wedding I also met Julie for the first time. She told me, "There were days when I didn't think Brad and I were going to make it. I always knew that I wanted to marry someone who would be not just a husband but also a supportive friend. That's why it used to feel so discouraging and insulting when Brad would start cutting me off with his constant advice and patronizing comments. I was afraid that if I just let Brad talk down to me like that it would eventually erode my self-esteem and make me feel trapped in the marriage. But now Brad rarely does that to me when we're having a conversation. Now he usually listens like a good friend and helps me find my own strength and my own way of solving the issues that come up in my life. I feel like he's become a best friend instead of someone who was trying to control me or put me down. It's a great feeling to come to him with a problem and know that he's really there for me."

Action Step #3: *Think of small and large things you can do in your own way to protect others*

An additional step for heeding the call of *"Lo tirtza-akh"*—"You shall not let a spirit be crushed"—is to find out how you can help locally, nationally, or internationally to give support to organizations that are doing outstanding work to prevent harm or save lives. Most people don't usually think of charity or good deeds as a way to live up to the Sixth Commandment, but in fact many murders, suicides, and painful cruelties are prevented each year by nonprofit and volunteer efforts by people not so different from you or me.

For example, near where I live and probably near where you live there are numerous violence-prevention organizations that need volunteers just a few hours a month or financial contributions that can be as small as a few pennies a day from your pocket change. These organizations clearly make a difference in preventing human spirits from being crushed, battered, or killed. I'll list just a few of the ways you can take action to prevent harm in your corner of the world. Perhaps these suggestions will spark your own good ideas on how you would like to contribute to the saving of vulnerable souls.

A. *You can give money or donate a few hours a month of your time to an organization that works to save lives.* For instance, in Los Angeles there's a remarkable program in which former gang members who have been permanently disabled or disfigured by gang violence visit and speak at elementary and junior high schools to warn young people of the dangers of getting involved in violent gangs. Supporting a group like this or some other organization in your community that reaches young people *before* they get pulled into lives of violence can save many young men and women. If you don't know of any organizations in your area, just ask your child's teachers or your clergy for their suggestions on how to contribute to violence prevention.

B. *You can help raise money or give some time or good ideas to an organization that focuses on preventing domestic violence.* There are child-abuse prevention programs in which teenage dads and moms are taught parenting skills and anger-management techniques. There are phone hot lines, shelters, and counseling programs for battered spouses, abused children, and mistreated elderly people, as well as for batterers. Near where I live there is even a new volunteer service that sends supportive counselors to sit with battered partners in court to help them stay courageous and not drop the charges or minimize the facts regarding violent spouses or lovers who need to be put in jail with stiff sentences. If violence that crushes the spirit of small children, frail elderly people, or frightened partners touches your heart, there are many places where you can make a difference.

C. *You can give a weekly or monthly donation or offer your expertise on a volunteer basis to an organization that helps people find work and get their lives back on track.* In most communities, there are numerous volunteer and low-fee services to help people who have lost their jobs. These services help people reeducate themselves, improve their job skills, develop better résumé-writing and job-interview skills, and give them coaching and counseling to boost their spirits. In the Talmud it says that taking away a person's livelihood not only crushes his or her spirit but also is tantamount to murder. Similarly, the twelfth-century scholar Moses Maimonides taught that the highest form of charity is to help someone become self-supporting and able to care for themselves and their loved ones without relying on charity. So when you support a job-training service or volunteer to help people who have lost their jobs, you are essentially living up to the suggestion of the Sixth Commandment not to let someone's spirit be crushed or killed.

D. *In your daily life, you can treat people you meet in a way that strengthens them in spirit through your genuine interest or respect.* How you talk to your family members and friends can make the difference between whether they feel battered by life or encouraged to face each day with dignity and optimism. In addition, there are many teachings in the Bible about the importance of treating each stranger you meet as a human being worthy of respect. I'm not saying you should go up to strangers with a patronizing or false sense of sincerity, but if you can find in your heart a genuine curiosity and respect for each individual you meet in life, you will most certainly have touched more souls than you can imagine.

To give you some idea of the power of treating a stranger with dignity and respect, I want to pass along a story told by Episcopal archbishop Desmond Tutu of South Africa, who won the Nobel Prize for his long-term efforts against the crushing economic and racial policies of his country prior to the 1994 change of government. When asked what was one of the formative experiences of his life, Tutu replied, "One incident comes to mind immediately. When I was a young child I saw a white man tip his hat to a black woman. Please understand that such a gesture was completely unheard of in my country. The white man was an Episcopal bishop and the black woman was my mother."

WHY EVEN A SMALL DONATION OF TIME, MONEY, OR RESPECT IS WORTHWHILE

There is one other story that I want to include about how much even a small amount of caring or dignity can help a person whose spirit is at risk of being crushed. I've heard this tale from both Jewish and Christian sources, and its message of inspiration can apply to anyone, regardless of background or beliefs. Most recently, I heard this story told by a member of my congregation who volunteers a few hours each week to spend time with and run errands for housebound AIDS patients. It's the story of the little girl and the starfish.

Once there was a little girl who was at the beach with her somewhat cynical and jaded grandfather, a man who had seen one too many instances of human cruelty. Along the shoreline the girl watched closely as a delicate starfish, which had washed up on the sand, struggled to move back into the water in order to survive.

The little girl picked up the starfish and gently placed it back in the salt water, where it safely floated away. But as she and her grandfather looked along the shoreline they saw there were hundreds of delicate starfish that had also washed onto the sand. As the girl bent down and picked up a second starfish to place it gently back into the water, the grandfather remarked, "What's the point in picking up these starfish? There are so many of them you can't possibly make a difference."

The little girl thought for a moment. Then she replied, "It does make a difference to each one that I help."

Each day there will be chances to offer support or discouragement to the fragile spirits you meet. Whether this chapter has inspired you to heal some part of your own spirit or to make sure you treat with respect someone else's spirit, I hope you will recognize that your actions do make a lasting impact on each person you encounter. It's an enormous responsibility to take seriously how you treat the people in your life, and a great joy to know you have acted with caring, warmth, and love.

7

THE SEVENTH CHALLENGE

How to Elevate Your Sexuality to Greater Sacredness and Fulfillment

The Seventh Commandment from the Book of Exodus contains useful, important insights into how to have a better sex life. This may surprise people who think that spirituality and sexuality are irreconcilable opposites. As a psychological colleague once told me, "The way most people compartmentalize their lives, sex is at one extreme and holiness is at the other." Or as a client once explained, "I don't want to think about God when I'm getting hot and heavy with someone. That would make me feel guilty and uncomfortable."

The Seventh Commandment *unites* spirituality and sexuality by suggesting that a profound erotic intimacy can be attained only by having a spiritual connection and long-term commitment to another human being. The words from the Scriptures simply say, "You shall not commit adultery," but over the centuries many scholars have interpreted these words as a directive toward appreciating the rich spiritual potential inherent in our sexuality.

IT DEPENDS ON HOW YOU DEFINE SEX

Even in the sexually progressive 1990s, many people still think of sexuality as something dirty or shameful. In recent urban slang, intercourse is even called "doin' the nasty." The biblical term for sexual intimacy is the Hebrew word *yada,* which means to know. It doesn't mean to know or meet someone briefly or superficially, but to know that person as a full human being, as a complex and wonderful soul mate.

According to Rabbi Michael Gold, author of *Does God Belong in the Bedroom?* "The Torah uses the term yada—'to know'—to indicate a sexual relationship. Sex is thus considered more than a mere biological act; it involves intimate knowledge shared by two human beings." Or as described by Rabbi Roland Gittelsohn in his book *The Extra Dimension,* "It is more than a linguistic coincidence that the Bible uses yada—to know—for intercourse. Our ancestors knew that coitus on the human level was meant by God and nature to be something more than just physical contact and release. It involves two individuals *knowing* each other—respecting and caring for each other deeply in both physical and spiritual dimensions—loving each other maturely enough to desire a permanent sharing of their lives."

A similar view is expressed by Father Morton Kelsey, a priest and best-selling author, who describes in his book *Caring: How Can We Love One Another* this process of "knowing someone" as follows: "One of the deepest desires of human beings is to be whole, unitary, one, in touch with all of one's self, both the masculine and feminine sides. Falling in love is an almost sacramental way of achieving this desired wholeness. Yet ideal people do not exist. When we discover that the other person is quite different from the ideal person we were hoping for, then a *real* relationship can begin between two people. When we come to the disillusioning realization that the person we love is different than we thought or wanted, we can either call off the relationship *or we can set about the business of knowing ourselves and the other person in reality and starting to truly love each other.*"

THE QUEST FOR TRUE INTIMACY

Instead of seeing the Seventh Commandment as a rigid restriction against having sex with someone new, consider for a moment whether it might be suggesting something more intimate and profound. "What if?," the Seventh Commandment seems to be saying. "What if you truly put your heart and soul into your primary relationship and treated your partner with as much attention, respect, and excitement as you would treat someone you were courting or trying to seduce? What if you put so much creative thought and compassion into your relationship with this one special person that neither of you felt neglected or in need of something more?"

The underlying message of "You shall not commit adultery" is that getting to know your partner fully is crucial to finding sexual fulfillment. This connection has been explored by many biblical scholars throughout history. For instance, in the thirteenth century, a highly influential book published in Spain, called *Iggeret Ha-Kodesh* (translated as *The Holy Letter*), presented a spiritual approach to elevating one's sexuality. Scholars disagree about who wrote *The Holy Letter;* many claim it was written by the great scholar and mystic Moses Nachmanides, although most agree the writer is unknown. In either case, this essay on the spiritual richness of sexuality from the Middle Ages recommends the observance of a mutual respect that is more enlightened than the advice in many twentieth-century books on sexuality.

The medieval Jewish author wrote, "When engaging in the sex act, you must begin by speaking to her in a manner that will draw her heart to you, calm her spirits, and make her happy. Thus your minds will be bound upon one another as one, and your intention will unite with hers. Speak to her so that your words will provoke desire, love, will, and passion, as well as words leading to reverence for God, piety, and modesty.

"A man should never force himself upon his wife and never overpower her, for the Divine Spirit never rests upon one whose conjugal relations occur in the absence of desire, love, and free will. One should never argue about sex and certainly never strike her on account of sexual matters. Rather act so that you will warm her heart by speaking to her with charming and seductive words. Also speak of matters that are appropriate and worthy, so that both your intention and hers will be for the sake of eternity.

"A man should not have intercourse with his wife while she is asleep, for then they cannot both agree to the act. Do not hurry to arouse her until she is receptive. Be calm, and as you enter the path of love and will, let her orgasm come first."

In the twentieth century, numerous Christian writers also discuss sexuality in terms of mutual respect and spirituality. A best-selling Protestant guide to lovemaking by Clifford and Joyce Penner, entitled *The Gift of Sex,* explains, "Sex is not something we 'do' to someone, neither is it something we do 'for' someone. . . . Sex is a 'with' experience. We must allow ourselves the right to receive pleasure. God has already given us that right. Sexual decisions must be made in an atmosphere of freedom and openness. There has to be the freedom to express what we want, what we need, what feels good, and what feels bad. In working out problems, negotiation based on each person's having an equal vote will also often be a necessary dimension to the communication."

Most Christian scholars and ministers isolate this human need for mutual respect as the reason behind the prohibition against adultery. For example, the authoritative *New Interpreter's Bible,* which includes the work of both Protestant and Catholic theologians, gives the following interpretation of "You shall not commit adultery":

"The Seventh Commandment points to the recognition that sexuality is enormously wondrous and enormously dangerous. The wonder of sexuality is available only if it is practiced respectfully and under discipline. The danger of sexuality is that it is capable of evoking desires that are destructive of a person and of communal relations. In its fullest interpretation, the command against adultery envisions covenantal relations of mutuality that are genuinely life-giving, nurturing, enhancing, and respectful. Such a notion of long-term trust is treated as almost passé in a narcissistic society preoccupied with individual freedom and satisfaction."

The Marriage Encounter movement within Catholicism sponsors weekends for couples who want to connect their spiritual lives with their sexual lives. One of the leaders, Father Chuck Gallagher, says, "Marriage Encounter starts with the basic premise that marriage is a love affair between two people who are totally and irrevocably committed to one another. It is two people who have chosen to share a lifetime of mutual self-discovery and self-revelation."

To Protestant scholar Walter Harrelson of Vanderbilt University, the "sin" of commiting adultery is *not* that sex is dirty but rather that being dishonest or manipulative is disrespectful of one's partner. Harrelson writes, "The commandment against adultery simply embodies enormous wisdom and power. Sexual activity by its nature aims at the sharing of life and love with the partner. The chief thing is that human beings commit themselves to one another honestly, truthfully, and lovingly, avoiding deception, exploitation, and irresponsible conduct of any kind. One acid test is evident: Is the [extramarital] relationship one in which I find pleasure at the expense of someone else? Exploitation of human beings is wrong and inadmissible."

In a world where many people tell big or small lies to get someone into bed, the Seventh Commandment seems to be saying, "Don't be sneaky, manipulative, or superficial with something as wonderful and sacred as your sexuality. It's a gift that deserves special care."

THE CHALLENGE TO ATTAIN "HIGH MONOGAMY"

In addition to Jewish and Christian teachers, many secular psychological and spiritual experts speak about sexuality as the challenge of getting to know one person intimately and building a lifetime of deep soulful connection. Acclaimed journalist and aikido expert George Leonard wrote a controversial book about the difficulties and joys of seeking "high monogamy," which he described as a challenging adventure in which two partners in a long-term relationship seek a spiritual path together that builds a creative, transformative love.

Claiming that high monogamy was a more fulfilling choice than an open marriage or having affairs, Leonard writes, "It's easy to link multiple sexual partners with personal change and monogamy with personal stasis. This can at times be true; but extramarital affairs or the pursuit of recreational sex are *far more likely to be associated with the avoidance of change.* After superficial erotic novelty has faded and the ego has had its full run (all the life stories told, all the sexual tricks displayed), *then* the adventure of transformation and a deeper eroticism can begin. But it is precisely at this point that most of us are likely to lose our nerve and leap into another bed, where we can once again tell our stories, display our tricks, do anything rather than see ourselves clearly and start doing something about it. Casual recreational sex is a diet of fast food served in plastic containers. Life's feast is available only to those who are willing and able to engage life on a deeply personal level, giving all, holding back nothing."

BUT WHAT IF YOUR EYES OR YOUR IMAGINATION START TO WANDER?

Even if you find the concept of lifelong passion and deep knowing with one special person an attractive goal, obstacles can still get in the way. For example, one of the great controversies about the Seventh Commandment is whether or not having lustful thoughts about someone besides your primary partner is adultery or not.

Many people recall that during the 1976 presidential campaign the devout former governor of Georgia Jimmy Carter was asked by an interviewer for *Playboy* magazine about the public's perception that Carter might be a "rigid, unbending" president because of his strong religious values.

The candidate answered, "We were taught not to judge other people. I wouldn't condemn someone who looks on a woman with lust . . . I've looked on a lot of women with lust. I've committed adultery in my heart many times."

That comment sparked a huge controversy. Some people were upset that a presidential candidate was talking publicly about lust and adultery. Others thought Carter was speaking from the heart about the complexity of being spiritual and being human. Dr. William Wolf of the Episcopal Divinity School in Cambridge, Massachusetts, commented, "It sounds to me like good theology and good honest human experience brought together."

Some Protestant denominations debate what Jesus meant in Matthew 5:27–28 when he said, "You have heard it was said 'Do not commit adultery,' but I tell you that anyone who looks at a woman lustfully has already committed adultery with her in his heart." Some would argue that this means staring at a person or fantasizing about someone is the same as committing adultery. To others, there is a substantial difference between having a sexual thought and carrying out a sexual affair.

Writing in the magazine *Christianity Today,* R. Kent Hughes and John H. Armstrong, members of the Protestant clergy, explained the difference as follows: "It appears in Matthew 5 and in James 2 there is no essential difference between mental adultery and the actual physical act. To the contrary, we believe, in concert with the historical interpretation of the church, that physical manifestations of lust are greater sins because of the damage they do to both the person who sins and the ones sinned against. Physical adultery is a great sin because it breaks the covenant of marriage. It violates another's body. It may prove to be grounds for divorce. Mental adultery does none of this. Jesus' intention in Matthew 5 was not to reduce adultery to the level of lust, but to show that lust would destroy the soul as surely as adultery."

WHAT TO DO ABOUT LUSTFUL THOUGHTS

If you were raised in a Catholic, Protestant, or Eastern Orthodox church that equated lustful thoughts with sin, bear in mind that the intention was to point you in the direction of building a respectful and long-lasting relationship. In most churches and denominations, forgiveness for lustful thoughts is always possible if you admit the thoughts to yourself and to God. According to Episcopal minister William S. Stafford, a professor at Virginia Theological Seminary and the author of *Disordered Loves: Healing the Seven Deadly Sins,* "Lust makes people look for love in all the wrong places and to miss the mark of loving as God loves—wholly. Yet vigilance against lustful thoughts is less important than bringing into our hearts the stories and images of God's wisdom and love. Meditate on God's faithfulness in love and on God's longing for justice, the sort of love that freed His beloved people from slavery. And seek forgiveness in Jesus Christ, whereby God forgives and accepts us wholly."

In Judaism, the contrast between lustful thoughts and adulterous actions is viewed somewhat differently. On the one hand, Judaism recognizes that sexual thoughts can become obsessive, distract you from your purpose in life, and lead to affairs that harm marriages. Many Jewish writings contain strong warnings not to let your private thoughts and inclinations turn into harmful actions. According to most Jewish scholars and interpreters, however, having brief lustful thoughts is no cause for alarm or shame. Just as recent psychological research studies by Harold Leitenberg of the University of Vermont and Kris Henning of the University of South Carolina Medical School have shown that 95 percent of people think of sex at least once a day, so has Judaism acknowledged that lustful thoughts are bound to enter one's mind.

According to Rabbi Joseph Telushkin, author of *Jewish Wisdom,* "With considerable realism, the ancient rabbis saw sexual thoughts as omnipresent: Rabbi Isaac comments, 'Even during the time a man is in mourning, his impulse is apt to overcome him.' In a much later period, a man is reputed to have asked the eighteenth-century Baal Shem Tov, the founder of Hasidism, how a person could discern a true religious leader from a false one. The Baal Shem Tov answered, 'Ask him if he knows a way to prevent impure thoughts. If he says he does, he's a charlatan.' "

The Baal Shem Tov also is reported to have offered another way of coping with the lustful thoughts that can distract your mind, especially when your eyes see an extremely attractive person. According to the legend, the founder of Hasidism told his followers that instead of resisting or feeling ashamed for having a brief lustful thought it is better to appreciate the God-given beauty of that individual. By refocusing your thoughts back on the Creator and the beauty of God's creation, you can elevate your sexuality from lust to a renewed appreciation for the holiness of all things.

WHAT IF YOUR DISTRACTING THOUGHTS ARE HARMING YOUR RELATIONSHIP?

As a psychologist, I hear almost daily from men and women who are having affairs, are close to having an affair, or are wrestling with hard-to-dismiss fantasies about someone other than their primary partner. In psychotherapy, the lustful thoughts are not viewed as harmful per se. These thoughts become windows into the person's psyche, indicating an underlying problem, worry, or longing in his or her life.

For example, if a client tells me he fantasizes about a younger lover I might ask him to discuss his feelings about growing older. Or, perhaps, he is coming to terms with regrets over his earlier social or sexual awkwardness. Quite often the fantasy is less about the attractive person currently desired and more about the client wanting to regain a sense of youthfulness, aliveness, control, or freedom he or she has never fully enjoyed. My job as a therapist is not to make a moral judgment about the person for having a sexual fantasy but to guide him or her to use this desire as valuable information about his or her life, just as we would analyze an interesting dream or creative wish, to find out what pain or unfinished business underlies the fantasy and needs to be addressed.

In nearly every case, the outcome is *not* that the person goes out and has an affair but rather that the fantasy turns into a wake-up call to attend to something that is out of balance or missing from his or her life. We then devise a practical course of action that remedies the real problem, which often includes making important improvements in this person's primary relationship.

To see how this type of self-analysis works, take a moment to think about your own most recent or frequently recurring lustful fantasies and consider the following possible issues:

1. If you keep fantasizing about lovers who are much younger than you, you may want to talk to a counselor, a friend, or a clergy member about your mixed feelings regarding growing older, your desire to be a guide or mentor for someone who is young and impressionable, or your regrets about not being more loved or sexually comfortable when you were in your teens or twenties. Instead of acting out your fantasy on a vulnerable human being, you can learn a great deal about what's stirring inside your psyche if you use these fantasies for self-analysis about your inner life.

2. If you keep fantasizing about someone who is much older or who seems to be more successful at life than you are, this could be an important opportunity to write in your journal, talk with a friend, or seek counseling about your secret desires to be nurtured and cared for by someone on whom you can lean. Or it could be a desire to find a supportive mentor or coach who

can guide you in an important growth phase of your life, rather than a sexual partner or a physical relationship.

3. If you tend to fantasize only about men or women who are married, in committed relationships, or in some other way are unattainable, then you may want to explore why you are unable or unwilling to fall in love with someone who can reciprocate fully. Do you feel you deserve to be loved? Do you need time to heal from a prior painful relationship? Do you somehow feel safer when you know you won't have to build an actual relationship with all its complexities? Do you want to say *the other person* wasn't available?

4. If you keep fantasizing about someone who seems more fun and lively than your long-term partner, it may be an indication that you secretly desire to regain the excitement and freedom you once enjoyed with your spouse but don't know how to recapture those lost feelings. You and your partner would do well to find a counselor, a book, a workshop, or a creative friend who can help you brainstorm on ways to put the fire and enjoyment back into your relationship. One book to consider is *Hot Monogamy*, by Dr. Patricia Love and Jo Robinson, which offers specific guidelines on how to rebuild the excitement in a long-term committed partnership.

We human beings are complicated psychologically and, especially, sexually. Unfortunately, when people feel guilty, ashamed, or secretive about their sexual desires, they are usually too uncomfortable to purchase a helpful book or to talk about the problem with a counselor who could help them explore the underlying issues, although they sometimes still act on these desires. Examining and making conscious your lustful thoughts and sexual fantasies can lead to personal insights about yourself and new understandings of how to make a more fulfilling relationship.

"IT SCARED ME HOW QUICKLY I BEGAN OBSESSING WITH THOUGHTS ABOUT GINNY"

Grant has been married for twenty-two years to a wonderful woman named Julianne, and they have four children. Grant told me, "I had a few affairs early in our marriage, but then my wife began feeling upset about my inattentiveness to her. I decided to stop fooling around because I didn't want to destroy what Julianne and I have built together. But last month I was on a business trip and I met an incredible woman named Ginny who's not only a lot better looking than Julianne but also so much more full of life. It scared me how quickly I began obsessing with thoughts about Ginny. I haven't been sleeping well. I can't seem to concentrate at work. And my wife and my kids are beginning to complain that I seem distant and a little edgy lately.

"I don't know if my wife suspects anything, and I would hate to put her through another round of lies, guardedness, and sneakiness. Don't get me wrong—I haven't even touched Ginny, but I can't stop thinking about her. I worry that I'll lose everything if I let myself get involved in another affair. At the same time, I'm terrified that I might be making the biggest mistake of my life if I don't pursue this amazing woman."

As in most cases like this, Grant thought the reason for coming into therapy was to help him decide whether or not to have an affair. But in counseling we discovered in the first few sessions that his challenge was much deeper than that. When I asked Grant to talk about his life prior to meeting Ginny, it became clear that he had been feeling unhappy and edgy for several years. He was worried about the fact that his sexual interest for his wife had been declining, and he had experienced a few incidents of being unable to maintain an erection. He had deep frustrations with the dead-end job and exhausting schedule he had fallen into at work. He also worried about getting older and had been somewhat depressed during the three months since his remaining parent, his mother, had died of cancer.

Over the next few weeks, Grant and I discussed how to improve his frustrating situation at work. We also did some grief and loss counseling about Grant's parents and his own fears of getting older. Then we began to focus on the declining sexual interest he had experienced with Julianne.

When I asked Grant whether he had ever enjoyed sex with his wife, he assured me that for many years he and Julianne had had a good sex life. He felt that Julianne was a fun and compassionate lover. As with many men who are tempted to stray, Grant's loss of desire for his wife seemed to be occurring for reasons that were not her fault. Grant simply felt tired from his job, fearful about the future, and curious about whether some new woman might be able to reignite the spark he once felt about sex and life in general.

I asked Grant, "If there were some way for you to feel alive, youthful, hopeful, and very excited about being with Julianne again, would you be interested?" Grant looked a little surprised, almost as if I were saying something unrealistic or unattainable. "How could that be?" he asked. "We've been together more than twenty-two years. The excitement just can't last that long."

I asked him, "Would you be willing to try a somewhat unusual exercise that might change your outlook?" Grant smiled and said, "It depends on how unusual."

During the next few sessions I taught Grant how to use a Tantric Yoga breathing and visualization exercise to generate more sexual excitement and change his attitude toward sex with Julianne. Based on ancient techniques that are found in the Kundalini tradition of Hinduism as well as the mystical Kabbalistic teachings of Judaism, this exercise is to be done in three steps at least once a day for ten to twenty minutes. You can experiment with them on your own or with a partner:

1. Find a quiet room in which you will be undisturbed and make sure the phone is off. Sit in a comfortable position either in a chair that supports good posture or in a Yoga cross-legged position on the floor if that is comfortable for you.

2. Sit for a few minutes and let your thoughts pass across your mind without judging any of them. Slowly and gently breathe in and out five times, deep enough to relax you but not so deep that you hyperventilate. With each inhalation, visualize a warm golden light moving from the base of your spine up through your heart and into the top of your head. As you exhale, feel the energy as the golden light moves back down the spine through your heart to your buttocks and genitals. Inhale again while visualizing this golden light traveling up along the spine through the heart and up to the top of the head. Then exhale as you imagine the light moving back down your spine to your pelvic area.

3. Once you get a sense of the breathing and you begin to imagine golden light moving up and down your spine, do five more inhalations and exhalations. This time, imagine this warm golden light passing through your heart and surrounding you

and your long-term partner. You might imagine the warm golden light healing the two of you or surrounding the two of you as you embrace inside your heart. On the inhalation, imagine the warm golden light coming up from your pelvic area to surround you and your partner inside your heart. On the exhale, visualize this warm golden light traveling down from the top of your head to embrace the two of you inside your heart.*

The first few times Grant tried to do this spiritual exercise he noticed his thoughts kept wandering. That's normal when anyone first attempts to do a meditation or visualization exercise. Gradually, however, as Grant did the exercise one or two times a day for the next several days, he described a series of feelings that were quite powerful. According to Grant: "I was skeptical at first because I've never been very good at meditating and I'm not a very spiritual person. But as I sat there breathing slowly in and out while imagining a warm golden light surrounding Julianne and me inside my heart, tears started to roll down my face. I had forgotten just how much I love her. There was a lot of energy moving up my spine and a tingling sensation at the top of my head. Part of me wanted to stop, but I kept going and the tears kept streaming down my face—almost like I'd opened a reservoir of unexpressed love I've been keeping locked away inside."

While each individual has a slightly different experience with this exercise, most do report a deep feeling of warmth and connection. In addition, Grant began to understand that the "reservoir of unexpressed love" he kept inside was not about Ginny or some other exciting individual he might meet this year or the year after. I've found repeatedly that most people make the mistake of thinking that their intense sexual feelings are about the other person. But in fact nearly every spiritual tradition has taught that the true source of these feelings of love is the Divine energy you possess deep in your heart. You get to decide how you want to express the deep reservoir of love that is a gift you have within you.

* For more information about breathing and visualization techniques from the Hindu tradition of Tantra and Kundalini Yoga or from Jewish Kabbalistic teachings that can help unite the spiritual and sexual aspects of your primary relationship, please see the Sources section at the back of this book.

As I explained to Grant, "You need to decide whether you want to share that profound source of loving energy with your longtime partner, Julianne, or with your current infatuation, Ginny. But don't think it's Ginny who is the true source of your intense sexual feelings. Or that your tiredness from work and the other stresses in your life means that you're no longer able to be sexual with Julianne. You possess a deep capacity to love and be loved. What you experienced during the breathing and visualization exercise is how much you are able to feel that intense love when you are surrounded by light with Julianne in your heart."

Over the next few weeks, Grant and Julianne began to discuss in counseling and on their own some ways to put more excitement and fun into their family life and their sex life. Specifically, they worked on three issues that had been missing from their relationship for many years but that were not too difficult to bring into their daily life. These were:

- Relaxed and comfortable sex talks. As a therapist who has counseled numerous couples, I've noticed that most people wait until they're in an argument or they're tired and upset before they start talking about what they like and what they don't like about their sex life together. Instead of having these important conversations at the worst possible times, I recommend to couples that they set aside a few hours on a weekend for a long walk, a picnic lunch, or a romantic private dinner in which they calmly and comfortably take turns imagining what they would like to change or add to their sex life together. Rather than shouting accusations at each other during a late-night argument, having these romantic and relaxed conversations about sex can be the beginning of a new phase of better communication about your sexual likes and dislikes.

When Grant and Julianne took a walk along the water on a Saturday afternoon and talked about what they used to love about their sex life and what they would like to add to make it more exciting again, Grant later said he felt "I was once again talking with my best friend and lover. It was like we were young and hot and adventurous again. It's sad that for all these years we never really set aside time for a creative brainstorming conversation about what we both like and want to improve about our sensuality together."

• Taking turns as choreographers. One of the things Grant wanted to change about their sex life is that he felt Julianne always waited for him to initiate and choreograph their sexuality. But when he started complaining, "You never initiate," Julianne corrected him and explained, "Sometimes I do subtle or not-so-subtle things to turn you on. But you don't seem to want to lie back and let me choreograph the dance for a while. You usually take charge pretty quickly, and I don't want to fight with your energy, so I let you. But that gets in the way of finding out what would happen if you truly surrendered for a while and let me slowly explore my own way of making things happen."

As a result of that conversation, Julianne and Grant decided to set aside at least one night a week in which Julianne was the "choreographer," gently guiding their sexual moves and build-ups. As Grant later admitted, "I had no idea that I was part of the reason why Julianne never seemed to initiate things. Once she explained it to me, though, I feel very lucky that I'm with such a creative and sensual partner."

• Taking the expectations and goal orientation out of their sexuality. The final issue that helped make their sex life more enjoyable than ever is that Grant and Julianne decided to stop seeing each sexual encounter as a goal-oriented agenda that had to include orgasms, habitual routines, and even an erection each and every time. Instead they began to look at each sexual connection between them as a chance to play, relax, roll around, laugh, feel turned on, or just feel close to each other. As Grant described it, "Knowing that we weren't pressured to have an orgasm each and every time has made our lovemaking so much more intimate and playful. Realizing that Julianne doesn't care whether I have an erection all the time has made me so much less performance oriented and more sensual with her. We've discovered what only longtime friends and lovers get to experience—that we can keep growing, changing, and exploring our sexuality with each other and that there is always so much more intense love waiting to be expressed. These past few months have been more passionate and exciting than any other time in our relationship."

While not every couple does as well as Grant and Julianne in reenergizing their relationship after one of them has almost had an affair, I have found that in the vast majority of cases a great deal of progress can occur if one or both partners are committed to making the relationship more alive again. It takes time and good communication for the sparks of love and the mutual enthusiasm for life to be reignited. In your own life, if an important relationship begins to decline or falter, do whatever it takes to uncover what's holding you and your partner back from reaching the intimacy and excitement of which you are capable. Throwing away all that you've built together usually isn't necessary if you take steps to revitalize the relationship.

WHAT HAPPENS IF THE TRUST IN A RELATIONSHIP GETS BROKEN?

The highest estimates of adultery were given by controversial author Shere Hite, who used a variety of informal and unscientific survey techniques to come up with the surprising figure that three-quarters of all men and more than half of all women have affairs. Additional high numbers came from a 1970s survey of *Cosmopolitan* magazine readers, which said that 54 percent of married women had had at least one affair. Another study, by Morton Hunt, which focused primarily on white upper-middle-class respondents, claimed that 42 percent of the men and 25 percent of the women surveyed had engaged in adultery. More recently, Samuel and Cynthia Janus found in a survey that one-third of all married men and one-quarter of all married women had been involved in an extramarital relationship.

A more scientific and carefully selected sampling of the entire U.S. population conducted in 1991 by the National Opinion Research Center suggests that each of the above estimates was overstated because of biased sampling techniques.

In the more carefully performed research from the National Opinion Research Center, which was reported in many major newspapers and is spelled out in detail in a book by Father Andrew Greeley called *Faithful Attraction,* the following estimates were obtained:

- Approximately 9 percent of married women have affairs.
- Approximately 11 percent of married men have affairs.

Whether you believe the true number is 10 percent or 50 percent, millions of men and women each year have to sort out their feelings about someone whom they trusted and loved but who lied to them at least once about whom they went to see and for what purpose. Yet even when trust is broken in a relationship, the vast majority of these individuals still desire to stay together. How do they do it?

According to Frank Pittman, M.D., a psychiatrist and family therapist who wrote the excellent book *Private Lies: Infidelity and the Betrayal of Intimacy,* "Most betrayed men, like most betrayed women, hunker down and do whatever they have to do to hold their marriage together. A few men and women go into a rage and refuse to turn back, and then spend a lifetime nursing the injury, but that unusual occurrence is no more common for men than for women. Marriage can survive either a husband's infidelity or a wife's, if it is stopped, brought into the open, and dealt with. I have cleaned up from more affairs than a squad of motel chambermaids. But infidelity is very messy."

Some couples get divorced, while others attempt to stuff the painful feelings away until they flare up again months or years later. Dr. Pittman and most other experts in the field recommend ending the outside relationship as soon as possible and bringing it out into the open rather than continuing to do anything that is sneaky, dishonest, or manipulative. Then, you need to deal with the underlying reasons that prompted one or both partners to stray. Only by facing and sorting out complex emotions and painful issues can a couple turn a hurtful infidelity into a chance for the relationship to deepen and grow.

THE ROAD BACK FROM A BETRAYAL OF TRUST

If you and your partner are looking for ways to recover from a painful incident of broken trust or the keeping of secrets that have put up a wall between you, I recommend you speak to a spiritual counselor, a psychotherapist, or a marriage and family counselor or pick up a copy of an excellent guidebook called *After the Affair: Healing the Pain and Rebuilding Trust When a Partner Has Been Unfaithful,* by clinical psychologist Janis Spring, Ph.D.

Dr. Spring suggests that one of the first steps of rebuilding is to decide how you want to view the affair that has affected your relationship. She advises, "Some of you may not want to risk starting over and exposing yourself to further hurt or disappointment. Turning your back on a damaged relationship may be the simplest or most sensible solution, one that frees you from the tyranny of hope. But it may also be a way to escape growing up, facing some bitter truths.

"If you choose to reconnect to each other, you may in time come to see the affair not merely as a regrettable trauma but as an alarm, a wake-up call. You may eventually discover that you needed a nuclear explosion like an affair to blow your previous construction apart and allow a healthier, more conscious, and mature version to take its place. I encourage you to enter the process of rebuilding, to challenge the hurt, and to see what you're capable of producing together."

"I Feel Like She's Taken Twelve Years of Hard Work and Thrown It Away"

Following three years of knowing each other in college, Marissa and Stan got married during graduate school and made an exciting life with two careers, three children, and a wide circle of friends. No one ever expected either of them to have an affair. According to Marissa, "Everyone thought we were the perfect couple."

None of their friends knew that Marissa was lonely. She explains, "I always thought that there must be something wrong with me for not being happy with my marriage. I had so much, and yet I felt very unfulfilled. It wasn't until I began going out for lunch with a work colleague named Evan that I began to sense what was missing in my marriage."

Marissa found in her frequent lunch partner a good listener and the supportive friend she'd never had in her marriage to Stan. As Marissa admitted later in counseling, "Stan is a very opinionated and driven professional who is always trying to be right and wanting to be in control in every conversation. He has never been able to sit calmly and just listen without trying to tell me how to do things quicker, better, or more like his way of cutting to the bottom line and skipping the feelings part. That's also how he was in bed. Stan knows what he wants and he knows how to take the quickest route to get there. Need I say more?"

Like many women and men who enjoy having a friend who has some of the qualities missing from one's spouse, Marissa had to decide whether to keep the friendship with Evan nonsexual or to let it cross the line into an affair. As Marissa recalls, "I knew in my gut it would be a mistake to go to bed with Evan, but one afternoon when we were taking an especially long lunch break we started holding hands. Then Evan kissed me and pretty soon we were no longer just friends."

According to many experts on infidelity, the need for a good listener who later becomes a sexual partner is one of the most common reasons for an affair. Quoting once again from family therapist and author Frank Pittman, M.D., "More often people are not seeking an alternative to their marriage, but a supplement to it. They just want a friend for whatever they aren't getting at home. Some people don't realize they can have friends of either gender without having to sexualize the friendship or keep it hidden or see it as a threat to their marriage. So they sexualize the friendship, and turn it inadvertently into something quite different from its original function. The sex was not the purpose for the relationship but merely the seal of the friendship."

A few months after Marissa and Evan began adding secretive sex to their lunchtime get-togethers, Stan began to suspect Marissa was having an affair. When he confronted her and demanded to know if she'd gone to bed with Evan, Marissa claims she felt backed into a corner, and so she lied and said, "Absolutely not."

Stan wasn't sure whether to believe her, and with each passing day his suspiciousness increased. The tension and the distance between them grew, until almost a year later Stan began having an affair with his former secretary.

By the time Stan and Marissa both heard through talkative friends about the other's affair, an enormous amount of resentment and distrust had accumulated. Stan moved out and hired a well-known aggressive lawyer to help him file for divorce. Marissa found an attorney with an even more ruthless reputation to defend her. Until their minister recommended mediation and counseling, which is when I first met them, neither of them felt willing to consider the possibility of a reconciliation.

In their first counseling session, both Stan and Marissa did what many couples do after one or both partners have been caught in an affair: they both tried to prove who was the more wounded victim. Stan was furious that Marissa had lied to him repeatedly for almost a year, when he'd begged her to tell him truthfully about her feelings for Evan. With tears in his eyes, Stan said, "I feel like she's taken twelve years of hard work and thrown it away." Marissa was furious with Stan for "once again being completely self-righteous and arrogant without any interest in hearing the other side of the story."

During the next few sessions they began to explore their options: to get divorced, to separate temporarily, or to try to rebuild the relationship gradually while living under the same roof. During their fifth counseling session, Stan and Marissa began to admit to themselves and each other that they didn't really want a divorce. For Stan it was a question of the children, as he insisted, "I just don't want our kids to have to juggle two households and two rival stepfamilies." For Marissa it was a question of not wanting to give up on their marriage. She explained, "I still think we have what it takes to make this relationship more fulfilling for both of us. But it's going to take some work on both of our parts, and I can see now that my affair with Evan was an easy but damaging way of avoiding the issues I need to confront with Stan."

Over the next few months in counseling, they began to make progress toward repairing the painful issues that had been brought to light by their extramarital affairs. Marissa began to work hard on her own habit of keeping her resentments locked inside, of not being willing to discuss with Stan what was frustrating her or to help him be the kind of friend she needed. Stan began to work on his own habit of being arrogant and talking down to Marissa and not taking her feelings seriously.

In addition to addressing the specific tensions of their particular relationship, Marissa and Stan also worked in counseling on four important issues that apply to any couple who wants a way to heal and recover from a painful affair. If you or someone you know is seeking a reconciliation after a betrayal of trust, these are the steps that are essential for turning an adulterous crisis into an opportunity for growth:

1. Careful medical monitoring. In this age of AIDS and many other sexually transmitted diseases, couples need to know realistically if their partner has gotten infected during an affair. Since some of these illnesses incubate for a while before becoming detectable, Stan and Marissa needed to agree to *several* regular medical tests before they could be assured that their health was not in jeopardy. I've found that if one or both partners refuse to get tested medically, it's extremely difficult to start rebuilding the sense of trust and caring that is the foundation of a relationship.

2. A clear understanding of why the betrayal occurred. Marissa and Stan needed several counseling sessions to identify and explain to each other the reasons why they had looked for emotional support and sexual excitement from someone outside the relationship. When discussing these issues with your partner, there are two ground rules to keep in mind. First, the conversation is for both of you to understand how to prevent it from happening again; the purpose is not to blame or shame the other person for what happened already. Second, it's important that each partner look carefully at those personal, internal vulnerabilities that could cause one to be drawn to an affair that on some level one knows would be harmful and destructive. During such an examination about individual vulnerabilities, Marissa discovered for the first time that she'd always been somewhat private and secretive in her life. Growing up with two controlling parents and a bossy older sister had made her put up a wall that had unfortunately carried over into her marriage with Stan. Marissa resolved to begin opening up more to Stan and to make sure she didn't settle for a secretive friendship with Evan or anyone else as her only outlet for talking about her daily needs and feelings.

When I asked Stan to focus not on what Marissa had done to him but what had drawn him into having an affair, he also discovered something interesting about himself. Stan admitted, "I guess there's a part of me that's insecure and wants to be in control much of the time. When I saw that I couldn't control Marissa, I went pretty quickly back to my former secretary, who had always been very timid and compliant. Maybe what I need to learn is that being in a relationship with Marissa can't be about control. I've got to learn how to give up a little bit of my power if I'm going to be able to make this marriage a success."

Instead of blaming each other and getting defensive, both Marissa and Stan had begun taking the important step of looking at their own vulnerabilities that had led to their seeking an affair.

3. A realistic plan for what to do the next time either partner is tempted to stray. This is a crucial step. Instead of insisting, "I'll never be tempted again," both partners need to think about and commit to exactly what they will do the next time they are unhappy and looking for someone else, or what they will do if they are approached by someone outside the relationship who's looking for a secret lover.

In Marissa and Stan's case, they made a vow to talk to each other in front of a counselor as soon as either of them felt the slightest urge to stray again. Other couples have agreed to talk to their minister, priest, or rabbi to help them refocus on their primary relationship. Another couple vowed they would go on a secluded vacation in a romantic setting the next time either partner was tempted to stray. Two of my close friends told me they make sure each time they are even slightly tempted to get involved with someone else that they take those "courting" and "flirting" energies and bring them back to their primary relationship, so that they court and flirt instead with their long-term partner. Yet another couple made a promise to each other that they would enroll in a workshop for couples to revitalize their relationship if one or both of them started feeling dissatisfied or tempted to look elsewhere. I have found with many couples that it's extremely useful to have a prevention agreement like those listed above already in place before trouble arises. Then if one or both of you are feeling the urge to pursue someone else, you can begin rebuilding your primary relationship *before* things get worse.

4. An admission that it will take time and numerous honest conversations to regain some if not all of the trust and goodwill that was diminished by the affair. While some couples pretend they can kiss and make up, or have sex and be done with the entire incident, relationship experts point out that it takes years to rebuild the good feelings and sense of security a relationship

once had. Knowing that it is a slow and careful process to discover how the affair has affected both of you and what insecurities have been stirred up can help you go slow and not rush to any conclusions. This appreciation of the gradualness of regaining trust can help you avoid the emotional roller coaster of shaky reconciliations and multiple breakups.

For Marissa and Stan, it took at least three years before the full sense of trust, playfulness, and security returned to their marriage. During that time, Stan worked hard on becoming less controlling and a better listener. Marissa worked hard at becoming a more open and honest human being, willing to risk telling Stan her needs and feelings in a gentle way rather than storing them up until they were huge and unmanageable. A few months ago, I received a postcard in the mail from Stan and Marissa. They had gone on a second honeymoon and had promised each other they were making a new commitment to "love, honor, and cherish each other." While it is a definite challenge, one can make a relationship that grows and flourishes for a lifetime.

8

THE EIGHTH CHALLENGE

Accomplishing Your Goals Without
Mistreating Other People

Most people discover in their adult years that integrity and highest values are not always easy to maintain. At work, in relationships, and in stressful family situations, it can be extremely difficult at times to live up to our good intentions. Occasionally, we are forced to make painful choices between what we know is right and what is expedient.

A few years ago a client of mine named Ruth told me, "All my life I've tried to be honest and caring. But at my job recently they've been 'downsizing,' which is an odd way of saying they've been firing people who've given their heart and soul to this company. At first I thought I was going to be one of the people laid off, but then I learned from my boss that my task would be even more distressing. He said it's my responsibility to find a way to cut half the staff and still keep our department running. I feel like some sort of executioner, only in my case I know personally the men and women whose lives will never be the same after we force them out."

An old college friend named Trevor ran into a similar struggle for integrity last year when he moved into a beautiful home. As Trevor took out his checkbook to pay the moving van crew, the driver commented, "You've got a great house here. How'd you ever afford it?"

Trevor told me later, "At that moment I felt a twinge of guilt. Here was this hardworking man looking at a home he probably never would be able to afford. I almost felt like I must have done something shady or immoral to be so fortunate. It got me thinking about how I've cut a few corners and probably been a little dishonest at times in my work. Even though I try to act with integrity, on a few occasions I have done some questionable things in order to be successful. I wish it weren't so, but sometimes I feel a little dishonest and afraid of being found out."

THE SEARCH FOR WHOLENESS

The words of the Eighth Commandment, "You shall not steal," at first seem to be about nothing more than taking someone else's property. Yet the actual Hebrew words found in Exodus 20 address something far more complex than thievery. This ancient spiritual teaching shows clearly how we can act with integrity.

The word *integrity* comes from the Latin *integritas,* which means to be whole or complete. In Hebrew the word for wholeness and completeness is *shalom,* which also means peace between people and peace within oneself. In Arabic, the word is *salaam.* Whatever your spiritual tradition calls this sense of wholeness and peace, it is the goal of most spiritual people. The Eighth Commandment directs us to this inner peace.

GOING DEEPER

To understand the wisdom of this useful teaching, however, you need to go beyond the common interpretation, "You shall not steal," to get to the layers underneath. There are many ways to steal in life besides going up to a store, a home, or a person and taking something without paying.

Rashi, a sage in eleventh-century France, and Samson Raphael Hirsch in nineteenth-century Germany, describe the Eighth Commandment as a warning against "stealing someone's freedom." In ancient times, that usually meant kidnapping and selling someone into slavery. In modern times, examples of stealing someone's freedom can include: a supervisor who breathes down your neck, is extremely controlling, or treats you like a servant; a possessive lover who gets demanding and dictatorial when his or her partner spends time with an old friend; a parent, lover, or friend who won't let you have any time alone; an overbearing parent who refuses to let a grown child make decisions or have an independent life.

In addition to this interpretation, many scholars suggest that the Eighth Commandment is a warning against deception and manipulation. As early as the second century, Rabbi Ishmael argued that "the worst kind of thief is someone who uses deception to steal the good opinion of people." In the twentieth century, a similar interpretation is given by Rabbi Nosson Scherman in *The Stone Edition Chumash,* a highly influential guide to the Book of Exodus developed by Mesorah Publications of Brooklyn, New York, which says under the Eighth Commandment, "To win someone's gratitude or regard through deceit is a form of thievery."

It might be a politician who lies to steal your vote, a salesperson or advertiser who misrepresents a product's attributes to win the sale, or a friend or co-worker who pretends to be on your side while secretly working against you. When someone uses deception or manipulation to steal your trust, it not only hurts in the present moment but it can make you less likely to trust or be open to potentially good things in the future as well.

Dr. Lewis Smedes, a Protestant scholar and professor of theology and ethics at Fuller Theological Seminary in Pasadena, California, offers a similar emphasis on deception and broken trust as the key teaching of the Eighth Commandment. Smedes suggests, "The commandment confronts a modern culture which accepts greed as a style of self-affirmation. Recognizing the difference between stealing and dealing is a lost art. We still know that when a thug snatches a woman's purse, he is stealing; we are not sure whether or not a creative ad writer who woos money from people by seductive lies is stealing. We know that a burglar who takes a poor family's television set is stealing; we are not always sure whether a company is stealing when it exploits a poor nation's resources."

STEALING SOMEONE'S SELF-WORTH

Some rabbis, ministers, priests, and scholars have suggested a different interpretation of the Eighth Commandment, which says that to be rude to someone, to treat any human being in a demeaning way, or even to fail to respond to a greeting is a theft of a person's self-respect. If you ever have been on the receiving end of someone's coldness or indifference, or have ever been in a good mood until someone treated you like you didn't exist, then you have some idea what it means for someone to steal your self-worth.

Interrupting someone in conversation is another type of stealing of self-worth. Especially if the person speaking needs to be heard and understood, the abruptness of a sudden interruption or a sarcastic and demeaning "Get to the point already!" can be quite jarring. In some families, one person repeatedly cuts off other family members. In some relationships, the inability or unwillingness of one partner to listen patiently to the other can be the cause of numerous fights or even a breakup. The phrase commonly used for this habit of cutting people off in conversation is "stealing the floor." There's no prison sentence or monetary fine for it, but from a spiritual point of view it's thievery nonetheless.

Another type of deception that is stealing occurs far too often in academic, literary, corporate, and creative circles when co-authors, research assistants, and important sources of information are not acknowledged. Plumping up credentials by refusing to acknowledge the hard work and contributions of others is commonly referred to as "stealing the credit." People who monopolize the glory or pretend to be the originators of something that was primarily another's idea are essentially thieves.

Many scholars also point out that mistreating the people who work for you is like stealing their self-worth. In his excellent book on how to have integrity in your work life, entitled *Being God's Partner: How to Find the Hidden Link Between Your Spirituality and Your Work,* Jeffrey Salkin suggests that it's stealing to take advantage of an employee, to hold up someone's wages, or to fail to pay someone what they deserve for a job.

DISCOVERING THE LINE BETWEEN CLEVERNESS AND DUPLICITY

Finally, one additional interpretation of the Eighth Commandment reveals the complexity of how to accomplish what you want in life without deceiving or mistreating other people. To understand this particular interpretation, you need to know a little bit of Yiddish, the language based on Hebrew, German, and several Slavic tongues that for centuries was spoken by Jews in Eastern Europe and that has contributed many words to the English language, including *schlepping* (carrying a heavy load), *chutzpah* (nerve or assertiveness), and *schlemiel* (a victim or fool).

The biblical wording in the Book of Exodus for the Eighth Commandment says, *"Lo tig-nove."* The word *lo* means no or don't. The word *tig-nove* has as its Hebrew root the word *gonnif,* which in Yiddish usage has both positive and negative meanings. In his best-selling book *The Joys of Yiddish,* Leo Rosten explains that *gonnif* can mean a thief, a crook, someone who is dishonest in business, or a shady, tricky character it would be smart not to trust. Yet *gonnif* can also mean a wonderfully clever person, a wise or precocious child, or a person who outsmarts an inflexible bureaucracy.

Rosten explains that if you speak of someone admiringly with a lilt in your voice and say, *"What* a gonnif," it means you are appreciating how cleverly this person can outsmart the system and take advantage of a loophole. At times in life, cleverness is appropriate. On the other hand, if you say disapprovingly with a disgusted tone of voice, "What a *gonnif,"* it means you are talking about someone who hurts people, who deceives them, or who looks out for his own interests at the expense of others. That one word—*gonnif*—can mean brilliant cleverness or cruel insensitivity, depending on whether the feelings of others are considered and respected.

Therefore, when the Eighth Commandment says *"Lo tig-nove,"* or "Don't be a gonnif," it isn't telling you to feel guilty for being clever, ambitious, assertive, or successful. It does warn you that there's a line between cleverness, ambitiousness, or assertiveness and unfairly hurting someone else. The biblical words telling you not to steal or be deceitful also challenge you daily to decide whether you want to seek a life of integrity and wholeness. The Eighth Commandment forces you to choose consciously whether you want to settle for a life of getting what you think you want and never be at peace because you know in your heart that you stepped on a few too many people along the way.

MAINTAINING YOUR INTEGRITY EVEN IN DIFFICULT SITUATIONS

If you decide to take the Eighth Commandment seriously and make a commitment to yourself (and possibly to God) to live more compassionately and responsibly, four key principles can help you live with greater wholeness and integrity in your daily life:

Integrity Principle #1: *Take time to make conscious decisions. When you are faced with a tough dilemma, don't settle for a quick solution that hurts you or hurts someone else. Take some extra time and ask for assistance to see if there is another alternative that will combine much better what you need and what will avoid hurting others.*

As a psychologist I have watched too many people rush into important decisions. Rather than deciding in haste and regretting the decision later, give yourself time to think fully through the ramifications your decision will have on yourself and the people around you. If you can, take time to consult with your most trusted friends, family, clergy members, or therapist.

Think back on the tough decisions you've made in your life. Did you make sure to take enough time and get advice? In your work life, did you ever do something questionable because you didn't want to disappoint your boss? If you'd had more time, would you have been able to come up with a better solution? In your sex life, did you ever feel rushed into saying yes to something, only to find the next day you wished you'd said no? In your family life and friendships, did you ever agree to go along with a misguided plan?

Professor Teri Bernstein, who teaches business and personal ethics at Santa Monica College near Los Angeles, has a theory about why most people settle for shortsighted solutions that compromise their ethics. She suggests, "Most people instantly come up with only two options—one that is self-sacrificing and one that is self-centered and hurts others. In my courses, I try to teach students to look at every dilemma as a chance to find that third option—the one which takes your needs into account and also avoids hurting other people. It often takes creative, nonlinear thinking or several diverse viewpoints to come up with that third option, but it's important if you want to maintain your integrity."

For a good example of the need to find a creative third option, let's return to Ruth's dilemma, mentioned at the beginning of this chapter. Ruth was faced with her supervisor's request to develop a plan for "downsizing," or reducing by 50 percent, their department's staff. At first, Ruth told me she could imagine only two drastic options. Either she would have to tell her boss, "I refuse to do your dirty work and fire all these people. I quit." Or she could be a loyal employee and design a program that insensitively got rid of numerous women and men. When I asked Ruth to brainstorm with me on what might be a more creative third option, she and I came up with several possibilities.

One possibility was to offer several employees the opportunity to job-share with flexible hours and a shorter workweek until business picked up again. Instead of firing people, the company could keep those who were able to work fewer hours. A second possibility was to design a compassionate and helpful program for assisting people in finding new jobs. I suggested to Ruth that she speak with a few local experts on outplacement counseling and job retraining to see what affordable options were available to help the displaced employees make an easier transition back into full employment. A third possibility was not only to redesign Ruth's department but also to work with other departments in the company to see who might benefit from some of the talented people that Ruth's boss wanted to fire.

After Ruth spent a few days researching the costs and details of these three options, she presented them to her boss. As she told me later, "I wasn't completely successful in saving *every-one's* job. But I did feel a sense of satisfaction that I had helped numerous people stay employed. Plus I helped establish a supportive and practical series of counseling options for those we absolutely had to lay off."

Integrity Principle #2: Confront your own habits of being sneaky, deceptive, or insensitive.

We all have certain situations in which we slip into deception and dishonesty. Think about your own behavior at work, in relationships, in family conflicts, or in raising children, and notice which of the following situations and tendencies challenge you:

- Do you tend to get impatient and interrupt?
- Do you sometimes cut corners or take what you need from a situation and lie to cover up what you've done?
- Are you sometimes rude or cold to people, especially those who you perceive as below you in status or intelligence?
- Do you ever exaggerate or misrepresent your credentials or your contribution to projects in order to impress people?
- Do you occasionally find yourself doing things you know are unkind, immoral, or illegal in business because you haven't been able or willing to develop better options?
- Do you ever feel as though you are "faking it" or doing whatever will get people to like you?
- Do you sometimes become controlling, possessive, or restrictive of someone, even though he or she would probably act responsibly given a little more slack?
- Do you sometimes take advantage of people's innocence, niceness, or trust?

My goal in asking you to look at these questions is *not* to make you feel guilty, but rather to help you see where in your life you need to make careful efforts to bring your behavior in line with your values. You can begin working on these issues as soon as right now or you can make them your top priorities during Lent, Ramadan, the Jewish High Holidays, or whenever you tend to examine your spiritual progress.

In order to change these habits, it helps to understand that at one time in your early life you probably needed to act this way. Quite often I have found when counseling people that they formed dishonest or sneaky behavior in order to survive in their families of origin. For example, if you grew up with an extremely controlling or easily upset parent, you probably learned to be secretive in going about your life in order to grow beyond that restrictive environment. As an adult, you need to become conscious of these habits, recognize them as inappropriate, and develop other attitudes and behavior that do not compromise your integrity or hurt other people.

Overcoming an Old Habit

I recently counseled a very creative computer-software designer named Edwin who came into therapy because his girlfriend, Claire, and his business partner, Michael, had each complained to Edwin that he tended to be secretive and a little bit dishonest with them.

Specifically, in his relationship with Claire, Edwin pretended to be content to go along with whatever Claire wanted to do together but later would get impatient and resentful. Yet he insisted that Claire always got her way and he never got what he wanted in the relationship. In his computer-software partnership with Michael, Edwin usually let Michael call the shots, but would later become resentful and rebellious.

As Edwin admitted during counseling, "I usually try to be nice, and I let other people make most of the decisions. But then I start to feel frustrated that things are turning out wrong." As a result, Edwin had become short-tempered, sometimes cutting Claire off in conversation or putting her down for little things. Edwin had also begun to feel rebellious at work and recently had failed to let Michael know about an important new customer whom Edwin was thinking about keeping for himself.

I asked Edwin to explore exactly how he had learned to keep things to himself and act so cautious around people who were more decisive and up-front. Edwin explained, "When I was little both my dad and my mom were extremely opinionated and insistent. I never got to have things my way, and I learned there was no point in speaking up because they always had the last word."

After several months of counseling, Edwin was able to break his habit of being overly compliant. Edwin had to learn slowly that, unlike his parents, Claire and Michael *did* want to know what Edwin needed and they weren't going to dominate him if he started speaking up earlier—*before* he became resentful. Even though it took a while to change this lifelong habit, Edwin gradually began to speak up sooner and let others know how he felt about things.

Today, Edwin is still somewhat soft-spoken and polite, but his self-confidence and happiness have grown enormously. Recently, an incident arose in which Edwin had to decide whether to tell Michael that he disagreed with his somewhat dishonest strategy for landing an important new customer. Edwin not only spoke up to Michael, he helped Michael develop an honest and forthright way of winning this important customer.

Integrity Principle #3: Anticipate when doing the right thing will be unpopular.

Principled action sometimes causes people to turn against you. If your boss is unethical and you refuse his or her mandates to behave in the same style, you will have problems. If you are a stockbroker who refuses to go along and churn the accounts of your clients, some colleagues will resent your honesty. If you are an attorney who refuses to inflate the number of billable hours charged to your clients and you work for a firm that loves to overcharge, then you may be held back from partnership or other perquisites of the job. Or if you work for a company that routinely overprices its charges for government contracts, you might anger your supervisor by not going along with the deception.

To protect yourself in practical ways in situations in which your honesty and integrity may disrupt your life, family, and career:

- Find out who else in your company behaves ethically. Try to cultivate enough allies who will back you up if you're ever mistreated for your decency.
- Document in writing whenever your proper behavior is criticized, mocked, or impeded by someone else.
- Take time each day to pray, meditate, or read inspiring writings that will support your inner strength no matter how isolated or lonely you get.
- Find or start a support group of people who share your principles and commitment to acting with compassion.
- Become active in your industry or professional association so that you can cultivate important allies and get emotional support for whatever ethical battles are taking place where you work.

"I Don't Know How Much Longer I Can Hang in There"
A client of mine, Charlene, went to law school years ago because she wanted to make a positive contribution to society. But when jobs were hard to find she became an attorney specializing in

representing corporations involved in insurance litigation. After a painful divorce, in order to support her two children she needed to keep her job.

As Charlene told me when she first came for counseling, "Hardly a week goes by in which I don't have at least one moral dilemma. Whether it's doing something dishonest to help a corrupt client or having my boss insist that I need to start charging more to meet our quota for billable hours, I'm constantly being asked to compromise my values. The worst challenge so far happened recently when one of the senior partners told me I needed to act more 'ladylike' around a certain corporate client who seems to be intimidated by any woman who walks into the room. I don't know how much longer I can hang in there, but I've also got a mortgage to pay and two kids to put through school."

In counseling, Charlene and I worked on alleviating the emotional and psychological stresses from her job, and on the spiritual issues raised by her work. Over the next few weeks, Charlene began to take the steps listed above to strengthen her ability to act ethically. She began reading spiritual texts and meditating for a half hour each morning to clarify and support her sense of well-being; she started to cultivate allies at work who shared her values; and she joined a professional support group of women attorneys from various firms where she made several new friends and important contacts.

Six months after she had first come in for counseling, Charlene heard from one of the women in her professional support group that a position was opening up at another firm. Charlene applied for and got the job, which involved doing the type of consumer-advocacy work she had always wanted to practice. While there have been a few moral dilemmas at her new job, Charlene reports, "It's a lot better here because at this new firm I don't have just one or two allies but a dozen or more people who share my values. It's so much easier making healthy decisions when I'm surrounded by caring people. Finally, I'm in a place where I don't have to hold my nose half the time."

Integrity Principle #4: Share a portion of what you have with people who have less.

Many of the scholarly writings about the Eighth Commandment point out that not only shouldn't we steal from other people but that we have a spiritual obligation to the corollary of the Eighth: make sure that others don't need to steal in order to feed or clothe their families. This idea of shared responsibility for the hungry and poor in our midst is found in several places in Exodus and Leviticus, as well as in many other teachings since that time. Leviticus, chapter 19, explains the Eighth Commandment in detail as the key to finding fulfillment and satisfaction in a stressful life of hard work.

In Leviticus, chapter 19, verse 11, the Eighth Commandment is repeated as "You shall not steal; you shall not deal deceitfully or falsely with one another." Verses 9–10 read, "When you reap the harvest of your land, you shall not reap all the way to the edges of your field, or gather the gleanings [the things left behind] of the harvest. You shall not pick your vineyard bare, or gather the fallen fruit of your vineyard; you shall leave them for the poor and the stranger." In other words, we have a duty to others to make it easy and nonshameful for a poor or hungry person to enjoy a portion of whatever we create. Without having to beg for help, those who are in serious need can be provided for by the rest of us. Each of us has an obligation to give a portion of our money, our products, or our creative gifts to people who might be hungry, homeless, or unable to afford what we have to offer. The reason for this generosity is explained in similar terms by Jewish, Christian, Muslim, Native American, and other spiritual traditions.

In Judaism, there is a humbling suggestion: "A person should meditate on the fact that life is like a revolving wheel, and in the end a person, or one's children, or one's grandchildren, may be reduced to taking charity. One should not think, therefore, 'Should I diminish my income by giving it to the poor?' Instead, one should realize that one's property and creative gifts are not one's own, but only deposited with you as a trust to do with as the Depositor [God] wishes."

Many Catholic and Protestant writers and members of the clergy have also written that our work and our rewards belong to God and not to us alone. For instance, a recent chapter on the Eighth Commandment written by Protestant Reverend Robert Schuller of Garden Grove, California, says, "If you believe in the God who believes in you, then you'll believe that God gives to you—and to every person—some idea, some dream, some desire to achieve or acquire. Your duty is to see this as a divine opportunity entrusted to the care and keeping of your imagination, your ingenuity, and your hard work. You must seize the moment, develop the possibility, and return your accomplishment as a gift to God, worthy to be an offering of thanksgiving to the God who entrusted the treasured opportunity to you."

In Islam, there is also a strong sense of justice and compassion for the poor. The Quran insists that the human desire for acquiring wealth or status must be balanced by fair play, a sense of honor, and the annual "poor due" distribution of a portion of one's holdings to those who are in need. According to Islamic teachings, not giving to the poor essentially breaks the flow of how money and divine gifts are to be distributed. Holding back on what you owe the poor is like blocking an artery of circulation and clogging a vital passageway.

Many Native American tribes believe that sharing your wisdom and your gifts with each person of the community is a natural duty. As described by Bear Heart, a Native American healer in New Mexico who wrote *The Wind Is My Mother,* to share what you have and what you know with others is beneficial to your own soul as well. He explains, "To be replenished, we need to keep emptying ourselves to receive more. In that way, we become vessels, holding up one hand to receive the blessings and then opening up the other hand so that we become channels—letting those blessings flow into the lives of others."

CHANGING FROM AN ATTITUDE OF INSUFFICIENCY TO A FEELING OF FULLNESS AND GENEROSITY

After years of counseling people from all economic circumstances, I can assure you that very few human beings ever feel satisfied from what they do for a living. Even if someone has a huge income, he or she usually has sizable debts, risky projects, or internal fears that cause an ongoing feeling of insufficiency and stress.

Yet whenever someone follows the advice in Leviticus 19 to "set aside the gleanings of your harvest" and shares his or her gifts and opportunities with others who happen to be having a hard go of it, a powerful sense of wholeness and completeness results. Instead of feeling you'll never have enough, gradually your mind starts to notice that by repeatedly sharing with others you have more than you thought and more than enough.

A traditional Jewish saying is "Even a poor person who survives on charity should give regularly to charity." In other words, no matter how little you have, there is a powerful liberating feeling that comes with being generous and helping others on a habitual basis. It's particularly good for your psyche to give regularly to charity and do volunteer work if you've been fired, laid off, or are going through a hard emotional time. Instead of feeling insufficient and cut off from the world, you will find yourself feeling useful and appreciated.

Many spiritual traditions encourage setting aside and giving to the needy at least ten percent (a tithing) of your income or creative gifts. As Reverend Robert Schuller points out, "You will never feel poor if you are rich enough to give away ten percent of whatever you earn. No matter how slight or slim your income, you'll never feel the embarrassment or shame of poverty as long as your mind and mood are stirred to philanthropy. This kind of stewardship is the secret of financial peace of mind."

In his analysis of the Eighth Commandment, Rabbi Isaac Klein offers a similar viewpoint: "Whatever we have, we only hold in stewardship, in trust from God. It is significant that there is no word in Hebrew for beggars or alms. The Hebrew equivalent, Tzedakah, which we say when talking about giving to the poor, actually means righteousness or right doing. According to our doctrine, the poor have a right to be supported by those who are more fortunate because the more fortunate are only stewards for what belongs to God."

The Talmud says, "One who wishes to donate [generously] should not give more than a fifth of one's income, lest one comes to be in need of charity." Rabbi Joseph Telushkin explains these figures as follows: "The psychological wisdom in specifying minimum and maximum donations to charity is twofold. It encourages people to give more than they would otherwise. I have noticed that people who give two or three percent of their income to charity usually think of themselves as generous. And it enables sensitive people who have donated the requisite amount to enjoy their possessions without guilt."

Besides giving money, there are many other ways to share your gifts with people who need them but can't afford to pay for them. You could devote a percentage of your time to volunteering or reserve a percentage of your product line or creative energies for projects that might not make a huge profit but can make a positive difference. For instance, when I worked for Doubleday Publishing Company in the 1970s we devoted a part of each list of new publications to children's books with positive and multicultural themes that rarely made a profit.

"I Began Feeling Good About My Life Again"

A somewhat spiritual patient of mine with a dry sense of humor, Jeremy currently works as an accountant for a midsized firm. He had come into counseling because he was frustrated and burned out after years of working for several high-pressure financial-services companies.

Jeremy told me, "A long time ago I actually believed it might be nice to have a secure, well-respected profession like accounting to help me pay for my son's designer athletic shoes and my daughter's orthodontia. But the longer I've worked and the more I've risen to higher echelons of number crunching at various firms, the more empty I've felt."

Three months before he came in for counseling, Jeremy lost his wife, Marianne, to cancer. As a result of her death, he said, he felt especially frustrated with his long hours and what he called "the yearly deluge of new tax regulations and loopholes that I have to learn and utilize so that my corporate clients can write off all sorts of stuff you and I can only dream about."

During the four months that I saw Jeremy in counseling he did some extensive grieving and also explored ways in which he could assist causes that would bring him a stronger sense of meaning and satisfaction. Specifically, Jeremy began volunteering a few hours a month to help two nonprofit organizations with free financial advice. One was related to the cancer that took his wife and the other developed after-school arts programs for inner-city children. He also worked with the senior partners at his financial-services company to develop a pro bono (for the public good) service. This free and low-fee segment of the firm would allow the staff to spend a few hours each week doing taxes and financial planning for low- and middle-income people who normally could not afford the advice of a top financial-services professional.

On the day Jeremy completed his therapy, he told me, "Finding a way to give back to other people has meant more to my daily satisfaction than all the years I've been working at making a living. I used to dread getting up in the morning and commuting to work because it was so much of the same old, same old. But once I started to see a higher purpose for all this number crunching I began feeling good about my life again."

Living with greater integrity and wholeness is a goal that many people feel is out of reach or no longer relevant in these competitive times. But as these examples and guidelines from the Eighth Commandment illustrate, it's extremely rewarding when you find a way to be moral and compassionate in situations where previously you were oblivious or numb. Living with integrity is one more way to awaken the sparks of light within your soul and to feel a greater sense of spiritual richness.

9

THE NINTH CHALLENGE

Reducing Gossip and Hurtful Talk in Your Daily Life

One of the most misunderstood and overlooked of the commandments is the Ninth, which is usually translated, "You shall not bear false witness against your neighbor." The commandment might at first consideration seem to apply only to making false statements in a court trial, as it urges each of the trial participants: "Don't falsify evidence. Don't lie on the witness stand. Don't let your prejudices about someone influence how you talk about them in court." It's the commandment that says to anyone involved in a legal dispute, "Don't lie or exaggerate, because we can't have a decent system of justice or a cohesive society if people make false accusations or cook up phony evidence against each other."

Some scholars have suggested, however, that if the commandment simply had to do with testifying in court, the Hebrew would begin with the phrase *"Lo ta-eed,"* which would mean "Don't *testify* falsely against your neighbor." But that's not what it says in the Bible. The Hebrew text in the Torah is *"Lo ta-ahneh,"* which translates as "Don't *answer, respond,* or *repeat* against your neighbor," and it applies to far more situations than how to behave in a legal trial.

For many centuries, scholars and commentators have analyzed the Ninth Commandment to understand what is meant by "Don't repeat against your neighbor." Most experts interpret the meaning as "Don't lie or exaggerate when you talk about other people," "Don't gossip about other people," or "Guard your tongue and refrain whenever possible from saying harmful or private things about other people."

From a psychological perspective, this Ninth Challenge of "Don't repeat against your neighbor" suggests that if we hear something negative or embarrassingly private about someone else *we will feel tempted to repeat it,* but by doing so we might in fact harm that person. Joining in negative talk about someone at work or in social situations is also potentially hurtful.

HOW DID GOSSIP MAKE THE TOP TEN?

When I first began studying the additional and deeper meanings of the Ten Commandments, I remember wondering, "How did gossip make the top-ten list?" One can certainly see that murder, stealing, and adultery deserve to be in the top ten. But gossip? Today, gossip is the economic fuel that drives the business of TV news and talk shows, book publishing, magazines, and radio. Where would we be without juicy gossip? Even the financial columns and political analysts these days rely on gossip and rumors as the basis for predicting crucial trends. Is it possible that the Bible is outdated or simply wrong when it says, "Don't gossip"?

TAKING A NEW LOOK AT THE HABIT OF TALKING BEHIND SOMEONE'S BACK

Gossip is a complicated issue, and I'm not referring to the supermarket tabloids that announce movie stars' affairs, their tantrums, addictions, and love children.

To understand what gossip means to you personally, consider that all it requires is one individual where you work, where you go to school, where you worship, or in your neighborhood spreading a dishonest or exaggerated negative story about you. It might take this person only five seconds to spread some dirt about you, and then it might take you five months, five years, or the rest of your life to regain the respect and trust you lost because of the gossip your colleagues, congregants, or neighbors heard.

Gossip is so widespread and common that most of us barely notice the extent to which it exists in our lives. Think about your own daily encounters with gossip for a moment. At work, do you know of a group that gets together over lunch, in the copy room, at the water cooler, on the phone, or through faxes or E-mail to trade juicy stories about people in the office? At your church or synagogue, does a rumor or piece of gossip about a prominent congregant or about the private life of the minister, priest, or rabbi travel at the speed of light? In your neighborhood or in the building where you live, if someone is getting divorced, having an affair, or having trouble with their kids, is it kept private or does the news spread like wildfire?

Many good people have been personally or professionally harmed by someone else's loose tongue. For example, which of the following have *you* experienced either in your own life or in the life of someone you care about:

- In the past did you ever get unfairly teased by classmates or were you ever the butt of cruel comments or snide gossip because of some way in which you were different from the majority?
- In your circle of friends, relatives, co-workers, or colleagues, do you ever feel uncomfortable because someone has a big mouth or likes to spread rumors or belittling stories about you or others?
- Have you ever been in a work or social situation in which an adversary or competitor actively set out to harm you with a story that was exaggerated or untrue?
- Have you ever felt hurt or betrayed because a close friend, roommate, romantic partner, or family member divulged something embarrassingly personal about you to people whom you felt had no business hearing such private stuff?

LIKE FEATHERS IN THE WIND

There's a famous Hasidic story that describes beautifully how hard it is to repair the damage from gossip and rumors spread about a good person. In this tale a student has been saying hurtful things and spreading untrue gossip about his teacher. But eventually the student feels guilty, goes to the teacher, and asks for forgiveness.

The teacher suggests, "If you want to make amends for what you've done, I recommend taking several feather pillows, cutting them open, and letting the wind disperse the feathers."

The student does as he was told and returns to the teacher, who says calmly to the student, "Now, there's one more step. Go out and gather up all the feathers."

The student replies, "But how can I do that? It's impossible. The winds have scattered them in every direction."

The teacher explains, "Now you're beginning to learn about the power of words. Once you have started or repeated a hurtful rumor and it spreads in all directions, it is very difficult to try to undo all the damage."

A CONTROVERSIAL REQUEST

It's one thing to desire that other people not gossip about you, but how willing are you or I to stop gossiping or sharing private information about the people with whom we live, work, go to school, or go to church or synagogue? Guarding one's tongue is not an easy thing to do, especially if you only feel mildly interested in doing so.

To begin to understand how difficult and controversial this Ninth Challenge is for most people today, ask yourself the following question: What would be your first reaction if someone told you, "Keep your mouth shut when friends, neighbors, co-workers, or relatives ask you for the inside dirt about someone else"?

The first reaction of most people to being told not to gossip is "Forget that! This is a free country. I can say whatever I want."

There's a funny story about a new preacher who gives her first sermon to an already established congregation. The sermon topic is the Ten Commandments, and as the new preacher discusses "Honor thy father and mother," the congregants seem impressed and say to one another, "Now, that's great preaching." When the new preacher starts talking about "Thou shalt not murder" and "Thou shalt not steal," the congregants are nodding in agreement and whispering to each other, "Excellent preaching! Very moving!"

But when the preacher gets to talking about the Ninth Commandment and suggests, "If we want to build a stronger sense of community and partnership, we've got to stop gossiping about each other and saying things behind each other's backs," a vocal member of the congregation whispers loudly to the next person, "Now the preacher's gone from preaching to *meddling*."

Human beings do not take very kindly to someone trying to reduce or eliminate their "inalienable right" to gossip and talk trash about other people. It feels to many people like censorship, rigidity, or unnecessary prudishness. I have heard many intelligent and compassionate people say of the Ninth Commandment's request to stop gossiping, "That's unnatural. It's just not going to happen. Gossiping is not something that people are willing to give up anytime soon."

IF YOU DO CUT BACK ON GOSSIP, WHAT MIGHT YOU BE GIVING UP?

I need to warn you that if you decide to take seriously this Ninth Challenge and you successfully reduce the amount of gossip, backstabbing, and hurtful talk you allow in your daily life, you might be giving up a lot. There are several psychological reasons why human beings love to spread rumors, and if you cut back on gossip, you might feel a twinge of remorse. Just like someone who cuts back on chocolate or rich desserts for health reasons, you might feel a bit deprived and edgy at first. This feeling of awkwardness or discomfort might last until the new habit of less gossip becomes more familiar to you.

People gossip because it gives them:

• A sense of feeling equal to people they've put on a pedestal. If you can gossip about the private dirt of British royalty, American millionaires, stunning supermodels, or your sister-in-law whose house is so immaculately clean, it can give you a sense of relief; you may think, "Hey, maybe I'm not so bad off after all."

• A sense of revenge against people who have mistreated them. When you pass along hurtful talk about an unpleasant boss, ex-spouse, former friend, or current rival, it lets you ventilate some of the resentment you've stored inside.

• A sense of bonding for groups that have a common adversary or ideological opponent. Quite often you'll hear conservatives trying to find and spread dirt about liberals, or liberals seeking and dishing dirt about conservatives. As left-wing journalist Andrew Kopkind wrote in his book *The Thirty Years War* about why he took great pleasure in gossiping about a specific reactionary politician, "Gossip serves as justice in a corrupt world."

• A sense of voyeuristic pleasure that is socially permitted. You'd get arrested if you tried to sneak a peak into the bedroom of Antonio Banderas, Kevin Costner, Sharon Stone, or Cindy Crawford to see what his or her sex life is like. But if you pick up *People* magazine, *Us*, or *Entertainment Weekly*, you will receive a "no felony, no misdemeanor" dose of gossip and sensual information about these and other stars.

• A sense of satisfaction from pretending to be an "expert" about issues and private information they only know partially. Many people feel smart, powerful, and "in the know" when they gossip, even if they are passing along half-truths and items for which they only possess the most superficial portion of the whole story. An old Spanish proverb says, "The person who knows only a little says very much." Even with partial information, however, you might feel proud to be the first person on your block or in your office to have a juicy piece of gossip no one else has heard yet.

• A subtle way to enforce codes of behavior. In any family, group, or organization, one of the ways to keep people informed about "what's acceptable" and "what's shameful" is by gossiping and snickering about anyone who's crossed the line into what the enforcers feel is socially unacceptable behavior. By saying hurtful things about the rebellious outsider, the family, group, or organization implies to its members, "Don't be like him or her, because then we'll gossip about you, too."

WHAT BENEFITS MIGHT YOU RECEIVE FROM CUTTING BACK ON GOSSIP?

My goal in writing about the Ninth Commandment is *not* to turn you into an uptight, no-fun, can't-laugh-at-a-joke kind of person, but to offer you some spiritual and psychological reasons for cutting back on gossip and hurtful talk in your daily life. And you may find that this reduction serves a useful purpose in your personal and professional activities.

In my own life and in counseling many others, three major benefits have become apparent for cutting back on gossip.

Benefit #1: Cutting back on gossip is one of the best ways to see whether you intend to live according to the Golden Rule.

If you say something hurtful or negative behind someone's back or far beyond their earshot, the odds are slightly in your favor this person will never know exactly who said it. So if you are the kind of person who likes getting away with things and who doesn't feel bad about doing to others what you wouldn't want done to you, then gossip and snide comments may seem an effective way of letting off steam and not getting caught.

On the other hand, if you think of yourself as someone who tries to live up to the Golden Rule, then gaining control of the urge to gossip becomes an excellent experiment to see how well you intend to live up the statement "Love your neighbor as yourself."

The Golden Rule is first stated in the Book of Leviticus, chapter 19, verse 18, as "Love your fellow as yourself, for I am the Eternal One." Later it was explored in depth by the great teacher Hillel, who in the first century B.C.E. was asked by an impatient student to summarize the essence of Judaism while the student stood on one foot. Hillel's famous response to this bold request was "What is hateful to you, don't do to your neighbor. The rest is commentary . . . now go and study."

As described in the Book of Matthew (19:16–19), when Jesus of Nazareth was asked, "Rabbi, what good thing must I do to receive eternal life?," Jesus replied, "Why do you ask? . . . If you want to enter life, keep the commandments . . . and love your neighbor as yourself." In the Book of Romans (13:9), the disciple Paul adds, "The commandments are summed up in one sentence, 'You shall love your neighbor as yourself.' "

Most people have a vague sense that they agree with and would like to live according to this Golden Rule. It seems useful both for how we'd like to handle our personal relationships and how we'd like the rest of the world to treat us. Yet living up to the Golden Rule depends on a deep sense of empathy for another person's discomfort, which many people are unable to do when they're feeling angry, competitive, or self-righteous. It takes an active shift in perspective to be able to ask yourself, "Can I stop myself from divulging something hurtful to someone else, even if it is only another person and not myself who will feel the hurt?" or as the Muslim mystic Al-Ghazali suggests, "If you want to know the foulness of something, consider how you shun it and despise it *when someone else does it to you*. For you do not realize the foulness of your vices from your own case, but from someone else's."

So ask yourself, is the principle of "Don't do unto others that which you find objectionable" a value that you care about or that you've tried to teach your children? If so, then you can begin to view gossip as an especially challenging opportunity to see how closely you're abiding by the Golden Rule.

Benefit #2: Guarding your tongue against saying hurtful things is one way of improving the karma or consequences of your actions in this lifetime.

From a Buddhist, Hindu, or Zen perspective, there are three types of Karma, or consequences, that play out in our lives. These include the consequences we are working out in this lifetime because of actions from previous lives (Prarabdha-Karma); the consequences we will face in future lives because of past lives (Sanchita-Karma); and the consequences we will face in the future because of our current actions in this lifetime (Agami-Karma).

Bad-mouthing other people behind their backs falls under the category of Agami-Karma, the future consequences we can prevent or worsen right now depending on how we control or indulge *our current harmful inclinations and desires*. In essence, from a Buddhist, Hindu, or Zen perspective, if you guard your tongue and avoid bad-mouthing people you create less future pain for yourself and those you love. On the other hand, if you give in to the urge to spread gossip, you create painful consequences for the future.

A similar Talmudic saying teaches, "Gossip is like a three-pronged tongue which injures the spirit of three people: the person about whom the gossip is said, the person who listens to it, and *also the person who says it.*"

Regardless of your religious affiliation, if you tend to believe that how you treat others comes back to you, then gossip and rumors can't be thought inconsequential or escapable. Talking behind someone's back may temporarily seem like a way to get away with something, but if you believe in spiritual consequences or wounded souls then you may be setting yourself up for future pain. And if you find a way to cut back on gossip and hurtful talk, you will then gain some control over improving your Karma or the well-being of your spiritual self.

Benefit #3: Questioning and contradicting the gossip or generalizations you hear about groups of people who are different from you is an important act of social responsibility and fairness.

The most harmful speech is racism and sexism. Complicity or silence in the face of such malignant speech is also harmful. Once again, the Golden Rule applies. If someone were bad-mouthing *your* race, ethnicity, gender, or religion *behind your back,* would you want the bystanders to speak up for you, to keep silent, or to join the insensitive gossip about your group?

Questioning the negative things people say about others not only benefits the target of the hateful talk, it also prevents the hurtful remarks from lodging in the minds of anyone present. For a moment, think about the false generalizations or stereotypes to which you were exposed when growing up. Have you been able to question and overcome these initial generalizations, or do they still affect your reactions to other people?

Repeating even *seemingly positive generalizations* about a group can be hurtful or cause tensions. For example, saying, "All Asian-Americans are good in math" can cause resentment against Asian-Americans or embarrassment and pressure for those Asian-Americans who do not in fact fit the stereotype.

Or saying "Jews don't have an alcoholism problem" is a false generalization that can cause an increase in the shame and desire to avoid seeking treatment in those Jewish men and women who do struggle with a drinking problem.

By actively questioning stereotypes you accomplish three things:

- You make the person who is telling hurtful things about a group think twice before maligning other people.
- You prevent bystanders from accepting slander as truthful.
- You make sure you don't internalize and later repeat lies or hurtful remarks.

Each of us faces the awkward challenge from time to time of confronting someone who makes a racist, sexist, or prejudicial remark. Do you let it slide, or do you say something and risk making waves? If you do speak up, what is the best way to do so?

On the day of the Oklahoma City bombing, rumors were spreading that the Alfred P. Murrah Federal Building had been blown up by "Arab terrorists." Although it seemed possible the rumor spreaders could be right, I had an uncomfortable feeling in my gut that these rumors were based on stereotypes and fear.

At a meeting, when a colleague said, "This is exactly the kind of thing Arab terrorists are going to be doing throughout North America," I felt I had to say something. Trying to remain appropriate to the tone of a collegial meeting, I asked the other person if he had any basis for his comments. He seemed surprised that someone was questioning him. He coughed, cleared his throat, and tried to look authoritative as he said, "Well, everyone knows what these people are like."

That started a conversation in which several colleagues admitted they, too, were uneasy about the rush to judgment and the hurtful generalizations about Arabs being tossed about in the media and in private circles during the first hours after the Oklahoma City bombing. Pretty soon the rumor spreader was outnumbered and it became clear none of us was going to believe his rumor or his stereotyping.

Now, some people reading this might say, "Why get all concerned? If someone gets insulted or stereotyped and they're not even in the room, how are they going to be hurt?" Yet experts who have studied the nature of prejudice and discrimination know that unconfirmed and unconfronted rumors spread *behind people's backs* cause long-lasting, negative perceptions and harsh judgments. In a society where several million Arab-Americans are viewed by many with suspicion and false stereotypes, some people have argued that Arab-Americans are the last ethnic group in the United States about whom people still get away with saying hurtful remarks.

As a Jew who grew up being taught repeatedly, especially during the Passover story each year, "Our ancestors were strangers in a hostile land and we need to open our hearts to all who are minorities in our own lands today," it doesn't sit well with me when I hear any group being stereotyped or maligned. I share the belief of many Jews, Christians, Muslims, and other Americans that none of us is truly free until everyone is treated with fairness and respect. The words of Reverend Martin Niemoller, a Christian minister in Germany who strongly opposed the Nazi regime and was jailed in the 1930s, come to my mind whenever I'm in a situation where another group is being maligned:

"First they came for the Socialists and I did not speak out—because I was not a Socialist. Then they came for the trade unionists and I did not speak out—because I was not a trade unionist. Then they came for the Jews and I did not speak out—because I was not a Jew. Then they came for me—and there was no one left to speak for me."

Even though it may not be socially correct or polite to speak out against prejudiced statements, the Ninth Commandment challenges us to stop those who would spread rumors or incite prejudice against people who are at risk of being mistreated in order to live together as a community.

The terrorists who killed all those children and federal office workers in Oklahoma City were white Americans, not Arabs, not foreigners. Yet for many hours after the bombing, anti-Arab sentiment flared throughout the country. The Islamic Center in Los Angeles received more than a dozen harassing phone calls. A bullet was fired through the window of a mosque in Indianapolis. Many Muslims who are United States citizens reported obscenities and accusations being hurled at them. An American citizen with an Arab-sounding name was taken off a flight in London and flown back to the United States for questioning. At a mosque in Los Angeles, an Islamic man praying to Allah was quoted as saying, "We prayed for those who are innocent victims of the disaster in Oklahoma City and we also pray that America will keep its tradition of accepting other faiths and other creeds."

Sometimes it can be awkward or lonely to speak out against prejudice, but in many cases all it takes is one person to question a toxic belief for the truth to become clear to the hearts and minds of witnesses and listeners. Even if the words of hate are not about you or your group, defusing the harm those words can cause is still worth the effort of speaking up in opposition.

HOW EXACTLY DO YOU CUT BACK ON OTHER TYPES OF GOSSIP AND HURTFUL TALK?

Most people have little or no desire to become mindful and careful in their speech, which makes your own challenge to cut back on gossip even more difficult. Fortunately, scholars and teachers have been studying this issue and offering spiritual, practical guidance for many centuries. In the nineteenth century, a Lithuanian rabbi named Israel Hacohen Kagan wrote an extensive classic text on reducing gossip in your life. His book title, *Hofetz Hayim* (The One Who Loves Life), is from Psalm 34, which says:

> *Who is the one who loves life,*
> *whose desire is for years of goodness:*
>
> *If you guard your tongue from evil*
> *and your lips from deceitful speech.*
> *If you avoid cruelty and do good,*
> *if you seek peace and pursue it.*

Hofetz Hayim was later updated in a 1975 book called *Guard Your Tongue* by an Orthodox rabbi named Zelig Pliskin, and is used around the world as a guide for mindful, conscious speech. In 1993 a Reform rabbi named Stephen Wylen wrote a book called *Gossip: The Power of the Word* to make the teachings of *Hofetz Hayim* more accessible to less traditional men and women. Most recently, in 1996 Rabbi Joseph Telushkin published a highly acclaimed book for Jews, Christians, Muslims, and others on how to speak carefully and responsibly. This easy-to-read guide to becoming a more loving individual is called *Words That Hurt, Words That Heal: How to Choose Words Wisely and Well.*

Based on these writings and on many other scholarly sources, I've come up with the following brief practical reflections for meeting the Ninth Challenge in everyday situations. They are helpful in making sure you don't cause harm with your words.

Reflection #1: *If you are about to say something personal about someone and it might be hurtful or invasive for that individual, ask yourself, "What is my intention here . . . to do good or harm?"*

In most religious and spiritual practices, slowing down and noticing your own intentions is a key step. In Hebrew the word for intention is *kahvahnah,* and many feel the essence of the Jewish way (or *halakhah*) is to make sure we're not run by lower instincts but by *higher intentions.* In the Buddhist, Hindu, and Zen traditions, your inner *intention* is that which matters in the long run, and it matters more than the external result of an action in determining whether you are producing good or bad Karma. Christian teachings also emphasize that which you intend in your heart. In Romans (2:14–16), it's explained that "what the law requires is *written on your heart*" and that "God will judge the secret thoughts of all."

An important first step for applying the Ninth Challenge to your daily life is to slow down each time you're about to spread gossip and ask yourself, "Are my intentions good or am I seeking to do something sneaky, vengeful, or egotistical here?"

Reflection #2: *Recognize that the issue is not whether the gossip is true or false. Will your words likely produce harm or good?*

Many people who spread hurtful gossip make the mistake of saying, "Well, I wasn't at fault. I was only passing along the truth about that person." But if you seriously desire to stop hurting people with your words, you need to understand that even truthful statements can be hurtful if taken the wrong way or if spread to the wrong person. For example, you might say casually to a friend, "Jane is great in bed" or "Bill is terrible with money" and these statements might feel true to you, but you can see almost immediately that Jane and Bill might be harmed by your words, especially if Jane's current lover or Bill's financial partners become upset as a result of hearing these unnecessary disclosures about the past.

Reflection #3: Treat nearly everything said to you as a secret that's entrusted to you for safekeeping, rather than as a juicy piece of gossip to spread.

If you start out by assuming everything is confidential, then you will err on the side of avoiding harm instead of causing harm. If you do feel there is a compelling reason to share someone else's personal information with others, that, for instance, you feel this information can help another person or can prevent some other harm, you can always go back to the person who spoke to you and ask her or him if it's all right to pass along what was told to you in private.

Reflection #4: Carefully select an honorable person with whom you could share private things, to whom you could ventilate or complain confidentially.

Choose the right listener for your words as a measure to prevent gossip, and notify people that you are speaking confidentially when you want information kept secret. You will be successful at stopping many rumors and types of gossip.

Reflection #5: Think seriously about when silence is a mistake.

The Ninth Challenge is *not* about censorship or passivity, but rather about how to build a sense of community that includes discretion, respect, and mutual caring. In any community of people, there are bound to be situations in which it is extremely appropriate and healthy that you speak up and share certain private facts and bits of information. Scholars studying the issue have listed several examples of when you would be preventing harm and doing a necessary good by cautiously and responsibly passing along private details, such as:

A. If someone is about to get married or move in with someone that you know to be violent, abusive, or already secretly married, you have an obligation to tell the person what you know, but clarify what is the factual basis of your comments and what is still unclear, rumored, or not yet observed directly.

B. If you are giving a job reference, a financial character reference, or some other opinion that can specifically prevent harm or loss for someone, you should speak up but be careful to discuss the actions of the other person in descriptive terms ("this is what I saw" and "this is what I was told but cannot prove") rather than judgmental terms ("he is a _____" or "she is a _____"). You should also let the other person know that yours is but one opinion and not necessarily the whole picture about that person.

C. You should report crimes to the proper authorities or speak out to prevent a crime, such as reporting a violent threat, suspected child abuse, or elder abuse, but be sure to describe only what you observed as fact and clarify what you are passing along based on secondhand rumor or speculation.

D. You certainly have the right to point out or correct someone's misbehavior (including a child's), but do so to the person directly rather than going behind his or her back to someone else whenever possible. Be sure to make your corrective comments in a tone that respects the dignity of that person and addresses his or her wrongful *behavior* but doesn't judge or shame his or her *character.*

E. Be quick to confess your own misdeeds and oversights, and attempt to correct any wrongs you committed directly to the person you may have hurt.

Reflection #6: Be willing to let people know you aren't available for gossip or bad-mouthing others, even if that makes you temporarily less "popular."

You don't need to be self-righteous or obnoxious about this. You can say, "I'd rather not comment," "I try not to say anything personal I can't guarantee is true," or "I'm not comfortable judging someone's character." If you say it with humility and warmth rather than a haughty sense of self-importance, you probably won't be ostracized for your integrity. But if you do find that certain cliques and gossipy individuals resent your unwillingness to play by their rules, you will also find many other women and men who respect you for your discretion. Even if you lose a few gossipy friends, certain other people will seek you out for friendship based on the warmth and respectfulness you've shown.

NOTICE YOUR GRADUAL IMPROVEMENTS

At first glance, these guidelines may appear difficult or hard to sustain in the light of the strong human desire to gossip. That's why I call them guidelines for experimenting with this important challenge and not commandments you absolutely must follow 100 percent of the time. In fact, in *Guard Your Tongue* Rabbi Pliskin quotes a scholar who wrote, "Even if someone has learned the laws of Loshon Hara ["evil tongue"] in their entirety, he definitely will not be able to observe them to their fullest extent without constant review."

Paying attention to your gradual progress on this issue is for most spiritual people a lifelong process. In Buddhism, where Right Speech is one of the eight steps of the path toward enlightenment, the first task is to *notice* your speech and what it reveals about your character. Instead of resolving right off to speak with complete integrity, the Buddhist approach says to be mindful and notice how often each day you find it necessary to deviate from the truth, to chatter, gossip, slander, or verbally abuse. You are especially urged to notice when your verbal put-downs are covert—when subtle, belittling, "accidental," or tactless remarks and barbed wit reveal the underlying harm of what you are saying about other people. As you can see, paying close attention to your speech will give you tremendous insights into your own moods, character, and integrity.

If each year of your life you become more mindful and successfully cut back 10–50 percent from the gossip and hurtful talk you used to engage in, that would be a significant improvement. It would also be a huge accomplishment with far-reaching positive consequences for many people.

A Woman of Verbal Brilliance

To give you some idea of what can happen if you begin applying the Ninth Challenge to your daily life, I'd like to tell you about a fascinating woman named Rita, who came to me for counseling after being laid off from her job as a university instructor. Rita is a highly intelligent, very articulate woman who enjoyed working as an associate professor of literature at a nearby university. Unfortunately, her verbal brilliance sometimes got her in trouble in her career and in her personal relationships.

As Rita explained to me, "At my previous job, I was the rising star in the department for a while, making friends and always being in the middle of departmental gossip and strategy sessions. People often seem to be attracted at first to my sarcasm and my ability to poke fun at human foibles, especially when we gossiped behind certain tenured professors' backs."

She admits, however, "Sooner or later I wound up saying the wrong thing about someone who couldn't take a joke that got back to the person. At this last job I was in a meeting with several colleagues and we were exchanging vicious stories about the director of the department, a major bozo with an ego the size of Alaska. Little did I know his best friend, who was in the room at the time, would decide to go and quote me in great detail to the boss. I was ostracized for several months and eventually laid off."

Rita also got in hot water during her marriage to a man she had met during graduate school. "My ex-husband used to listen to me bad-mouthing my colleagues and friends so much that he began to comment, 'Rita, I wonder what you say about *me* behind my back.' In truth, I said some pretty funny but somewhat cruel things about my husband over the years and several of the most hurtful things got back to him. I don't think that's what caused our divorce, but it certainly didn't help build trust or comfort between us."

As I explained to Rita during one of her initial sessions, my therapeutic goal in working with her was *not* to suppress her wit or her verbal brilliance. These gifts are what make her a lively soul at any social or work gathering. I did want to help

Rita discover the discretion that would help her judiciously apply her verbal gifts.

In therapy, we discovered Rita's verbal skills and sarcasm were related to the anger she had stored inside from being raised with two favored siblings—her older brother, "the doctor," and her younger sister, "the stunner." Rita was the middle child. Not quite as academically successful as her brother and not nearly as physically attractive as her sister, Rita had relied on her verbal skills as her major claim to fame. Yet with so much anger stored inside, her wit had become increasingly caustic over the years.

When I offered Rita the guidelines on gossip listed above, her first reaction was "Sounds great for someone else, but not for me! I've always survived by being a verbal warrior, and if you take away my barbed tongue, what will I have left?"

Over the next few weeks, however, Rita began to work on channeling her anger into more positive outlets and finding healthier ways to let off steam besides her old habit of saying hurtful things with her brilliant but somewhat self-defeating tongue. She slowly agreed that the goal was to keep her excellent sense of humor but to stop turning it against other people.

When Rita then began experimenting with these guidelines in her daily life, she found, "I get a good feeling when I stop and consciously choose which people I want to verbally skewer and which people I want to keep quiet about. I'm no angel and I still have quite a big mouth, but I've managed to become a lot more pleasant to live with and work with since I made the decision to get some control over what I say and how I say it."

A few months ago, Rita landed a job at a prestigious college and began dating an interesting man she met at a literary-sites tour of Europe. As she told me during a brief follow-up visit to my office, "I don't want to mess up with these two good situations. If it means I have to watch what I say and not be so brutally funny all the time, I'm willing to give it a try. I used to be completely identified with my smart mouth, but now I think I'm opening up my heart and my gentleness after all these years."

If you seriously desire greater integrity and decency in your life, are you willing to start by how you deal with gossip and hurtful talk? As I mentioned before, it may feel awkward at first to keep to yourself a juicy piece of gossip for which you might be the first person on your block to know something private and shocking. But if you do begin to make conscious choices by asking yourself, "Am I creating harm or good with my words?," it can set the tone for how you want your life to be and open up the possibility of a life based on respect and right speech.

10

THE TENTH CHALLENGE
The Way to Feel Good About What You Have

Have you ever wished you could have the face, the figure, the good health, or the physical stamina of someone else? Have you ever desired to have as nice a home, a family, or social get-togethers as one of your neighbors, friends, or relatives? Have you ever looked at someone else's financial security, successful creative project, or well-behaved children and felt a twinge of envy?

The Tenth Challenge addresses an interesting desire in human psychology, namely our desire for what we don't have and our lack of appreciation for or dissatisfaction with what we do have. Based on the Tenth Commandment from the Book of Exodus, which says, "You shall not covet," this spiritual lesson directs us to learn to handle the natural human tendency to become jealous or discouraged about what other people have. Yet most people don't think of themselves as being envious or jealous *until it hits them by surprise.* For example, here are some comments from people I've counseled. See which of the following sound like you or someone you know:

- "I usually felt pretty good about my appearance until my spouse began flirting with someone at work who's a stunner, and then suddenly I started noticing everything that's less than perfect about my looks."
- "I always thought I was smart enough to make it in the world until I got to graduate school and found myself jealous of how much these people knew and what superior training they had."

- "I never thought much about keeping up with the Joneses until my younger sister bought a house much bigger than ours and I started to notice little things I don't like about where we live."
- "I usually don't feel jealous of people except when I'm listening to other parents brag about their kids and I begin to feel uncomfortable about my two kids, especially how unmotivated and stubborn they are."
- "I know it's not a good idea to compare one's life to other people's lives, because it's only an illusion that other people are happier. But sometimes when my creative projects are stuck or when I feel stressed about money, I can't help wondering if other people have it a lot easier than I do."

The Tenth Challenge explores what to do when you notice you're comparing yourself to others and wanting what others have. Most people are ashamed of having these feelings, but in fact they are quite common. According to Sigmund Freud, "Jealousy is one of those affective states, like grief, that may be described as normal. If anyone appears to be without it, the inference is justified that it has undergone severe repression and consequently plays all the greater part in his unconscious mental life."

Jealous thoughts can flood your body with insecure feelings and painful self-doubts. For example, I once counseled a famous film director who sought therapy because he'd felt unhappy and somewhat depressed for much of his life. No matter what he accomplished, his critical, perfectionist mind (which made him a great director but was torture when he turned it on himself) would always find a way to invalidate his success. Most of the time *his feeling of dissatisfaction came from looking around at his peers* and wishing his films were a little more artistic or a little more financially successful. Like many creative people, he had suffered long bouts of frustration and had many insecurities, especially when he was between projects and unsure of when he would find work again.

Even though this film director was a caring and generous man, there were times when his sense of envy flared up, surprising him with its intensity. I will never forget the comment he made during an especially bad month for him; he admitted, "Every time a friend succeeds, I die a little."

A PERSONAL CONFESSION

When I heard that, my first reaction was empathic. What a difficult way to live, I thought, to have to read the trade papers *Daily Variety* or *Hollywood Reporter* and every time to feel sadness and anger at other directors' lucrative deals. That has to be a terrible drain on his energy, health, and creativity.

I didn't realize until recently that I, too, am capable of feeling that intense kind of envy or jealousy. I usually feel pretty satisfied with whatever goes well in my life and try to be open to learning from events that go badly. I rarely spend time wishing I were like someone else or envying what others have or accomplish.

For eight years, however, beginning in 1986, my wife, Linda, and I went through an extremely difficult ordeal trying to start a family. We learned we were both carriers of a rare genetic disorder called Tay-Sachs disease, which meant that each time Linda got pregnant there was a 25 percent chance the baby would die from this inherited illness. I learned a great deal about the pain of jealousy.

In 1987 we were excited to find out Linda was pregnant, but our hopes crashed when the fetus was tested and we were informed the baby would not live because of Tay-Sachs. In 1990 we had a second ray of hope when Linda got pregnant again, but Tay-Sachs turned up as well in the second pregnancy.

Then, in 1992, we spent several months getting to know a teenage birth mother in Iowa who was pregnant and had decided to make an adoption plan for her child with us. We took a red-eye flight to be there at the birth. We got to know her entire family. We had dozens of friends and relatives waiting for us back in Los Angeles, hoping we would be bringing the child with us on the flight home.

After the baby was born, the birth mother suddenly became indecisive. She kept telling us, "Don't go back to Los Angeles yet; I still might want to go forward with this." Then she would hedge and say, "I can't do it. I know I'm unable to raise this child, but I can't let her go."

For ten days she kept saying one thing and then the opposite. The indecision was torture for her and for us. Several counselors, lawyers, friends, and relatives were unable to help her make a clear decision. Finally, it became obvious she would never be able to let go and the adoption had to be called off. We went home childless again.

A few weeks later I attended a Thanksgiving dinner at which several cousins and other relatives were playing happily with their kids, including an adorable infant and three energetic toddlers. More than ever before in my life, I felt an enormous pang of jealousy and resentment. I finally understood what single people feel like when they're invited to a Noah's Ark–like wedding reception of mostly couples. I began to realize what makes jilted lovers so furious and out of control. Now I truly appreciated what my client the film director meant when he said, "Every time a friend succeeds, I die a little." As much as I didn't want to be jealous, I deeply resented that these cousins had healthy children and Linda and I were still unable to do so.

"TO WISH FOR LONGINGLY"

In Exodus 20, the Tenth Commandment reads, "You shall not covet your neighbor's house: you shall not covet your neighbor's wife, or his male or female slave, or his ox or his ass, or anything that is your neighbor's."

Covet is an unusual word. Yet the emotion is common. We wrestle daily with the desire to have things that are not ours. *Covet* means a lot more than just wanting something. According to the dictionary, to covet is to *wish for longingly.* Not lightly. Not passively or mildly. In English it means enviously to desire that which belongs to another. In Hebrew, the Tenth Commandment, "*Lo takhmohd,*" means, "Don't hold as precious or as a treasured possession something that doesn't belong to you."

Think about those times in your life when you deeply longed for something or someone, when you couldn't stop thinking about how badly you wanted this person, this goal, this dream of yours. To covet is to yearn with so much longing that you feel you'll never be complete and whole unless you satisfy this desire. It explains those moments in your life when you feel upset or frustrated at how unfair life is that you were deprived of something that someone else is enjoying so easily. To quote the philosopher John Locke, "Coveting or envy is an uneasiness of the mind, caused by the consideration of a good or desire, which has been obtained by one we think should not have it before us."

THE DANGERS OF WANTING
WHAT OTHERS HAVE

While mild, brief bouts of envy or jealousy are normal, when these feelings of jealousy persist obsessively or flare up with too much intensity, we become spiritually and psychologically incapacitated. As you look over the illustrations of what I mean by spiritual and psychological wounds due to envy, take note of when you or someone you care about have suffered in these ways:

THE SPIRITUAL PAIN FROM DESIRING AND COMPARING
Various spiritual traditions have different ways of describing what happens when we covet or desire what other people have. For example, in the Buddhist tradition the word for suffering is *duhkha,* and according to the Buddha's early sermons the essence of human suffering is "blind craving or desire." As described by Sylvia Boorstein, a Buddhist meditation teacher in Barre, Massachusetts, "Suffering is what happens when we *struggle* with an experience rather than accepting it or opening to our experience with a wise or compassionate response. I once heard someone say that enlightenment is the ability to say (and mean it) in any moment, 'Well, this isn't what I wanted, but it's what I got, so okay.' "

In Christianity there is a long history of statements that describe why desiring what another has can lead to unhappiness and dissatisfaction. In the fourth century, a priest named Claudian said, "The man who covets is always poor." In the fifth century, Saint Augustine wrote, "The devil is ruler of those covetous desires by which we long for all that passes away." In the seventeenth century, William Penn, the Englishman who helped found Pennsylvania as a Quaker colony, described how "covetousness is the greatest of monsters as well as the root of all evil."

I recently heard two modern Christian perspectives that I would like to pass along so you can decide for yourself which view appeals to your own personal beliefs. The first interpretation of "You shall not covet" was told to me by a Lutheran minister who warned against comparing ourselves to others and wishing our lives were like theirs. She said, "The problem of wanting what someone else has is that it puts us at odds with God's plan for us. God puts on our plate exactly what we need to work on in this lifetime, and if we're always looking enviously at someone else's plate we get distracted from what God has given us."

The second interpretation, also by a woman minister but from a Congregational denomination, disagrees with the first. This second minister told me, "I don't believe that 'God puts on our plate exactly what we need to work on in this lifetime' because that would imply victims of an earthquake, a flood, a war, or a rape are being given exactly what God up on a throne doles out to each individual as reward or punishment. That seems like a simplistic and old-fashioned view of what God is and does."

She explained, "A more modern view is that God is the ongoing force of creation in the universe who sets all things in motion, including natural law and human free will. It may *feel* like God intervenes, tests, deprives, or punishes us sometimes, but I believe those are human interpretations of events set in motion by nature, by our choices, by chance, or by the choices of others. Our lives are a combination of free choice and chance, but always with the comforting, strengthening *Presence* of God within and around us."

This second minister then offered, "With regard to envy and the passion of wanting what others have, I believe that our passions have a purpose. God created all things, including emotions, for a purpose. Problems arise when our passions become unbalanced.

"I believe that when balanced, the purpose of envy is to motivate us to change one's situation, to move forward in life, to allow us to see and reach for the many possibilities offered by God's creation or to celebrate our collective wealth and seek out a deeper relationship with the Holy.

"But when our envy or passion for something gets out of

balance, it can be immobilizing, debilitating, and destructive to relationships. Too much envy or desire can move us backward rather than forward—it narrows our vision to the objects of obsessive desire, which can lead us to blame God for our deprivation and separate ourselves from the Holy. God created us as passionate beings not to become obsessive or stuck but to survive, evolve, and grow toward the Holiness to which we are capable."

This same theological question—Does God keep track of how much is given to us and how much is given to our neighbors?—is addressed not only in Christianity but also in Judaism, Islam, and many other religions as well. Within each tradition, some say God doles out the joy and suffering to each individual, while others say God is the source of creation, connection, and compassion within and around us but does not cause us to have or not have things that are controlled by nature, chance, or human choices.

THE ESSENTIAL HUMANNESS OF WISHING YOU COULD BE LIKE SOMEONE ELSE

Judaic teachings appreciate how common it is to lose sight of one's own purpose and gifts in life because our anxious minds tend to dwell on "Why can't I have what this other person has?" According to the Jewish sages and writings, the Tenth Commandment is referred to as the "most inward of the commandments" because it addresses our most secret desires, longings, and self-criticism. One commentary describes how "the human heart is pained" when we let our desires run wild or start feeling bad about who we are because we are looking at our neighbor's successes with longing.

A story from the Jewish mystical tradition that has always touched me deeply captures the essential spiritual pain caused by comparing ourselves to others and feeling inadequate as a result.

The story is about a man named Zusya, who lived during the eighteenth century and aspired to become a great teacher. But sometimes Zusya was simply good or mediocre or, like the rest of us, capable of having a bad day when nothing seemed to go right.

There are many stories about Zusya's struggle to become a wise teacher and to live according to the teachings he was sharing with others. But the most memorable story about Zusya is what happened when he was dying and he asked God to help him make sense of his imperfect life.

Zusya asked God, "Please tell me, why wasn't I more like Moses, the greatest teacher in our tradition." God replied, "Zusya, that's not the question. The question is *not* why weren't you more like Moses, but *why weren't you more like Zusya.* That's what I want to know."

Zusya never understood or lived up to his own potential because he was longing to be like someone else. That's so human, to look around and wish we could be like someone we admire, or to wish we had what someone else has, or to lose sight of our own path in life because we are looking to someone else for clues and guidance.

The Psychological Pain from Desiring and Comparing

An entire book could be written on the psychology of envy, but I'll simply list a few of the most important negative psychological results to help you begin to recognize what a serious physical, emotional, and spiritual deficit envy causes:

1. Envy increases your daily stress or anxiety levels and ties in to an underlying feeling of insufficiency or self-criticism.

If you were raised by parents or other relatives who said, "Why can't you be like So-and-so," or who implied that no matter what you did it wasn't good enough, there is a high likelihood that you carry these painful messages inside you to this day. You might feel anxious or stressed on a daily basis because you are still secretly trying to win their acceptance, even if you're no longer in close contact with them or they're no longer alive. No matter how successful you are in your adult career or relationships, you might still be feeling the pressure to be like someone else or to live up to an unreasonable expectation of who your family wanted you to become.

One of the most important psychological insights of the twentieth century came from Dr. Karen Horney, a psychoanalyst who quarreled with Freud's views in the 1930s and '40s. Horney demonstrated in her research and therapy work that two of the major causes of human psychological distress are: (A) When we compare ourselves unfavorably against an idealized sense of who our families wanted us to become; and (B) When we compare ourselves against an unrealistic goal we ourselves invented to compensate for the feeling that no matter how hard we tried, our families never quite seemed satisfied. In either case, to disregard your own true self and to keep desiring the lifestyle or success of someone you are not is to set yourself up for severe unhappiness.

2. Comparing and desiring leads to mood swings and physical symptoms of illness.

If you have fallen into the habit of looking enviously at others and wishing your life were more like theirs, your daily moods and physical health may be affected. Every time you start to feel clear and focused on your goals, you can easily be knocked off center by someone else criticizing your approach or by hearing about someone else's most recent triumph. Or you can lose sight of your own tasks and be bogged down in procrastination if you have a habit of getting distracted by envious thoughts about what other people are doing or accomplishing.

Studies show that this daily roller coaster of trying to focus on your own goals and then getting pulled down by envious feelings can also contribute to many physical symptoms. For example, recent research from the field of psychoneuroimmunology (which measures how thoughts and moods affect the immune system and healing processes) has demonstrated that feelings of low self-worth and the belief that others have it better than we do can dramatically affect the production of T cells and other crucial components of our immune systems. This research suggests we are far more susceptible to a variety of ailments and far less able to recover from certain disorders when we are mired in feelings of inadequacy, loss of control, and bitterness.

Studies also show that high blood pressure, heart problems, stomach and digestive disorders, skin ailments, and back problems are sometimes related to feelings of envy, hostility, bitterness, and dissatisfaction. How you deal with this Tenth Challenge can affect not only your psychological health but also your physical health and longevity.

3. Too many comparisons might be affecting those you love in unintended ways.

Even if you promised yourself, "I'll never do to anyone else what was done to me as a child," it's quite common for people to say unintentionally or imply to their kids, spouse, or co-workers, "I wish you could be different" or "I wish you were more like someone else."

If you notice yourself feeling impatient or judgmental about the people you love or wishing they could be different from who they are, you might need to stop and ask yourself, "Is this how I want to treat those I care about? Do I really want to wound them with the same kind of comparisons I grew up with as a child?" Learning how to control your own covetous and comparing impulses will help improve not just your own health but also the health and well-being of those you love.

THREE HEALTHY STRATEGIES YOU CAN USE TO HANDLE ENVY AND COMPARISONS

Now we come to some possible solutions. How exactly do you stop the habit of coveting, comparing, and desiring what other people have? How do you begin to live a life that feels more satisfying? How do you walk the fine line between desiring important goals that can and should be pursued and not obsessing or becoming bitter about plans and dreams that remain out of reach?

Strategy #1: Sometimes you need to take your envious feelings seriously and ask yourself, "Is this a wake-up call?"

Even though most of us feel embarrassed for having an envious or covetous desire, in fact the right strategy sometimes is *not to suppress your jealous feelings but to honor them and turn them into something positive*. The jealous desire you feel inside might be trying to motivate you to follow through on a worthwhile goal that eluded you in the past but that is still within your reach, if you are willing to stretch a bit more this next time.

In spiritual terms, your envious desire might be a spark of intuition, a sign that you need to pursue this goal or dream with extra passion and a new sense of purpose and commitment. In psychological terms, if you repress or feel ashamed of your desire for something it will then persist and become an obsession;

but if you take control of your envy or desire and transform it into something positive and constructive, then you will no longer be obsessed by it.

For example, two years ago a woman named Suzanne came to see me for counseling on why she had been unsuccessful at relationships and how she might improve her chances of finding someone who would be suitable for marriage. During her first session, she admitted with some embarrassment that she felt jealous and resentful whenever one of her friends or co-workers got married. She confided, "I feel ashamed that these feelings of jealousy come up whenever I hear someone else has found a great relationship. I wish I could just be happy for them and not feel so frustrated that it hasn't happened for me."

She had tried to ignore or suppress these jealous feelings, but the more she resisted them the more they persisted in making her feel depressed, sluggish, and unable to do anything positive to improve her chances at a relationship.

In counseling the strategy we took was *not* to downplay or disregard her jealous feelings but to take them seriously. I asked Suzanne, "What if those feelings could be transformed into a positive force in your life? What if these painful thoughts of 'Why is it happening right for everyone except me?' could be a wake-up call that motivates you to try some new ways of finding a great relationship?"

Suzanne's reaction was positive, and during the next several sessions we gained some valuable insights into why she had so much trouble in relationships and what psychological and spiritual blocks were preventing her from achieving her dream of a quality love relationship. We also began to explore what she might do differently this time.

In the past, Suzanne had been very passive in seeking a relationship. She was too embarrassed to tell her friends, relatives, and co-workers exactly what kind of man she was looking for and she was unwilling to try other methods for meeting someone. As a result of taking her strong jealous feelings seriously, she was a little less embarrassed about telling her friends, relatives, and co-workers exactly what kind of man she didn't want and what kind she did want. She also began placing ads in a reputable publication and responding to those that most closely described the kind of person she was seeking.

I had told her when she first began looking for a partner, "You may have to see several frogs before you find a prince." In fact, she went out with seven or eight dreadful guys before she finally found a man whose sensitive heart and brilliant mind were exactly what she was seeking. After seven months of getting to know each other, they became engaged and were recently married.

I truly believe that if Suzanne had simply hid in shame from her envious feelings she would still be waiting passively for Mr. Right to appear. Turning painful feelings of jealousy into specific positive, active steps and confronting inner psychological and spiritual blocks invariably improves your overall life. The Tenth Challenge directs us inward to self-knowledge as the ultimate challenge—and one that it is necessary for us to meet in order to become more adept at integrating the other nine lessons in our lives.

This strategy of facing painful covetous feelings and using them to change one's life works with a variety of issues. One businessman who came into counseling after nearly declaring bankruptcy used this approach to help himself break his focus on other people's successes and to turn the energy generated by those jealous feelings into specific steps for doing a better job at helping customers, cutting costs, and making his own business a lot more profitable. I also recently worked with a woman who is recovering from a damaging stroke and had been feeling depressed by how much mobility she had lost, as well as how frustrating it was to see how much easier everyone else was getting around. By using her jealous feelings as a wake-up call she has become much more motivated and successful at her daily rehabilitation regimen. Instead of feeling ashamed for wanting more mobility, she has used those passionate emotions to fire up her spirit and improve her mobility at a rate far superior to what her doctors had predicted.

This strategy also proved useful with the film director I mentioned earlier who had been feeling depressed and dissatisfied with his life. When I urged him to see his jealous feelings as a wake-up call to become an even better director, he was reluctant at first but then decided to give it a try. He and I began to brainstorm about how he could revive and get financial backing for one of his most artistic and heartfelt creative projects, which had been shelved a few years earlier because of an executive shake-up at one of the studios.

Instead of letting his jealous feelings lead him back into depression, we were actively turning them into sparks of motivation to help him be more creative and persistent. He enthusiastically reedited his film, carefully made an improved three-minute preview trailer for marketing purposes, and began to show it to possible sources of financing. Although it took several months of getting rejected before he found the right backers, he not only had the creative satisfaction of having his film produced, he also generated stronger financial returns for it than for any of his previous films.

As he commented during his final counseling session, "I always thought that if I wanted something badly and was jealous of people who seemed to have it, it meant I was greedy, selfish, or a bad person. But now I've learned that if something truly comes from the heart and is for a good purpose, then there's no harm in wanting it badly and working hard for it. It's not wrong to be passionate and persistent about something, especially when that kind of passion and persistence is the only way for certain good works to get done."

Strategy #2: Sometimes you need to let go of the longing for what you don't have and truly accept what is.

While Strategy #1 applied to those goals that deserve to be pursued with extra commitment, there are some desires that can't or shouldn't be followed. For example, if you have a craving for something unhealthy, self-defeating, or unrealistic, then the best strategy is not to fire up your passion for pursuing it but to learn how to let go of these unproductive longings. Or if you are feeling jealous of something another person has and it simply isn't meant to be yours, then you need to find some way to let go of the envy that is draining your energy and replace it with something else better suited for you.

There's an insightful quote about jealous longing that comes from the writer Joan Didion: "To cure jealousy is to see it for what it is, a dissatisfaction with self, an impossible claim that one should be at once Rose Bowl princess, medieval scholar, Saint Joan, Eleanor of Aquitaine, one's sister, and a stranger in a pink hat seen once and admired on the corner of 55th and Madison—as well as oneself, mysteriously improved."

Since none of us can be all things to all people, we have to let go of certain unrealistic longings and save our energy for those goals and dreams that we select as our top priorities. Unfortunately, many of us don't like to say no to any intriguing desires and goals, even if they detract from our ability to achieve our most important priorities.

For example, I once counseled a man named Bruce, a talented artist with an interest in textiles, graphic design, sculpture, and photography who had been unable to find substantial success in any of these fields because he kept trying to do all four of them. Like many multitalented individuals, Bruce didn't want to say no to any of his creative desires, and he refused to focus for very long or finish most of his good ideas. As a result, he found himself financially insecure much of the time, and he secretly resented people who seemed to have a much easier time picking a goal and sticking to it.

In therapy, we discussed how painful it was for him to keep having good creative ideas that he was unable or unwilling to finish or to build into a successful career. This frustration was compounded by the fact that Bruce grew up in a family where he was frequently compared to his older brother, Richard, a very successful real estate developer who, according to Bruce, has always been "a first-class manipulator and an all-around dishonest guy."

Bruce had come into therapy after his fiancée insisted he needed counseling to get his financial problems and self-defeating habits under control. What became evident in my second session with Bruce was that he carried a great deal of painful longing and jealousy inside himself about Richard. Bruce told me in that second session, "I've always had a secret dream that I'd somehow turn one of my creative projects into a huge financial success that would say to my family, 'See, I'm a somebody, too.' "

But that jealousy had caused him to keep jumping from one project to another, hoping to find the one perfect breakthrough that would undo a lifetime of painful comparisons.

In therapy we decided to work toward a more realistic goal, namely to let go of the desire to compete with his wealthy brother and to focus instead on his own path. Instead of taking on too many projects and failing to finish most of them, Bruce needed to build a career for himself and a life with his fiancée that was realistic, meaningful, and satisfying—and that didn't have the pressure to outdo his brother's success.

We began looking at which of his four interests—textiles, graphic design, sculpture, or photography—he was willing to pursue as a solid career choice and which should remain a hobby or secondary pursuit. After a few months of exploration and research, Richard decided to join a creative firm specializing in graphic design for textile manufacturers. He began focusing on completing his projects and saying no to ideas and whims that would have distracted him in the past. After two years of hard work and discipline, he has developed an impressive portfolio, a number of important contacts and loyal customers, as well as a feeling of satisfaction that he is able to enjoy a successful career as a working artist.

To achieve this, Bruce had to let go of two lifelong desires: his longtime urge to surpass his brother financially and his old habit of saying yes to every creative idea without having to focus or stick to any priorities. But as Bruce told me during his final therapy session, "I thought I would be losing something important if I gave up my drive to match my brother's success. Yet letting go of that painful desire has been one of the most liberating feelings of my life. I no longer wake up each morning comparing myself to my brother and coming up short. I actually have more energy and enthusiasm for my own projects and my own follow-through."

Another client who successfully used Strategy #2 for letting go of painful jealous feelings is a forty-eight-year-old accountant named Barbara who has two college-age children and who came to therapy after her handsome but very controlling ex-husband got married to a woman slightly older than Barbara's kids.

Barbara told me in her initial session that she was angry at herself for feeling as jealous and insecure as she had been since learning about her ex-husband's remarriage. She admitted, "I look in the mirror and I keep obsessively comparing myself to this woman, even though I know I don't really want to be like her. I don't even want to be married to my ex any longer. Yet I resent her and every young woman I see who can make heads turn the way she made his head turn."

For several sessions, we explored Barbara's goals for the second half of her life and her mixed feelings about her body, her attractiveness, and her relationships. Even though we made some definite progress in boosting her self-esteem, she still felt a lingering jealousy and bitterness stirring inside her and making her feel sluggish and depressed much of the time.

Something deeper than talk therapy was needed to help Barbara let go of her painful jealous feelings. So I discussed with her the fact that throughout history, certain spiritual and religious people have created personalized ceremonies and rituals to commemorate important transitions and new beginnings in their lives.

For example, in a recent book called *Four Centuries of Jewish Women's Spirituality*, authors Ellen Umansky and Diane Ashton describe how women over the centuries have created and participated in healing rituals to celebrate the turning points in their lives. Three of the most memorable chapters in the book explain how one woman created a meaningful ritual to honor the loss of a child, another woman created along with some close friends a ritual called Simchat Hochmah (Celebration of Wisdom) to honor her emergence as a wise older woman, while a third woman created a ritual with friends called Sitting Shiva (a Mourning Gathering) for a Lost Love when her sixty-three-year-old husband left her for a woman of twenty-three.

Since Barbara was somewhat active in the Jewish Feminist Center in Los Angeles and liked to participate in women's rituals around significant life events, I suggested that Barbara and several of her closest friends consult a rabbi and create a women's ritual that had two parts: the first a humorous and innovative letting go of the bittersweet feeling of watching an ex-husband marry a younger woman and the second part to commemorate Barbara's new life as a wise woman who has successfully raised her two adult children and now has new adventures to explore.

The planning and preparation for these rituals took several weeks, and then finally it all came together in a creative celebration for Barbara and twelve of her friends.

At the conclusion of her ritual event, Barbara wrote me a note in which she said, "I finally feel like I'm letting go and getting my strength back again. I'm excited about and able to open up to what's next in my life. Instead of holding on to the past and being weighed down by jealous feelings, I'm ready now for things that are new and more fulfilling."

Strategy #3: Sometimes you need to find a way to be patient and receptive in situations that aren't clear yet or that simply require more time.

While Strategy #1 applied to envious situations that definitely should be pursued and Strategy #2 dealt with letting go of jealous feelings that definitely shouldn't be followed, there is a third type of dilemma most of us face at different points throughout our lives: how to remain open, receptive, and healthy even when we're involved in a journey or project that is unclear or takes a very long time.

For example, how do you stay patient and open when you're feeling jealous of a colleague's promotion while you've spent years waiting for a promotion that you're not sure will come? How do you stay calm and focused when you're caring for an ailing loved one and you're resenting that other people are recovering while your loved one hasn't shown any signs of improvement? How do you stay sane when you've been trying to start a family or get a creative project sold and you watch other people having a much easier time of it? How do you keep from becoming irritable when you're trying to sell a house that has gone down in price or expand a business during tight financial times and you're forced to watch other people's projects move forward while you have to wait for months or years for the economy to change?

When a dream of yours has been stalled or stopped for years, how do you keep yourself from giving up hope or from screaming out loud, "Enough already! Give me an answer!"?

In the eighteen years since I moved to Los Angeles, I have met and counseled many creative people whose dreams of success were delayed for years while they waited for a stroke of good fortune. Staying patient, open, and healthy when each day might be a breakthrough or another rejection is definitely one of the great challenges of life.

Several years ago I counseled an unemployed actor named Keith whose case demonstrates Strategy #3 and how to apply it to goals and dreams that involve a lot of delays and extensive waiting. I hope his experience inspires you and gives you ideas for your own long-delayed dreams and wishes.

Keith is an amazingly talented actor who had much success in college and in New York theater productions. But four years after moving to Los Angeles for film work, he had obtained only a few tiny roles. His wife, Carol, and their three children were doing their best not to put pressure on him, but with all the pressure Keith felt inside himself it was only a matter of time before the frustrations from his career began to tear away at his home life.

Each time Keith saw another one of his friends hit it big in Hollywood, he felt torn up inside with feelings of envy, as well as a deep sense of embarrassment for feeling jealous and bitter. By the time he came for counseling, he was smoking two packs of cigarettes a day, arguing with his wife several times a week, and taking medication for high blood pressure and stomach problems.

In therapy, Keith was highly motivated to regain his health and save his marriage, so he made great progress in the first few months in several areas: he got two day jobs to help pay the bills (one doing parties for a catering firm and the other in phone sales); he successfully quit smoking; he changed his eating habits to get rid of his stomach problems; and he learned some anger-management techniques to reduce the number and intensity of his arguments with Carol.

But something deeper was still causing him a great deal of pain. Keith told me during one of his sessions, "I'm the kind of person who feels alive when I'm given the chance to use my God-given talent for acting. But when I'm not allowed to use my gift, I feel empty and frustrated. It's a pain that just won't go away."

So we began to brainstorm about possible ways for him to begin acting again, even if producers and casting directors continued to reject him. Keith got involved briefly in a small theater company that did one-act plays by new writers, but that also felt too intermittent and unsatisfying.

Then, after visiting his wife's grandmother in a nursing home, Keith came up with the idea of starting a traveling theater company that would do improvisational theater at several local nursing homes each month. Keith felt good about this volunteer use of his talent, and he looked forward to each of the events at the nursing homes.

As often happens when someone does work for free and comes alive during those volunteer events, a greater opportunity emerged. I have seen this phenomenon happen dozens of times for clients, friends, and relatives, as well as in my own life. When you are waiting for something that keeps eluding your grasp, I've found doing good work and making healthy contacts through volunteer activities more often than not open up a world of possibilities.

In Keith's case it happened during a fund-raiser he arranged for his nursing-homes project. At this entertaining fund-raiser, Keith performed magnificently for an audience that included a casting director who was there because her husband's grandfather was a resident of one of the nursing homes. As Keith tells the story, "This casting director saw me at my best and got me an important audition, which turned into my break as a film actor and led to several major roles that have finally gotten my career going."

In addition to using volunteer activities as a way to break out of a slump, Keith used two other methods for staying open, receptive, and healthy that I strongly recommend. For almost a year before his breakthrough, Keith and his wife were facing daily crises because of their financial problems and the illness of one of their children.

Three Good Things

One of the methods they used to stay positive on their difficult journey is something called Three Good Things. On any day that feels frustrating or stressful, one of the best ways to regain your sense of calm and openness is to set aside a few quiet minutes and say to yourself or to the person you live with: "Three good things that happened today are . . ."

When Keith and Carol first tried the Three Good Things exercise at night before going to bed, Keith reported, "It was difficult. Neither Carol nor I was in the habit of noticing anything good about each day because we were so caught up in our financial struggles and family crises. Our youngest daughter was undergoing treatments for a serious respiratory problem and everything was beginning to feel overwhelming."

Keith continued, "So that first night all I could come up with as three good things is that our other kids seemed healthy, the dishes were clean, and Carol's eyes still looked beautiful to me. And I think Carol took a while before coming up with three good things, which were that her cat had been playful and fun that morning, her walk at lunch had been relaxing, and the skin rash on her arm had gotten a little better. Not the most thrilling stuff, but we did feel a lot closer as a couple and a lot more positive about our lives from just that simple exercise."

Like most people who have used the Three Good Things exercise, Keith and Carol found that nearly every time they listed for each other three good things that happened on a given day (even an uneventful or a terrible day) their moods lifted from stressful to more relaxed, from feeling discouraged to feeling more open and positive.

In essence, what the Three Good Things exercise does is to cut through the jealousy, comparisons, and other discouraging thoughts that we accumulate each day in our minds. By taking a few moments to notice and verbalize that indeed there were at least three good things that day, we can change a tendency toward sluggishness and discouragement into a positive feeling of gratitude and appreciation with which to end the day.

Something else that Keith and Carol used to stay patient, open, and receptive during their long wait for a paid acting job is a prayer that my wife, Linda, taught me years ago and that I have recommended to people from a variety of faiths for staying healthy during times that look bleak. Whenever Linda is faced with a frightening situation or an event that looks like it might be difficult or unpleasant, she takes a moment of quiet and says: "Please God, may I be open to something unexpectedly good happening here."

This prayer doesn't guarantee what will happen, but it changes the way you enter the situation. Instead of feeling fearful and expecting a disappointing outcome, you walk in with a sense of curiosity, openness, and receptivity, which are exactly the elements that increase the likelihood of something good happening. I have seen it work wonders hundreds of times in our life, and that's why I recommend it to others.

When Keith and Carol said this affirmation or prayer every so often during their long wait for a paid acting job, Keith noticed, "It caused a subtle change in my mood and my ability to connect with whomever I was meeting. Instead of feeling anxious or defensive walking into an industry party or an important audition, I could say this to myself and be a lot more relaxed and open. No matter how stressed Carol and I became during our hospital visits with our daughter, we would sometimes remember to take a moment and ask for help in keeping us open to the possibility of something unexpectedly good happening for us and our daughter. It almost always made a difference in how we felt inside and how we treated each other much better."

ONE FINAL FOLLOW-UP TO AN EARLIER CONFESSION

In closing, I'd like to refer back to the discussion earlier in this chapter in which I described the setbacks my wife and I encountered in trying to start a family. After two failed pregnancies and a failed adoption, we were feeling envious of others who had an easier time of it.

But instead of causing us to give up or become bitter, those eight years of disappointments opened us both up psychologically and spiritually to keep learning and growing as individuals and as a couple. With the help of supportive friends, relatives, and counselors who assisted us in turning each piece of bad news into another challenge to remain open and hopeful, we continued to pursue our dream of having children.

Today as I write this final chapter of *The Ten Challenges*, I am glad to be able to say that Linda and I did not give up trying. It took eight years of waiting, but finally we became the parents of a wonderful baby boy who has been a great source of joy and aliveness for us.

I urge anyone who is reading this book to consider the setbacks and disappointments in your own life not as an excuse to harden your heart with bitterness and jealousy, but rather as a challenge for opening up to lessons, creativity, and persistence beyond anything you have experienced before. My hope is that at the end of your life you won't be asking, "Why wasn't my time on Earth more like someone else's?" but instead you'll be feeling satisfaction from knowing that you lived the portion that was given to you with purpose and commitment.

FINDING THE WAY TO PEACE

You may have noticed while reading this book that the Ten Commandments are essentially about how to achieve peace and wholeness on several levels. On the deeply personal level, the Second Commandment (against idols) can help you avoid getting seduced by addictions and painful habits, while the Tenth Commandment (against coveting) teaches that in order to have inner peace—to feel good about yourself and your life—you may need to understand your own gifts more fully and stop longing for what others have.

On the interpersonal level, several of the commandments can help you find greater peace in your relationships: The Third Commandment (about not taking God's name in vain) can help you be less self-righteous and quick to anger with loved ones; the Fifth Commandment (about honoring your parents) can assist you in dealing with your mother and father; the Seventh Commandment (against adultery) focuses on improving your primary love relationship; and the Eighth (against stealing) and Ninth Commandments (against false witness) address how you deal with work associates, friends, and strangers.

Finally, there is another kind of peace that would be achieved if more people truly started following these ancient spiritual lessons—a peace between human beings of all races, religions, and differing viewpoints. If each of us fully appreciated the First Commandment (there is a God who cares), which says that we share one world with one Divine Source, how different life would be. If each person made a daily effort to follow the Sixth Commandment (don't murder) and not crush the spirit of those we encounter, the world would be a much better place. And if every week more people observed a Sabbath (the Fourth Commandment) to step back and look at the vision of a world in which everyone could have their basic needs met, can you imagine the kind of life we might create together?

Several years ago I attended a workshop on nonviolent peacemaking in which, ironically, an argument broke out between two contrasting groups. One group at the workshop argued that peace would come only if people learned how to meditate or pray each morning and devote their lives to the search for inner peace. The other group argued that peace would come only if people got more involved in improving the world —in the search for economic justice and peace between differing peoples.

Fortunately, one of the workshop participants got up and said, "If you study the greatest spiritual teachings of all time, such as the Ten Commandments, you will realize that peace comes from both directions." The search for inner peace and the quest for peace in the world go hand in hand. The overall impact of the Ten Commandments is to show us how being a good person in the world and finding a sense of spiritual wholeness deep within are intimately connected to each other.

On that note, I will end this book with a traditional prayer that asks for support in finding peace both in the world and deep within ourselves. The prayer, which in Hebrew is called Oseh Shalom, can be translated as follows: "May the One who creates peace in the heavens and on earth help us to bring peace to our world, to all the peoples of this world, and to the place deep within us that longs for wholeness. Amen."

GLOSSARY OF TERMS

Listed below are brief definitions of words used in this book that may be unfamiliar to some readers. For more extensive definitions of many of these words, see *The HarperCollins Dictionary of Religion,* edited by Jonathan Z. Smith, New York: HarperCollins, 1995; *Encyclopedia of Eastern Philosophy and Religion,* Boston: Shambhala, 1989; and *Encyclopedia Judaica,* New York: Macmillan and Jerusalem: Keter Publishing, 1972.

Agnostic Someone who believes there is insufficient evidence to say whether God exists or doesn't exist.

Aikido A spiritually based martial art developed by Ueshiba Morihei to harmonize oneself with the movement of the universe and to transform an attack into a nonviolent dance.

Allah The foremost name of the supreme being according to Islam.

Amidah The standing prayer in Judaism (because in most congregations one stands when reciting it), sometimes called The Shemonei Esrei (the Eighteen Blessings) or The Tefila, "The Prayer."

Baal Shem Tov (1700–1760) Rabbi Israel ben Eliezer was known as the Baal Shem Tov, "Master of the Good Name." He founded the Hasidic movement.

Bahai A religion founded in Iran in 1863 by Mirza Husayn ali Nuri, known as Bahaullah, that now has approximately two million members worldwide and describes in its scriptures an openness to all religions.

Buber Martin Buber (1878–1965), a Jewish philosopher from Germany who came to Palestine in 1938 and wrote well-known books on Hasidism, human relationships, dialogue, and the I-Thou relationship between people and between humans and God.

Buddha Means "Awakened One." Historically, Siddhartha Gautama lived in the sixth and fifth centuries B.C.E., renounced his upper-class upbringing at age twenty-nine, went through six years of deep spiritual quest, and at age thirty-five attained enlightenment, after which he spent forty-five years teaching what he had rediscovered.

Buddhist   Someone who studies the traditions of the Buddha, practices a Middle Path (avoiding the extremes of self-denial and self-indulgence), quests for Nirvana (the end of the suffering that plagues human existence), and follows the Buddhist precepts for ethical behavior.

Catholic   Refers to Roman Catholicism and can mean either someone who participates in the sacraments and beliefs of the Roman Catholic church or someone who grew up in a Catholic family or church and considers himself or herself Catholic.

Challah   A special loaf of bread that usually is braided and glazed. Traditionally served at Shabbat meals to signify that the Sabbath is different and more special than the other days of the week.

Ch'i   A Chinese word for ether, breath, matter-energy, vital energy, or life force, which is central to Eastern religions and medicine.

Conservative Jewish   A movement within Judaism that arose in the mid–nineteenth century in both Europe and the United States that accepts some changes in Jewish life because of Westernization, but attempts to keep essential aspects of Judaism, such as Hebrew prayers, kosher dietary laws, and Sabbath practice.

Covet   To desire what belongs to someone else, to wish for longingly.

Dalai Lama   The spiritual leader of Tibetan Buddhism. The current Dalai Lama, a Nobel Peace Prize winner in 1989, was born in Tibet in 1935 and has lived in exile in India since 1959, nine years after the Chinese takeover of Tibet.

Decalogue   Another name for the Ten Words or Ten Commandments.

Disciples   A student of a spiritual teacher, often refers to the followers of Jesus or to the Twelve Apostles.

Divine Presence   One of the many names for aspects of the One God, it refers to the in-dwelling light or energy, sometimes called the Shekhinah, that exists within and between beings.

Duhkha   A Sanskrit word in Buddhism for suffering, which arises because of desire and craving.

Eastern Orthodox   Refers to the Christian denominations such as Greek Orthodox, Russian Orthodox, Serbian Orthodox, and Romanian Orthodox, etc. and to those who believe or participate in the sacraments of the Orthodox church.

Egalitarian   Religious or spiritual practices that include women and men as equal participants, or that use prayer language that is not primarily male-oriented.

God's Names   Various Hebrew and English names are used for the One God in the Bible and in Oral Rabbinic teachings. In *The Ten Challenges,* I refer to several of these names, including the One, the Eternal One, the One who is and will always be, the Holy One, the Divine Presence, the Breath of Life, and Spirit.

Gonnif   A Yiddish word for a thief or a clever person.

Gregorian Chant   Odes or elegies sung to God without accompaniment as part of Roman Catholic liturgy.

Halakhah   Literally, to go or to follow the way, it refers to the legal side of Jewish practice and traditions.

Hasidism   A movement within Judaism that began in Poland and Lithuania in the eighteenth century with the Baal Shem Tov and is characterized by deep attachment to God, joyfulness, humility, and charismatic leadership.

Havurot   Literally means "friends," a gathering of people to study, pray, celebrate, or explore their spirituality together.

Hindu   One of the world's major religions, with over 650 million people in India and elsewhere. Literally means "one living near the Indus river." It has a diversity of forms and includes many Vedic ("received knowledge") writings, including the Bhagavad-Gita, the Upanishads, and the Mahabharata and Ramayana myths.

Holocaust   Literally means "a devastation or destruction by fire," it is often used to describe the horrific destruction of six million Jews and others by the Nazis during the period from 1933 until 1945.

Humanist   A person who focuses on human values, needs, and qualities. In the case of Erich Fromm, humanism sees religion as an opportunity not to impose an authoritarian code of behavior but to help people unfold and develop their highest human values.

Kabbalah, Kabbalistic   Literally means "the received wisdom," it refers to the esoteric and mystical teachings and writings of Judaism, which explore the origins and workings of the universe, the inner life, and the way to the service of God.

Kahvanah   The Hebrew word for intention or aim.

Karma   A Sanskrit word in Buddhism, Hinduism, and Zen meaning deed, action, ritual, result, or consequences.

Karma Yoga   A Sanskrit term from Hinduism, one of the four chief types of Yoga or path to union with God, it refers to selfless conduct in which every action together with its results are offered to God.

Klezmer   Lively and soulful folk music from European Jewry, often with clarinet, accordion, percussion, and violin.

Kundalini   The Sanskrit word meaning "snake" or "serpent power," it refers to the sleeping spiritual force in every human being, which lies coiled at the base of the spine and when awakened, rises through a series of energy centers (chakras) to find expression in spiritual knowledge and mystical visions.

Loshon Hora   A Hebrew term meaning "evil tongue," it refers to gossip, talebearing, and the problem of passing along negative speech even if the content is true.

Maimonides   (1135–1204) Moses ben Maimon, a scholar, physician, writer, and authority on Jewish law, he was born in Spain, later lived in Morocco, Israel, and Egypt, and he wrote major works on Jewish practice, faith, philosophy, medicine, and tradition.

Mitzvah   A commandment, a good deed, or a way of connecting to God.

Muhammad   (570–632) Born in Mecca, he was orphaned at a young age and rose from poverty to a life of spiritual leadership. He had his first revelations at age forty, founded the Islamic religion, and transmitted the Quran as God's message to humankind.

Muslim   Literally "one who submits to the will of God (Allah)," and to the practice of Islam in daily life.

Mysticism   Those who experience or seek to experience a direct, immediate connection with God or ultimate reality.

Native American   People and tribes whose ancestors lived in North America prior to Columbus.

Niebuhr, Reinhold   (1894–1962) An American Protestant theologian and minister known for promoting social action and for the Serenity Prayer later used in most Twelve Step meetings.

Niggun A wordless melody, often based on Hasidic custom, that when sung heartfully and repeatedly can elevate the soul.

Oral Rabbinic Tradition Authoritative interpretations of the Written Torah, which are considered by many to be as Divinely inspired or revealed as the Written Torah.

Orthodox Jewish Those who attempt to be Torah-true and who accept and observe as Divinely inspired the totality of the written and oral laws of Judaism.

Pentateuch A Latin word for the "law of Moses" or the first five books of the Bible: Genesis, Exodus, Leviticus, Numbers, and Deuteronomy.

Pogrom A Russian word meaning an attack with destruction, looting, murder, and rape, often referring to attacks on Jewish villages in Russia between 1881 and 1921.

Protestant Beginning with the Reformation in Germany in the early sixteenth century, it refers to the numerous denominations of Christians who are not followers of Roman Catholicism or Eastern Orthodoxy. Some of the major Protestant faiths are Anglican or Episcopalian, Baptist, Congregationalist, Fundamentalist, Lutheran, Methodist, Pentecostal, Presbyterian, Reformed, and Unitarian.

Quran Meaning "recitation," it refers to the revelations recited by Muhammad and believed by Muslims to be the word of God.

Reconstructionist Jewish A movement within Judaism that began with Rabbi Mordecai Kaplan (1881–1983), an American Conservative Jewish scholar and teacher, who argued that Jews are a community or a civilization rather than the followers of ancient law. Since the 1970s, Reconstructionism has become more spiritualist than in Kaplan's time, but still committed to change, community formation, and social action.

Reform Jewish A movement within Judaism, sometimes called Liberal or Progressive Judaism, that arose in Germany in the early nineteenth century, and that asserts the legitimacy of change within Judaism and supports a diversity of ways of practicing Jewish faith, traditions, social action, and community outreach.

Religious Science Sometimes called Science of Mind, it refers to the churches and members who study the teachings of Ernest Holmes.

Renewal, Jewish A twentieth-century movement within Judaism taught by Rabbi Zalman Schachter-Shalomi to bring a stronger spiritual and mystical sense into the prayers and practices of Reform, Reconstructionist, Conservative, and Orthodox congregations.

Right Livelihood A Buddhist teaching from the Eightfold Path about caring for one's appropriate work and doing one's work mindfully and lovingly as one of the steps to enlightenment.

Rosary A counting device often used as an aid in repetitive prayer, or in a series of prayers to Mary, usually with a knotted cord or a string of beads.

Rumi (1207–1273) Jalal al-Din Rumi, a Persian mystic poet and Sufi teacher, born in what is now Afghanistan, he wrote over three thousand love poems that speak of spiritual truths.

Saint Francis of Assisi (1181–1226) A Roman Catholic saint from Italy who was the son of a wealthy merchant, yet at twenty-two underwent a conversion to become extremely devout and ascetic. Best known for establishing an order of friars, preaching in various foreign countries, and exemplifying humility, he is often associated with a love of nature.

Sea of Reeds In Biblical Hebrew the Yam Suf. The actual Red Sea is a long, narrow strip of water separating the Arabian Peninsula from the northeastern corner of Africa (Egypt, Sudan, Ethiopia), but some scholars say the biblical crossing refers to the Red Sea while others say the Sea of Reeds is a lagoon on the shores of the Mediterranean Sea or one of several other narrow bodies of water nearby.

Secular Jewish Those within Judaism who focus more on family and social rituals, Jewish ethics, and history rather than on theology, religious law, or affiliation with a temple or synagogue.

Seventh-Day Adventist A Protestant Christian denomination that arose in early-nineteenth-century America focusing on when Christ would return and how practicing the Ten Commandments, and especially the keeping of the Sabbath on the Seventh Day, would speed his return.

Shehekhiyanu Prayer A prayer in Judaism that says "Blessed is the Eternal One, our God, Who has kept us alive, sustained us, and brought us to this season (or this moment) for good." It can be said when celebrating a new season, a new harvest, a happy occasion, or any gift God has given you, including the gift of a new day or a moment of appreciation.

Shekhinah In Judaism, the Divine Presence or the aspect of God that dwells or resides in the world, sometimes referred to as the light or energy that comes from God and exists within and between beings.

Shofar A ram's horn traditionally used at Rosh Hashanah (the Jewish New Year) and Yom Kippur (the Day of Atonement) to proclaim the sovereignty of God and to awaken people to examine their deeds and return to a more sacred way. (Maimonides, Yad, Teshuvah, 3:4).

Siddur Means "arrangement or order" of prayers, usually referring to a Jewish prayer book.

Sin Literally meaning "to miss the mark," can also mean to falter while performing a duty, to break a religious or moral law, or to mistreat or offend someone.

Soul As defined in the Bible, the Divine Breath that exists within a person, that animates the person, and that yearns for unity with God.

Spirit Used synonymously with Soul as the Divine Breath or Presence that animates a person and yearns for connection with God.

Spiritual A hard-to-define word that refers to the quest for a higher purpose, a sacred meaning in life, or a connection with God, or ultimate reality.

Sufi The mystical tradition in Islam, involving intense devotion to Muhammad and the Quran, as well as master-disciple relationships and, in some cases, ecstatic prayer known as "Whirling Dervishes."

T'ai-Chi A Chinese term literally meaning "Great Ultimate Boxing," it is a dancelike martial art exercise used for health and spiritual purposes to understand fundamental Taoist principles.

Talmud Literally meaning learning or study, it refers to the body of Jewish law, interpretation, practices, and tradition discussed orally by Rabbinic Sages for centuries and later recorded in the fourth and fifth centuries c.e. as sacred teachings.

Tantric Yoga A Sanskrit term meaning "to extend, span, or employ the tensions," it has different meanings and practices in Hinduism and Buddhism, but usually involves studying sacred texts and practicing certain types of meditation, healing, and purification rituals.

Taoist A traditional component of Chinese culture to liberate people from the mundane and reorient them toward the deeper, abiding realities of life, including but not limited to the study of the Tao te-Ching of Lao Tzu and the Chuang-tzu writings.

Tefillin Leather prayer boxes and straps that contain biblical passages and are worn by observant Jews on the hand and between the eyes.

Teshuvah The process of repentance, turning toward a more Godly direction, or opening one's heart.

Tikkun Olam The restoration or repair of the world, or in Hasidic Judaism the restoration of the broken vessels of light that shattered when God pulled back to create the universe.

Torah Literally "the teaching, doctrine, or instruction," it usually refers to the biblical books Genesis, Exodus, Leviticus, Numbers, and Deuteronomy, as well as the Prophets and Writings, but it can also refer to the Oral Torah and teachings of the Rabbinic Sages over the centuries.

Twelve Step Meeting A group meeting with anonymity that uses the Twelve Steps developed by Bill Wilson, the cofounder of Alcoholics Anonymous, to help a person understand and overcome a self-defeating habit (such as excessive drinking, drug use, gambling, spending, codependence, etc.).

Unitarian A modern liberal religious movement in Europe, Britain, and America that in some churches is Christian but does not believe in a Trinity, while in other churches is universalist and not Christian per se.

Vision Quest In some Native American tribes a ritual involving isolation, physical preparation, and/or deprivation and mystical visions that provides guidance to the individual and to the tribe.

Yiddish The language of European Jewry from medieval to modern times, derived from German, Hebrew, Slavic, and Romance languages.

Yoga An Indian practice of physical exercises, meditation, and concentration to yoke or join with higher knowledge, divine realms, or powerful actions.

Zen Buddhist   A school of Buddhism, especially as practiced in Japan, for using meditation to attain satori or enlightenment.

Zohar   Also called "The Book of Splendor," it is the central work in the literature of the Jewish mystical Kabbalah.

S O U R C E S

INTRODUCTION

page 2 The order of the Ten Commandments. Some Christian scholars and texts offer slight variations of the ten precepts found in Exodus 20. Throughout this book, I have used the standard Jewish list found in the Masoretic version from the tenth century C.E., using the translation into English published by the Jewish Publication Society in 1967. However, the Jewish and Christian versions are quite similar.

page 4 "For Jews . . . these ten spiritual teachings are part of a continually evolving set of guidelines." For most Jews the Torah has many levels of meaning. Traditionally, scholars of the Bible look not only at the written words but also at the oral rulings, interpretations, and stories that have emerged over the centuries. According to Avigdor Bonchek's book *Studying the Torah: A Guide to In-Depth Interpretation* (Northvale, NJ: Jason Aronson, 1996), there are four acceptable types of Torah commentary, consisting of P'shat (the plain sense of the text), Remez (the esoteric or subtle meaning), Drash (as in midrash, which is the homiletic, moral, or personal view of the underlying lesson), and Sod (the hidden, Kabbalistic, or mystical meaning). Throughout this book, I will be exploring what scholars over the centuries have said about the Ten Commandments from all four of these levels.

page 4 Jesus' saying to teach the commandments is from Matthew 5:19, *The New Jerusalem Bible;* the statement to "keep the commandments and abide in my love" can be found in John 15:10, *The HarperCollins Study Bible;* and the suggestion not to abolish but to fulfill the commandments is from Matthew 5:17, *The New Jerusalem Bible.*

page 4 The Five Precepts of Buddhism can be found in Huston Smith's *The Illustrated World's Religions* (New York: HarperCollins, 1994), p. 74.

page 5 The two books by Viktor Frankl are *Man's Search for*

Meaning (New York: Pocket, 1985) and *The Doctor and the Soul* (New York: Vintage, 1986).

page 6   The translation of *Ahseret Ha-deebrot* as "The Ten Words" or "The Ten Things" can be found in many sources, including the Talmud, Berachot 12a, Shabbat 86b, and *The Torah: A Modern Commentary,* edited by W. Gunther Plaut (New York: Union of American Hebrew Congregations, 1981), pp. 531, 539.

1.   THE FIRST CHALLENGE

page 14   For more on Sigmund Freud's views on religion, see his *The Future of an Illusion* (New York: Norton, 1961), pp. 26–42.

page 14   For more on the spiritual ideas of Carl Jung, see his *Man and His Symbols* (New York: Dell, 1964) and *Psychology and Religion: East and West* (Princeton, NJ: Princeton University Press, 1958).

page 14   For more on William James's observations about spirituality, see his *The Varieties of Religious Experience* (New York: New American Library, 1958) and *The Will to Believe* (New York: Dover, 1956).

page 16   "A God who cannot be seen with the eye nor heard with the ear" has been explored by many Jewish and Christian scholars, including the Baal Shem Tov, the founder of Hasidism, who is quoted in S. Y. Agnon's *Present at Sinai* (Philadelphia: Jewish Publication Society, 1994) as saying, "What is meant is not literally seeing or hearing but rather comprehending." Many other writers have speculated on a Divine Presence that communicates to humans as a "still small voice," a phrase that is found in the First Book of Kings 19:12.

page 17   The interpretation of the receiving of the Ten Commandments in a silent, intuitive way was first told to me by Rabbis Ted Falcon, David Cooper, and Mordecai Finley. It is also found in a fourteenth-century midrash (interpretation or seeking) by Netanel ben Yeshaya, entitled "Me'or Ha'afelah," in which the experience at Sinai is described as "Inner Vision." In the Zohar it says, "God spoke in a still voice because people must be filled with awe and silence to hear it" (*The Zohar*, translated by H. Sperling, M. Simon, and P. Levertoff, vol. 3 [London: Soncino Press, 1949], p. 245). The Zohar also suggests, "At first the sounds were not heard at all. Rather as the utterances came forth, everyone would greet each utterance by kissing it softly, lovingly. Only then would the commandment speak out and proclaim itself" (Zohar, Hadash, Exodus 41b). In other words, unless you have an open heart you won't hear the silent, intuitive message. Finally, there is a Talmudic midrash that each person heard in his or her heart only what that person was capable of hearing or understanding (Exodus Rabbah 28:6 and 5:9).

page 17 For more on "mitzrayim" meaning not only Egypt but also constriction or narrowness, see Ernest Klein, *A Comprehensive Etymological Dictionary of the Hebrew Language for Readers of English* (New York: Macmillan, 1987), chapter 1, or look up the root word *tsarah* or the plural *tsarot* in a Hebrew-English dictionary. This creative translation of the First Commandment was given at a study session I attended by Rabbi Ted Falcon based on "mitzrayim" meaning "a narrow way of seeing."

page 19 Benno Jacob's quote about the eternal covenant of love between God and humans is found in his *The Second Book of the Bible: Exodus* (Hoboken, NJ: Ktav Publishing, 1992), p. 545.

page 20 The statement about the receiving of the Ten Commandments in the wilderness and that it is intended for all peoples, including those not yet born, can be found in Exodus Rabbah 5:9, Tanhuma B, Shemot 22; in Gunther Plaut's *The Torah: A Modern Commentary* (New York: Union of American Hebrew Congregations, 1981), p. 529; and in Z'ev ben Shimon Halevi's *Kabbalah and Exodus* (Boulder: Shambhala, 1980), p. 111. It is also implied in Deuteronomy 29:13–14.

page 21 Rifat Sonsino and Daniel Syme, *Finding God: Ten Jewish Responses* (New York: Union of American Hebrew Congregations, 1986).

page 21 Anthony Wilhelm, *Christ Among Us: A Modern Pre-*

sentation of Catholic Faith for Adults (New York: HarperCollins, 1990).

page 21 Henri Nouwen, *The Way of the Heart* (New York: Ballantine, 1981).

page 21 Martin Copenhaver, *To Begin at the Beginning: An Introduction to the Christian Faith* (Cleveland: United Church Press, 1994).

page 21 Hassan Hathout, *Reading the Muslim Mind* (Plainfield, IN: American Trust Publications, 1995).

page 21 Annemarie Schimmel, *Islam: An Introduction* (Albany: State University of New York Press, 1992) and *Mystical Dimensions of Islam* (Chapel Hill: University of North Carolina Press, 1975).

page 22 Huston Smith, *The Illustrated World's Religions* (New York: HarperCollins, 1995).

page 22 Harold Kushner, *When Bad Things Happen to Good People* (New York: Avon, 1983).

page 23 Lynn Gottlieb, *She Who Dwells Within* (New York: HarperCollins, 1995).

page 24 Aryeh Kaplan, *Jewish Meditation: A Practical Guide* (New York: Schocken, 1985).

page 24 Rodger Kamenetz, *The Jew in the Lotus: A Poet's Rediscovery of Jewish Identity in Buddhist India* (New York: HarperCollins, 1994).

page 24 Henri Nouwen, *The Way of the Heart* (New York: Ballantine, 1981), pp. 59–60.

page 24 The quote about the soul is from *Meister Eckhart: Teacher and Preacher,* by Bernard McGinn (NY: Paulist, 1986), p. 285.

page 25 The poem excerpt from Rumi can be found in *The Essential Rumi,* translated by Coleman Barks with John Moyne (New York: HarperCollins, 1995, p. 122) and in *Birdsong: 53 Short Poems by Rumi,* translated by Coleman Barks (Athens, GA: Maypop, 1993).

page 25 The discussion about the Amidah or Standing Prayer suggesting each of us has an individual perspective about the one God is from *The Weekday Siddur: An Exposition and Analysis,* by B. S. Jacobson (Tel Aviv: Sinai, 1978), p. 215.

page 27 Anthony Wilhelm, *Christ Among Us* (New York: HarperCollins, 1990), p. 7.

page 28   For more on the Kabbalistic view of God's pulling back and broken shards of light existing in each of our souls, see chapter 5, "The Mysticism of Luria," *Finding God,* by Rifat Sonsino and Daniel Syme, op. cit., pp. 67–77. Also see *Tanya,* by Schneur Zalman of Liady, translated by N. Mindel (Brooklyn: Kehot Publication Society, 1973), and the chapter "Jewish Meditation: Healing Ourselves and Our Relationships," by Sheldon Z. Kramer, in Edward Hoffman's *Opening the Inner Gates: New Paths in Kabbalah and Psychology* (Boston: Shambhala, 1995), p. 230.

page 29   The statement by Jesus from the Book of James can be found in chapter 2, verses 14–17, *The Holy Bible: New International Version* (Grand Rapids, Michigan: Zondervan, 1984).

page 29   For more on Islamic views of giving charity, see John Esposito, *Islam: The Straight Path* (London: Oxford University Press, 1988), or Kurshid Ahmad, *Islam: Its Meaning and Message* (Ann Arbor, MI: New Era, 1976).

page 29   For more on Karma-Yoga, see Swami Vivekananda, *Karma-Yoga and Bhakti-Yoga* (New York: Ramakrishna Center, 1955), or Rick Fields, Peggy Taylor, Rex Weyler, and Rick Ingrasci, *Chop Wood, Carry Water: A Guide to Finding Spiritual Fulfillment in Everyday Life* (Los Angeles: Tarcher, 1984). The quote from the Buddha can be found in *Chop Wood, Carry Water,* p. 236.

page 30   The moderately positive correlation between involvement in a religious or spiritual community and overall well-being, sense of community, and marital satisfaction is from F. K. Willits and D. M. Crider, "Religion and Well-Being: Men and Women in the Middle Years," *Review of Religious Research* 29.3 (1988): 281–94.

page 30   The study correlating religious involvement with meaning and purpose, as well as reduced anxiety levels, is from L. R. Petersen and A. Roy, "Religiosity, Anxiety, and Meaning and Purpose: Religious Consequences for Psychological Well-Being," *Review of Religious Research* 27.1 (1985): pp. 49–62.

page 30   Other studies correlating attendance at religious services and duration of marriage, satisfaction with family life, and overall happiness can be found in I. Reed Payne,

Allen E. Bergin, Kimberly A. Bielema, and Paul H. Jenkins, "Review of Religion and Mental Health," in Kenneth I. Pargament, *Religion and Prevention in Mental Health* (New York: Haworth Press, 1992), p. 67.

page 30 The correlations between physical health and religious involvement are from Vanderpool and Levin, "Religion and Medicine: How Are They Related?" *Journal of Religion and Health,* 29 (1990): pp. 9–20.

2. THE SECOND CHALLENGE

page 35 "In traditional Judaism, the warning against bowing down to idols . . ." For an extensive discussion of this topic, see "Judaism and the Varieties of Idolatrous Experience," by Barry S. Kogan, in *Proceedings of the Academy for Jewish Philosophy,* edited by David Novak and Norbert Samuelson (Lanham, MD: University Press of America, 1992), p. 175, or Moshe Halbertal and Avishai Margalit, *Idolatry* (Cambridge, MA: Harvard University Press, 1992), especially the chapter "Idolatry and Betrayal," pp. 25–29.

page 35 "The special bond between God and us humans is like a marriage partnership." This issue is discussed in Exodus 34:15–16 and in Judges 2:17. Also, in many Jewish writings and teachings the Torah is viewed as the Ketubah (wedding contract) between God and us.

page 35 Bahya ben Joseph ibn Paguda's classic book *Duties of the Heart* has been recently translated by Yaakov Feldman. The quote I used is from *A Treasury of Jewish Quotations,* edited by Joseph Baron (New York: Crown, 1956).

page 35 Erich Fromm, *Psychoanalysis and Religion* (New Haven: Yale University Press, 1959).

page 35 The quote from Rabbi Ted Falcon is from a weekend spiritual retreat in Temescal Canyon, February 11, 1995.

page 36 The quote from Archbishop Ullathorne can be found in *The Book of Catholic Quotations,* edited by John Chapin (New York: Farrar, Straus and Giroux, 1956).

page 36 The statement from the Quran that says *shirk,* or idolatry, is the greatest sin in Islam is described in Karen

Armstrong's *A History of God* (New York: Ballantine, 1994), p. 149.

page 36 The story of Tan-hsia T'ien-jan using the statue of the Buddha as firewood is found in Ernest Kurtz and Katherine Ketcham, *The Spirituality of Imperfection* (New York: Bantam, 1992), p. 123, and in Ingrid Fischer-Schreiber, *The Encyclopedia of Eastern Philosophy and Religion* (Boston: Shambhala, 1994), p. 354.

page 37 The story of the Golden Calf is analyzed in W. Gunther Plaut's *The Torah: A Modern Commentary* (New York: Union of American Hebrew Congregations, 1981), pp. 641–49.

page 37 The quote from Martin Buber about the Golden Calf can be found in his *Moses* (New York: Harper Torchbook, 1958), p. 151.

page 39 The definition of *Israelite* as "the one who wrestles and strives with God" can be found in many sources, including Arthur Waskow's *Godwrestling* (New York: Schocken, 1978), p. 6.

page 39 Harold Schulweis's comment on dissent can be found in *For Those Who Can't Believe: Overcoming the Obstacles to Faith* (New York: HarperCollins, 1994), pp. 84–85; it is based on the midrash of the Golden Calf found in Exodus Rabbah 43:4.

page 40 The quote from G. I. Gurdjieff about moments of consciousness being short is from P. D. Ouspensky, *In Search of the Miraculous* (New York: Harcourt, Brace and World, 1949), pp. 116–17.

page 41 The shofar description is from the Code of Moses Maimonides, Yad, Teshuvah, 3:4, in *The Mishneh Torah Series* (Brooklyn, NY: Moznaim Publishing, 1989).

page 41 The quote from Father Andrew Greeley is found in *The Sinai Myth* (Garden City, NY: Doubleday, 1972), p. 118.

page 42 The quote about "monkey mind" is from David Cooper, *The Heart of Stillness: The Elements of Spiritual Discipline* (New York: Bell Tower, 1992), pp. 9–21.

page 43 The definition of *rakhaman* as womblike was first pointed out to me by Rabbi Amy Eilberg and can also be found in most Hebrew-English dictionaries.

page 43 The quote about the vision-quest healing ritual can be found in *The Wind Is My Mother,* by Bear Heart with Molly Larkin (New York: Clarkson Potter, 1996), pp. 230–32.

page 44   *The Big Chill,* written by Lawrence Kasdan and Barbara Benedek, directed by Lawrence Kasdan, Columbia/TriStar Pictures, 1983.

page 51   The traditional morning prayer for the body can be found in most Jewish prayer books. The translation I used here is a combination from *Gates of Prayer: The New Union Prayerbook* (New York: Central Conference of American Rabbis, 1975), p. 51 and *The Complete Artscroll Siddur* (Brooklyn: Mesorah Publications, 1990), p. 15.

page 51   The Islamic call to worship and the Opening Prayer, or Fatihah, can be found in Philip Novak's *The World's Wisdom: Sacred Texts of the World's Religions* (New York: HarperCollins, 1994), pp. 283, 297.

page 52   The prayer attributed to Saint Francis can also be found in Philip Novak's *The World's Wisdom,* p. 268.

page 53   The Serenity Prayer, by Reinhold Niebuhr, is in Philip Novak's *The World's Wisdom,* p. 277.

page 53   The Hasidic story of the man who knew how to say only "Amen" has been told to me by many rabbis, including Rabbi Ted Falcon of Bet Aleph in Seattle.

page 55   For more on Viktor Frankl's innovative ways of helping women and men find their purpose in life, see his *The Doctor and the Soul* (New York: Vintage, 1986).

3.   THE THIRD CHALLENGE

page 59   The comments by Rabbi Mordecai Finley were made during a study session at Congregation Ohr Hatorah in Los Angeles in March 1996.

page 60   Rashi, whose full name is Rabbi Solomon ben Isaac, warns against making false oaths in *Rashi Commentaries on the Pentateuch,* translated by Chaim Pearl (New York: Norton, 1970), p. 91.

page 61   The quote from Moshe ibn Ezra can be found in Benno Jacob's *The Second Book of the Bible: Exodus* (Hoboken, NJ: Ktav Publishing, 1992), p. 558.

page 66 The quote from *Ohr Hahayyim* can be found in *Sh'mos,* vol. 2 of *Torah Gems,* compiled by S. Ludmir (Brooklyn: S. Ludmir, 1992).

page 68 For more information about Brotherhood-Sisterhood USA, a summer workshop for teens on race, sexuality, and personal integrity, contact The National Conference, 1055 Wilshire Blvd. #1015, Los Angeles, CA 90017.

page 69 The biblical passage "Judge not, lest ye be judged" can be found in Luke 6:37 and Matthew 7:1.

page 70 *Gandhi,* written by John Briley, produced and directed by Richard Attenborough, and distributed by Columbia/TriStar Pictures, 1982.

page 70 For more on the "fight or flight" response in humans, see Philip Zimbardo's *Psychology and Life* (Glenview, IL: Scott, Foresman, 1985), p. 499.

page 71 The discussion of the phrase "Do not curse a deaf person" is based on Leviticus 19:14 and the interpretation of not using the gift of speech in a hurtful manner is given by Moses Maimonides in *A Maimonides Reader,* edited by Isadore Twersky (New York: Behrman House, 1972), pp. 434–35, and in detail in Joseph Telushkin's *Words That Hurt, Words That Heal* (New York: Morrow, 1996).

page 71 Carol Tavris, *Anger: The Misunderstood Emotion* (New York: Touchstone, 1989).

page 72 The research by Dr. Murray Mittleman and others on the danger of angry outbursts for heart patients was reported in the September 1995 issue of *Circulation* and in an article by *Newsday* reporter Jamie Talan, published in the *Los Angeles Times,* September 19, 1995, p. E3.

page 72 For more on how to use anger responsibly and not hurtfully, see Carol Tavris, *Anger: The Misunderstood Emotion,* op. cit.; Harriet Goldhor Lerner, *The Dance of Anger* (New York: Harper, 1985); and chapter 17, "Taming the Furies," in Aaron Beck, *Love Is Never Enough* (New York: HarperCollins, 1988), pp. 332–56.

page 76 For more on the Zohar's view of the Third Commandment as a way to honor God and deepen one's love for the Divine, see *The Zohar,* translated by H. Sperling, M. Simon, and P. Levertoff (London: Soncino Press, 1949), p. 268.

page 76   The quote from Goethe about using God's name in vain can be found in J. P. Eckermann, *Conversations with Goethe in the Last Years of His Life,* translated by S. M. Fuller (Boston, 1839), and in Solomon Goldman's *The Ten Commandments* (Chicago: University of Chicago Press, 1956), p. 155.

page 77   The story of the Baal Shem Tov saying the synagogue was filled with empty words has been told by many rabbis and can also be found in Robert Kahn, *The Ten Commandments for Today* (Garden City, NY: Doubleday, 1964), pp. 38–39.

4.   THE FOURTH CHALLENGE

page 84   The Shabbat interpretations of Rabbi Samson Raphael Hirsch can be found in *The Mystical Glory of Shabbath and Festivals,* by Matityahu Glazerson (New York: Feldheim Publishers, 1985), pp. 11–12.

page 84   The quote from Rabbi Mordecai Kaplan about Shabbat was originally written in his *The Meaning of God in Modern Jewish Religion* (New York: Jewish Reconstructionist Foundation, 1962).

page 84   The Kabbalistic view of the letters of Shabbat corresponding with the letters of Teshuvah can be found in Glazerson, *The Mystical Glory of Shabbath and Festivals,* op. cit., p. 17.

page 84   The Islamic view of the Sabbath (Yom Aljum'ah or the Day of Assembly) is described in W. Gunther Plaut, *The Torah: A Modern Commentary* (New York: Union of American Hebrew Congregations, 1981), p. 550.

page 84   The origins of the Christian Sunday worship service are discussed in Matthew 5:17; Luke 4:16; Revelation 1:10; in *The Earliest Christian Liturgy,* by Reverend Josef Maria Nielen (St. Louis: B. Herder, 1941), pp. 72–77, 342–43; and in the *Encyclopaedia of Religion and Ethics,* vol. 12, edited by James Hastings (New York: Scribners, 1922), pp. 103–11.

page 85   The quote from Martin Luther can be found in the chapter "Sunday: The Lord's Day as a Sabbath," by John Primus, in *The Sabbath in Jewish and Christian Traditions,* edited by Tamara Eskenazi, Daniel Harrington, and William Shea (New York: Crossroad, 1991).

page 85 The church publication stating the need for an inward day is from *The Lookout,* quoted in *The Encyclopedia of Religious Quotations,* edited by Frank Mead (Westwood, NJ: Fleming Revell, 1965), p. 389.

page 85 The Christian minister who said Sunday "belongs to God" is Samuel A. Jeanes, writing in *The Free Methodist,* quoted in Mead, *The Encyclopedia of Religious Quotations,* op. cit., p. 388.

page 85 Irving Greenberg, *The Jewish Way* (New York: Touchstone 1988), pp. 127–81.

page 86 The statement by Justin Martyr can be found in *First Apology 67,* quoted in *The Book of Catholic Quotations,* edited by John Chapin (New York: Farrar, Straus and Giroux, 1956).

page 86 The quote from Martin Luther on Sunday and eternal life can be found in Primus, *The Sabbath in Jewish and Christian Traditions,* op. cit.

page 86 Edythe Draper, *Draper's Book of Quotations* (Wheaton, IL: Tyndale House, 1992).

page 86 The quote from Zalman Schachter-Shalomi was made in a lecture by him I attended in Fort Collins, Colorado, July 1995.

page 87 Harvey Cox, "Meditation and Sabbath," *Harvard* magazine September-October 1977: pp. 43–44. Many thanks to the current editor, who found an old copy and sent it to me.

page 90 Ron Wolfson, *The Art of Jewish Living: The Shabbat Seder* (New York: The Federation of Jewish Men's Clubs and The University of Judaism, 1985).

page 91 The quote about Sabbath as a day of dignity for Christians can be found in *The New Interpreter's Bible* (Nashville: Abingdon, 1994), p. 846.

page 91 Irving Greenberg, *The Jewish Way,* op. cit., pp. 127–81.

page 91 Ron Wolfson, *The Art of Jewish Living: The Shabbat Seder,* op. cit.

page 91 Marc Dov Shapiro, *Gates of Shabbat* (New York: Central Conference of American Rabbis, 1991).

page 91 The quote from Dr. Arthur Green can be found in his two-page memo, *Toward a New Shabbat: A Modest Proposal* (Wyncote, PA: Reconstructionist Rabbinical College, 1995). Besides the four *Don't*s I listed, he also has four *Do*s.

page 95 David Cooper, *Renewing Your Soul: A Guided Retreat for the Sabbath and Other Days of Rest* (New York: HarperCollins, 1995), pp. 54–56, 126–28.

page 97 The story about Rabbi Judah and "the missing spice is the Sabbath" is told in Marc Dov Shapiro's *Gates of Shabbat,* op. cit., and in Genesis Rabbah 11:2.

page 97 Charlotte Forten, *The Journal of Charlotte L. Forten, May 28, 1854,* published in 1961, as quoted in *Quotations in Black,* edited by Anita King (Westport, CT: Greenwood Press, 1981).

page 103 Henry Wadsworth Longfellow, "Michael Angeleo," part I, stanza 5, as quoted in *The Encyclopedia of Religious Quotations,* op. cit.

page 103 For more on how to meditate or pray individually or in a group setting in your particular tradition, I recommend asking friends, teachers, clergy members, or other people you trust for their suggestions. In addition, a few books that are inspiring and useful include Aryeh Kaplan, *Jewish Meditation: A Practical Guide* (New York: Schocken, 1985); Mark Verman, *The History and Varieties of Jewish Meditation* (Northvale, NJ: Jason Aronson, 1996); Yitzchok Kirzner with Lisa Aiken, *The Art of Jewish Prayer* (Northvale, NJ: Jason Aronson, 1991); and Sidney Greenberg, *A Treasury of Thoughts on Jewish Prayer* (Northvale, NJ: Jason Aronson, 1989). For Protestant Christians, some possibilities are Richard J. Foster, *Celebration of Discipline: The Path to Spiritual Growth* (New York: HarperCollins, 1988), Jan Johnson, *Enjoying the Presence of God* (Colorado Springs, CO: NAV Press, 1996), Don Postema, *Space for God: Study and Practice of Spirituality and Prayer* (Grand Rapids, MI: CRC Publications, 1983), and Dallas Willard, *The Spirit of the Discipline: Understanding How God Changes*

Lives (New York: HarperCollins, 1991). For Episcopalian Christians, there is Kenneth Leech, *Soulfriend: An Invitation to Spiritual Direction* (New York: HarperCollins, 1992), and for Roman Catholics as well as other Christian denominations, many people highly recommend Henri Nouwen, *Making All Things New: An Invitation to the Spiritual Life* (New York: HarperCollins, 1981). For anyone interested in Buddhist meditation, three classics are Suzuki-roshi, *Zen Mind, Beginner's Mind* (New York: Weatherhill, 1970); Lawrence LeShan, *How to Meditate* (Boston: Little, Brown, 1974); and Joseph Goldstein and Jack Kornfield, *Seeking the Heart of Wisdom: The Path of Insight Meditation* (Boston: Shambhala, 1987). Finally, for an excellent book on meditation that draws on the wisdom from Judaism, Christianity, Buddhism, Hinduism, and Islam, see David Cooper's *The Heart of Stillness: The Elements of Spiritual Discipline* (New York: Bell Tower/Crown, 1992).

page 103   For more on how to do a Havdalah service at the end of the Sabbath, see *The Gates of Shabbat,* op. cit., pp. 62–70, or Lori Palatnik, *Friday Night and Beyond: The Shabbat Experience Step-by-Step* (Northvale, NJ: Jason Aronson, 1994), pp. 89–95.

page 103   The quote from Alice Walker can be found in *The Columbia Book of Quotations* (New York: Columbia University Press, 1993).

5.   THE FIFTH CHALLENGE

page 106   Harold Bloomfield and Leonard Felder, *Making Peace with Your Parents* (New York: Ballantine, 1985).

page 107   The reference to Simeon ben Yohai's statement about the difficulty of honoring one's parents is from *Midrash Tanhuma,* 'Ekev 2.

page 107   Walter Harrelson, *The Ten Commandments and Human Rights* (Philadelphia: Fortress Press, 1980), pp. 94–95.

page 107   Joseph Telushkin, *Jewish Wisdom* (New York: William Morrow, 1994), p. 147.

page 108   For the specific English definitions of the Hebrew word *cahbeid* (honor or heaviness), see Francis Brown, S. R. Driver, and Charles A. Briggs, *A Hebrew and English Lexicon of the Old Testament* (London: Oxford University Press, 1959), pp. 457–58.

page 109   The quote by Edwin Hubbell Chapin on forgiveness is found in *The Encyclopedia of Religious Quotations,* edited by Frank Mead (Westwood, NJ: Fleming Revell, 1965), p. 146.

page 109   The Yiddish proverb on why a slight from one's own kin hurts worse comes from *Leo Rosten's Treasury of Jewish Quotations* (New York: McGraw-Hill, 1972), p. 217.

page 109   Philo's quote "I forgive and forget" is from De Iosepho, section 239, and is quoted in Burton Stevenson, *The Home Book of Proverbs, Maxims and Familiar Phrases* (New York: Macmillan, 1948), p. 869.

page 109   F. Scott Fitzgerald's quote "forgotten is forgiven" comes from "Note-Books," *The Crack-Up,* 1945, and can be found in *The International Thesaurus of Quotations,* compiled by Rhoda Thomas Tripp (New York: Crowell, 1970), p. 226.

page 110   Paul Tillich's quote "forgiveness presupposes remembering" can be found in *The Eternal Now,* 1963, and is quoted in *The International Thesaurus of Quotations,* op. cit, p. 226.

page 110   Henry Ward Beecher's quote on forgiveness can be found in *The World Treasury of Religious Quotations,* edited by Ralph Woods (New York: Hawthorn, 1968), p. 337.

page 111   The dictionary definitions of forgiveness not being about ignoring or denying come from *Webster's New College Dictionary* (Boston: Houghton Mifflin, 1995), and *The Chambers Dictionary* (Edinburgh: Chambers Harrap, 1993).

page 112   The more confrontational approach to dealing with parents by Susan Forward that I warn against can be found in her book *Toxic Parents* (New York: Bantam, 1989), p. 238.

page 115   Michael Dorris, *A Yellow Raft in Blue Water* (New York: Holt, 1987).

page 121   The quote from Gur Aryeh ha-Levi on why the commandment regarding honoring parents was given specifically for aging parents can be found in *Melekhet Mahshevet* and is quoted in Francine Klagsbrun, *Voices of Wisdom: Jewish Ideals and Ethics for Everyday Living* (Boston: Godine, 1990), p. 198.

page 123   Some of the research studies on stress factors and coping strategies for taking care of aging or ailing parents can be found in Leonard Felder, *When a Loved One Is Ill* (New York: Signet, 1990), Barbara Silverstone and Helen Kandel Hyman, *You and Your Aging Parent* (New York: Pantheon, 1982), and Lissy Jarvik and Gary Small, *Parentcare* (New York: Crown, 1988).

page 124   The quote from Maimonides about delegating to others what you can't do yourself is from *The Code of Maimonides,* "Laws Concerning Rebels," chapter 6, section 10, and is also found in Francine Klagsbrun's *Voices of Wisdom,* op. cit., p. 200.

6.   THE SIXTH CHALLENGE

page 129   The quote on why the Sixth Commandment has been the most successful commandment is from *The Interpreter's Bible* (Nashville: Abingdon, 1952), volume 1, p. 986.

page 130   For numerous examples of the worldwide condemnation of the confessed murderer of Yitzhak Rabin, see the *New York Times* and the *Los Angeles Times,* November 5–30, 1995, which ran numerous articles, as well as the *Jewish Journal of Greater Los Angeles,* November 10, 17, and 24, which had extensive coverage of worldwide reaction.

page 130   The quote from Rabbi Yishmael about not killing the Divine Spirit that is in each person can be found in the *Mekhilta of Rabbi Yishmael,* edited by Jacob Lauterbach (Philadelphia: Jewish Publication Society, 1933).

page 130   The full definition of *Rahtz-akh* is found in Francis Brown, S. R. Driver, and Charles A. Briggs, *A Hebrew and English Lexicon of the Old Testament* (London: Oxford University Press, 1959) pp. 953–54.

page 130 The Talmudic connection between humiliating or shaming someone and killing someone can be found in *Baba Metziah* 58b, in *Aseres HaDibros: The Ten Commandments,* edited by Avrohom Chaim Feuer (Brooklyn: Mesorah Publications, 1981), and in *The Stone Edition Chumash,* edited by Nosson Scherman (Brooklyn: Mesorah Publications, 1993), p. 411.

page 130 The definition of shaming someone, *mahlbeen* can be found in most Hebrew-English dictionaries.

page 131 The quote from Harold Schulweis on "murdering" or eating at ourselves can be found in *For Those Who Can't Believe* (New York: HarperCollins, 1994), pp. 205–06.

page 132 The Talmudic statement that saving one life saves an entire world can be found in Mishna Sanhedrin 4:5.

page 132 For research studies on how painful traumas can lead to later problems if not processed sufficiently, see Judith Herman, *Trauma and Recovery* (New York: Basic, 1992); I. Lisa McCann and Laurie Anne Pearlman, *Psychological Trauma and the Adult Survivor* (New York: Brunner/Mazel, 1990); and R. Janoff-Bulman, "The Aftermath of Victimization," in C. Figley, *Trauma and Its Wake* (New York: Brunner/Mazel, 1985).

page 134 For more information on Parents Anonymous and where you can find one of the 2,100 chapters near you, call (909) 621-6184. Or to find a nearby parenting class, call your local community college or adult-education center.

page 134 For more information about recovering from childhood emotional abuse or earlier traumas, as well as lists of support group organizations, see Charles Sell, *Unfinished Business: Healing Adult Children Resolve Their Past* (Portland, OR: Multnomah Press, 1989); Jeremiah Abrams, *Reclaiming Your Inner Child* (New York: Tarcher/Putnam, 1990); and by Jim Mastrich and Bill Birnes, *Adult Children of Alcoholics' Guide to Raising Healthy Children* (New York: Collier/Macmillan, 1988). You can also call your local Psychological Association or the Association of Marriage and Family Therapists to ask for a referral.

page 138   Deborah Tannen, *You Just Don't Understand* (New York: Ballantine, 1990), pp. 52–53.

page 141   The Talmudic statement that taking away someone's livelihood is tantamount to murder can be found in *The Stone Edition Chumash,* edited by Nosson Scherman, op. cit., p. 411.

page 141   The statement from Maimonides that the highest form of charity is to help someone become self-supporting can be found in many sources, including Louis Jacobs, *The Book of Jewish Belief* (West Orange, NJ: Behrman House, 1984), p. 185.

page 142   The story about Archbishop Desmond Tutu can be found in Martin Copenhaver, *To Begin at the Beginning* (Cleveland: United Church Press, 1994), p. 248.

page 142   The story about the little girl and the starfish was related to me by Wendy Jo Block of Congregation Makom Ohr Shalom based on her work with Nechama-Jewish AIDS Service.

7.   THE SEVENTH CHALLENGE

page 145   Michael Gold, *Does God Belong in the Bedroom?* (Philadelphia: Jewish Publication Society, 1992).

page 145   Roland Gittelsohn, *The Extra Dimension* (New York: Union of American Hebrew Congregations, 1983).

page 145   Morton Kelsey, *Caring: How Can We Love One Another* (Ramsey, NJ: Paulist Press, 1981), pp. 126–27.

page 146   The controversy over who wrote *Iggeret Ha-Kodesh* (*The Holy Letter*) is described in Alan Green, *A Celebration of Marriage* (New York: Collier/Macmillan, 1987), pp. 87–88.

page 146   The quote from *Iggeret Ha-Kodesh* can be found in many sources, including Alan Green, *A Celebration of Marriage,* op. cit.; Aviva Cantor, *Jewish Women/Jewish Men* (New York: HarperCollins, 1995); and *The Holy Letter,* translated by Seymour J. Cohen (New York: Ktav, 1976).

page 147   Clifford and Joyce Penner, *The Gift of Sex* (Dallas: Word, 1981), pp. 342–43.

page 147   The quote about sexuality being wondrous and dangerous is from *The New Interpreter's Bible,* vol. 1 (Nashville: Abingdon, 1994), p. 848.

page 147   Chuck Gallagher, *Marriage Encounter* (Garden City, NY: Doubleday, 1975).

page 147   Walter Harrelson, *The Ten Commandments and Human Rights* (Philadelphia: Fortress Press, 1980), pp. 130–33.

page 148   George Leonard, *The End of Sex* (later retitled *Adventures in Monogamy*) (Los Angeles: Tarcher, 1983), pp. 155–56.

page 149   For a description of the controversy surrounding the 1976 *Playboy* interview by Robert Scheer quoting Jimmy Carter, see *Time,* October 4, 1976, pp. 33–34; *Newsweek* October 4, 1976, pp. 70–71; and *Christian Century,* Martin Marty, "About That Interview," October 6, 1976, p. 847.

page 149   The quote from Dr. William Wolf about Carter's comments can be found in *Time,* October 4, 1976, pp. 33–34.

page 150   The discussion of adulterous thoughts, written by R. Kent Hughes and John H. Armstrong, can be found in *Christianity Today,* April 3, 1995, p. 33.

page 150   William Stafford, *Disordered Loves: Healing the Seven Deadly Sins* (Cambridge, MA: Cowley, 1994), pp. 51–55.

page 150   For more on the Jewish view that occasional lustful thoughts are far less serious than actions, see Yehudah Hehasid, Sefer Hasidim, section 54, and Abraham David, Ezer Mikodesh 5A, Haezer 23:3, and Babylonian Talmud, Abodah Zarah 20a, which are summarized in Lawrence Grossman, "A Jewish Approach to the Pornography Issue" in *The Jewish Family and Jewish Continuity,* edited by Steven Bayme and Gladys Rosen (Hoboken, NJ: Ktav, 1994).

page 151   The research that 95 percent of people think of sex at least once a day is from Harold Leitenberg and Kris Henning, based on their examination of two hundred published studies spanning the past fifty years, as reported by Kathleen Kelleher, the *Los Angeles Times,* August 13, 1995, p. E1.

page 151 The quotes about sexual thoughts from Rabbi Isaac can be found in Babylonian Talmud, *Kiddushin,* 80b; here, I've quoted from Joseph Telushkin's *Jewish Wisdom* (New York: William Morrow, 1994), p. 132.

page 151 The Baal Shem Tov's suggestion to refocus your sexual thoughts back on the Creator is based on the Talmudic suggestion in TB *Abodah Zarah* 20a and is also described in Rodger Kamenetz's *The Jew in the Lotus* (New York: HarperCollins, 1994), p. 126.

page 153 Patricia Love and Jo Robinson, *Hot Monogamy* (New York: Plume, 1995).

page 155 For books that can give you more detailed information about sacred sexuality in Hindu Tantra and Kundalini Yoga, see Margo Anand, *Sexual Ecstasy* (Los Angeles: Tarcher, 1989); *The Encyclopedia of Sexual Wisdom,* edited by Rufus Camphausen (Rochester, VT: Inner Traditions, 1991); and Richard Craze, *The Spiritual Traditions of Sex* (New York: Harmony Books, 1996). For books that can give you more detailed information about sacred sexuality in the Jewish Kabbalistic teachings, see Alan Green, *A Celebration of Marriage* (New York: Collier Macmillan, 1987); Arthur Waskow, *Down to Earth Judaism* (New York: William Morrow, 1995); and Ruth Westheimer and Jonathan Mark, *Heavenly Sex: Sexuality in the Jewish Tradition* (New York: New York University Press, 1996).

page 159 Shere Hite, *The Hite Report on Male Sexuality* (New York: Knopf, 1981), and in *Women and Love* (New York: St. Martin's Press, 1989).

page 159 The *Cosmopolitan* estimates of adultery can be found in Linda Wolfe, *The Cosmo Report* (New York: Arbor House, 1981).

page 159 Morton Hunt, *The Natural History of Love* (New York: Anchor, 1994).

page 159 Samuel and Cynthia Janus, *The Janus Report on Sexual Behavior* (New York: John Wiley, 1993).

page 159 The National Opinion Research Center estimates of adultery can be found in *Society* May-June 1994: p. 9, and in Andrew Greeley, *Faithful Attraction* (New York: TOR Books, 1991).

page 160 The quote from Frank Pittman about marriages re-

covering from an affair can be found in "Beyond Betrayal: Life After Infidelity," in *Psychology Today*
May-June 1993: p. 32–38.

page 160 Janis Spring, *After the Affair: Healing the Pain and
Rebuilding Trust When a Partner Has Been Unfaithful*
(New York: HarperCollins, 1996).

page 162 Frank Pittman, *Private Lies: Infidelity and the Betrayal of Intimacy* (New York: Norton, 1989), p. 43.

8. THE EIGHTH CHALLENGE

page 168 For more on Rashi's interpretation of the Eighth
Commandment as "stealing someone's freedom," see
Pentateuch with Rashi's Commentary, edited by A. M.
Silberman (London: Shapiro, Valentine and Company,
1930), p. 105.

page 168 For more on Samson Raphael Hirsch's interpretation, see *Exodus,* volume 2 of *The Pentateuch,* translated
by Isaac Levy (New York: Judaica Press, 1971), p. 277.

page 169 The quote from Rabbi Ishmael about stealing "the
good opinion of people" can be found in *Mekhilta de
Rabbi Ishmael,* Mishpatim, Nezikin, 13, as cited in *The
Book of Legends from the Talmud and Midrash,* by
H. N. Bialik and Y. H. Ravnitzky (New York: Schocken,
1992), p. 657.

page 169 The quote from Nosson Scherman on using deceit to
win someone's regard can be found in *The Stone Edition
Chumash* (Brooklyn: Mesorah Publications, 1993),
p. 412.

page 169 Lewis Smedes, *Mere Morality* (Grand Rapids, MI:
William Eerdmans, 1983), p. 183.

page 169 For more on rudeness or demeaning behavior as
theft of someone's self-respect, see *Aseres HaDibros: The
Ten Commandments,* edited by Avrohom Chaim Feyer
(Brooklyn: Mesorah Publications, 1993) p. 57.

page 170 For more on interrupting as a type of stealing, see
Deborah Tannen, *You Just Don't Understand* (New
York: Ballantine, 1990).

page 170 For more on literary deception or stealing the credit for ideas, see Tanchuma Bamidbar; Magen Avraham to Orach Chaim 156; Yalkut Shimoni, II:960, as cited in *Aseres HaDibros,* op. cit., p. 57., and also Gary Vanden-Bos's excellent article on plagiarism and credit stealing, "Ethics and Etiquette in Publishing," *The Monitor,* March 1995, p. 15.

page 170   For more on mistreating employees as a form of stealing, see Jeffrey Salkin, *Being God's Partner: How to Find the Hidden Link Between Your Spirituality and Your Work* (Woodstock, VT: Jewish Lights, 1994), pp. 135–36.

page 171   For more on the Yiddish language and the Yiddish word *gonnif,* see Leo Rosten, *The Joys of Yiddish* (New York: Simon and Schuster, 1991).

page 172   The quote from Professor Teri Bernstein about choosing solutions with integrity was obtained from a direct interview on April 10, 1996.

page 178   The quotes from Leviticus 19:9–11 are from W. Gunther Plaut, *The Torah: A Modern Commentary* (New York: Union of American Hebrew Congregations, 1981).

page 178   The suggestion to consider life like a revolving wheel in which even the rich may be reduced to taking charity can be found in Solomon Ganzfried, *The Abridged Code of Jewish Law,* 34:1, as cited in Joseph Telushkin's *Jewish Wisdom* (New York: William Morrow, 1994), p. 22–23.

page 178   Robert Schuller, *Believe in the God Who Believes in You* (Nashville: Thomas Nelson, 1989), p. 201.

page 179   The Islamic views on charity come from the Quran and are described in Huston Smith's *The Religions of Man* (New York: Harper Perennial, 1958), p. 240.

page 179   Bear Heart with Molly Larkin, *The Wind Is My Mother* (New York: Clarkson Potter, 1996), p. 230.

page 180   The quote about poor people giving to charity is from the Babylonian Talmud, Gittin 7b, as cited in Joseph Telushkin's *Jewish Wisdom,* op. cit., p. 14.

page 180   Robert Schuller, *Believe in the God Who Believes in You,* op. cit., p. 220.

page 180   Isaac Klein, *The Ten Commandments in a Changing World* (New York: Bloch, 1944), 103–05.

page 180   The discussion of upper and lower limits for charity is found in Joseph Telushkin, *Jewish Wisdom,* op. cit., p. 18, and is based on Babylonian Talmud, Ketubot 50a.

9.   THE NINTH CHALLENGE

page 183   The view that *"Lo ta-eed"* means "Don't testify" while *"Lo ta-ahneh"* means "Don't repeat" is explained in *Aseres HaDibros: The Ten Commandments,* edited by Avrohom Chaim Feuer (Brooklyn: Mesorah Publications, 1993), p. 58.

page 183   Some of the places in which *"Lo ta-ahneh"* is described as "Don't answer, respond, or repeat" are *The Pentateuch,* translated and with commentary by Samson Raphael Hirsch (New York: Judaica Press, 1971), vol. 2, p. 277, and in *Haamek Davar,* as cited in *Aseres HaDibros,* op. cit., p. 59.

page 185   The Hasidic story about gossip spreading like feathers in the wind can be found in Stephen Wylen, *Gossip: The Power of the Word* (Hoboken, NJ: Ktav, 1994), and in Joseph Telushkin's *Words That Hurt, Words That Heal* (New York: William Morrow, 1996).

page 186   The story about the preacher who offends her congregation by telling them not to gossip can be found in Robert Kahn, *The Ten Commandments for Today* (Garden City, NY: Doubleday, 1964), p. 104.

page 188   Andrew Kopkind, *The Thirty Years War* (New York: Routledge, Chapman and Hall, 1995).

page 188   The Spanish proverb "The person who knows only a little says very much" can be found in David Carkeet's novel *Double Negative* (New York: Pocket, 1991).

page 189   The quote from Hillel can be found in the Babylonian Talmud, Shabbat 31a.

page 189   The quotes from Matthew and Romans are found in *The Holy Bible: New International Version* (Grand Rapids, MI: Zondervan, 1984).

page 190   The quote from the Muslim mystic Al-Ghazali can be found in Sisela Bok, *Lying: Moral Choice in Public and Private Life* (New York: Pantheon, 1978), p. 29.

page 190   The description of Karma consequences can be

found in *The Encyclopedia of Eastern Philosophy and Religion* (Boston: Shambhala, 1989).

page 191 The Talmudic saying that gossip also hurts the speaker can be found in Francine Klagsbrun, *Voices of Wisdom* (Boston: Godine, 1990), p. 74, and is based on the Babylonian Talmud, Arakhin, 15b.

page 193 Experts on discrimination and prejudice who point to the serious effect of things said when a group is not present to defend itself include Gordon Allport, *The Nature of Prejudice* (Boston: Addison-Wesley, 1979).

page 193 The view that many people feel they can say hurtful things about Arab-Americans with impunity has been suggested by Don Bustany and James Abourezk of the American-Arab Anti-Discrimination Committee and also by several non-Arab media experts I interviewed for a study in 1985.

page 193 For more on Reverend Martin Niemoller and his famous quote "and there was no one left to speak for me," see Joseph Telushkin, *Jewish Wisdom* (New York: William Morrow, 1994), pp. 536–37.

page 193 For more details about the anti-Arab incidents following the Oklahoma City bombing, see the coverage in the *Los Angeles Times,* April 20–24, 1995.

page 194 The books on compassionate speech are *Hofetz Hayim* (The One Who Loves Life), by Israel Hacohen Kagan (1873), Zelig Pliskin, *Guard Your Tongue* (New York: Aish HaTorah, 1975), Stephen Wylen, *Gossip: The Power of the Word* (Hoboken, NJ: Ktav, 1993), and Joseph Telushkin, *Words That Hurt, Words That Heal,* op. cit.

page 195 The Buddhist, Hindu, and Zen view of the importance of inner intentions can be found in Huston Smith, *The Illustrated World's Religions* (New York: HarperCollins, 1994), pp. 49, 75.

page 198 Zelig Pliskin, *Guard Your Tongue,* op. cit.

page 198 The Buddhist approach to being mindful about your daily words and gossip can be found in Huston Smith, *The Illustrated World's Religions,* op. cit., p. 74.

10. THE TENTH CHALLENGE

page 203 The quote from Sigmund Freud about jealousy can be found in "Certain Neurotic Mechanisms in Jealousy, Paranoia and Homosexuality," *Collected Papers* (New York: Basic, 1959), p. 232.

page 205 The definition of *"Lo takhmohd"* as "Don't hold as precious that which doesn't belong to you" was given by Rabbi Mordecai Finley, Makom Ohr Shalom Torah class, January 1995, and can also be found in Francis Brown, S. R. Driver, and Charles A. Briggs, *A Hebrew and English Lexicon of the Old Testament* (London: Oxford University Press, 1959).

page 206 John Locke, *Essay Concerning Human Understanding,* 1690.

page 206 The Buddhist definition of *duhkha* (suffering) as "blind craving or desire" can be found in *The Encyclopedia of Eastern Philosophy and Religion* (Boston: Shambhala, 1989), p. 96.

page 206 Sylvia Boorstein, *It's Easier Than You Think: The Buddhist Way to Happiness* (New York: HarperCollins, 1995), pp. 19–20.

page 206 The quotes from Claudian, Saint Augustine, and William Penn can be found in *The Encyclopedia of Religious Quotations,* edited by Frank Mead (Westwood, NJ: Fleming Revell, 1965).

page 207 The second minister, who explained how envy in balance can be motivating and in excess can be immobilizing, is Reverend Anne Gleaves Cohen of the Altadena, California, Congregational United Church of Christ; personal communication, February 24, 1996.

page 208 The Zusya story has been told by many rabbis and can also be found in Martin Buber's *Tales of the Hasidim* (New York: Schocken, 1948).

page 209 For more on the views of Karen Horney, see her *New Ways in Psychoanalysis* (New York: Norton, 1939).

page 210 For more on how bitterness, envy, and self-criticism harm immune systems, see S. E. Taylor, *Health Psychology* (New York: Random House, 1986), and D. Goleman and J. Gurin, *Mind Body Medicine: How to Use Your*

Mind for Better Health (Yonkers, NY: Consumer Reports Books, 1993).

page 214   Joan Didion, "Jealousy: Is It a Curable Illness?" *Vogue,* June 1961.

page 217   Ellen Umansky and Diane Ashton, *Four Centuries of Jewish Women's Spirituality* (Boston: Beacon, 1993); see in particular the chapters "A Ritual of Loss," by Penina Adelman, "Simchat Hochmah," by Savina Teubal, and "Sitting Shiva for a Lost Love," by E. M. Broner.

ACKNOWLEDGMENTS

Many people helped me write this book, and I wish I could give sufficient time and words to thanking each one personally. The comments and suggestions of hundreds of Jews, Christians, Muslims, Buddhists, Hindus, and others have inspired the words that are written throughout these pages.

I am especially grateful to my longtime friend and colleague Rabbi Marc Sirinsky of Temple Emek Shalom in Ashland, Oregon, who challenged me each time I said something incorrect and who guided me in finding primary sources for many of the ideas discussed in each chapter. My wife, Linda, and I were upset when Marc, his wife, Catherine, and their daughter, Zoey, moved from Los Angeles to Ashland, but the many phone calls and letters we exchanged about *The Ten Challenges* made the loss much easier.

Numerous teachers and friends also provided ideas and guidance to help me understand the deeper levels of the ancient texts. Lucky Altman of the National Conference not only answered my questions about Christian issues but also directed me to several other useful guides. Reverend Anne Gleaves Cohen of the Altadena Congregational United Church of Christ answered my numerous queries with great wisdom and caring. My beloved teachers, especially Rabbis Ted Falcon, Mordecai Finley, David Cooper, and Zalman Schachter-Shalomi, as well as Rabbis Amy Eilberg, Sue Levi Elwell, Laura Geller, Jonathan Omerman, Harold Schulweis, M. Robert Syme, Joseph Telushkin, Albert Vorspan, Abner Weiss, and Shawn Israel Zevit, have taught me that every spiritual question is a legitimate question and that our tradition is forever growing as each individual adds his or her sparks of wisdom.

I want to acknowledge the warm assistance on Islamic issues I received from Fawad Yacoob, Munir Shaikh, and Shabbir Mansuri of the Council on Islamic Education in Fountain Valley and Dr. Hassan Hathout of the Los Angeles Islamic Center. Additional insights on Christian viewpoints were provided generously by Reverend Ron and Colleen Wilstein of Park City, Utah, Sister Alexis Navarro of Immaculate Heart College in

Los Angeles, and all the people I met through Christian-Jewish dialogues.

Tremendous support and assistance came from the librarians and staff of several outstanding facilities, including the collections of Loyola Marymount University, the University of Judaism, Hebrew Union College, Fuller Theological Seminary, the Santa Monica Library, and the Beverly Hills Library; I am especially appreciative of the generous help and suggestions given to me by Rachel Glasser of the Sinai Temple Library in Westwood.

Several friends and colleagues expressed enthusiasm for the topic during the early phases of the project and offered thoughtful suggestions, including Teri Bernstein, Dr. Miriam Raviv, Peter Reiss, Dr. Rowland Shepard, Drs. Harold Bloomfield and Sirah Vettese, Dr. Amy Gross, Michael Stroud, Neil Van Steenbergen, Barbara Rotman, Janet Sternfeld Davis, Trudi Alexy, Nancy O'Donohue, Julie Simon, Dr. Patricia Birch, Rachel Ballon, Caty Konigsberg, Laurie and Joe Jacobs, Linda Waddington, Nick and Nancy Scanlan, Patty and Michael Melnick, Eli and Renat Amir, David Bayer, Dr. Susan Cross, Marti Leviel, Barbara Zheutlin, Dr. Janet Ruckert, and Dr. Janet Tunick. I especially want to thank my longtime friend Nancy Shapiro Pikelny of Chicago, who critiqued an early draft of the manuscript and offered much-needed support and guidance.

I was fortunate on this project to work with a very supportive and intelligent literary agent, Reid Boates, who along with his wife, Karen, gave me encouragement and good ideas from the start. I also want to thank Leslie Meredith, Andrew Stuart, Amy Zelvin, and all of the creative people at Harmony Books for their hard work on this project. Reid Boates told me I would like working with Leslie Meredith, an editor who is extremely wise and sensible, but I had no idea our creative collaboration would be as enjoyable as it was.

On a personal level, I want to thank my family for their love and support, especially Martin and Ena Felder; Helen Rothenberg Felder; Eddie Rothenberg; Bill and June Schorin; Jeff Schorin; Ruth Wilstein; Janice, Craig, and Erica Ruff; Andi Wagner Bittker; Ruthe Wagner; Ron Wagner; and my wonderful son, Steven Alon Schorin Felder. Most of all, I want to express my deep thanks and love to my wife and best friend, Linda Schorin, for her honest feedback, easy-to-hear criticism, and useful ideas, which have helped me on this and all my projects. Linda saw the importance of doing this book even when no one else did, and her vision made it possible.

There's one more thank-you I want to make. I am usually private when thanking God and shy about doing so in public, but the enjoyable time of research and writing on this topic has truly been a blessing. I hope my words bring honor and respect to the holy wisdom that was given so that we might draw closer to the Divine Presence. In writing this book I finally understand what is meant in the Book of Proverbs where it says, *Etz khayim heeh,* "It is a tree of life to those who hold it dearly."

INDEX

theft of another's self-worth and, 169–70
wholeness and, 168–69
Eliezer, Israel ben. *See* Baal Shem Tov
Emotions. *See* Psychological issues; *specific emotions*
Empowerment, 136–38
Entertainment, commercial, 91–92
Envy, 208–10, 211–22; *See also* Coveting; Jealousy
Eternal life, 189
Eternal One. *See* God
Ethical behavior, unpopular, 176–77
Ethnic groups, 68; *See also specific groups*
Exaggeration, 62–63
Exodus, Book of
  Eighth Commandment and, 168, 171, 178
  Fifth Commandment and, 108
  First Commandment and, 13, 17
  Fourth Commandment and, 82–83
  Golden Calf and, 38
  in Pentateuch, 229
  Seventh Commandment and, 144
  Sixth Commandment and, 130
  Ten Commandments stated in, 1, 4, 6
  Tenth Commandment and, 202, 205
Extra Dimension, The (Gittelsohn), 145

Faithful Attraction (Greeley), 159
Falcoln, Ted, 35
Falsehoods. *See* Ninth Commandment
False idols. *See* Idols, false; Second Commandment
False witness. *See* Ninth Commandment
Family, 27, 30, 122; *See also* Parents
Father, Son, Holy Spirit, 79
Fatihah (Islamic Opening Prayer), 52
Fear, of seeking help, 122–23
Feathers in the wind (Hasidic story), 185–86
Feelings. *See* Psychological issues; *specific feelings*
Fifth Commandment, 105–28, 223
  challenge of, 3
  parent-child relationship and, 107–8
  steps toward honoring parents, 108–28
  See also Parents
Fight or flight response, 70
Finding God (Sonsino/Syme), 21
Finley, Mordecai, 59
First Commandment, 13–33, 130, 223
  alternate translation of, 17
  challenge of, 2
  Exodus from Egypt and, 18

God's presence and, 22–27
personal response to, 20–22
skepticism about, 14–15
spiritual views and, 15–16, 28–33
traditional interpretation of, 19–20
understanding of, 16–17
Fitzgerald, F. Scott, 109
Food. *See* Meals
Food addiction, 133
Forgiveness, 108–16
  inability for, 115–16
  process of, 112–13
  self-discovery and, 113
  techniques for, 114–15
Forten, Charlotte, 97
Forward, Susan, 112
Four Centuries of Jewish Women's Spirituality (Ashton and Umansky), 217
Fourth Commandment, 9, 82–104, 223
  and benefits of Sabbath observance, 83
  and bringing joy to Sabbath, 87–89
  challenge of, 2–3
  dream vs. reality of Sabbath observance, 86–87
  meaning of Sabbath, 84–86
  steps for Sabbath observance, 90–104
Francis of Assisi, Saint, 52, 230
Frankl, Viktor, 5–6, 55
Freedom, personal, 168–69
Freud, Sigmund, 14–15, 203, 209
Freudian theory, 71
Friends, 27
Fromm, Erich, 21, 35, 227
Frustration, 136–38
Fund-raising, 141
Future of an Illusion, The (Freud), 14

Gallagher, Chuck, 147
Gandhi (film), 70
Gangs, 141
Generosity, 179–81
Genesis, Book of, 39, 85, 229
Gift giving, 178–79
Gift of Sex, The (Penner), 147
Gittelsohn, Roland, 145
God
  arguing/wrestling with, 39
  belief in, 2, 15–16, 17
  childhood image of, 15–16
  confession to, 43–48
  as Divine Presence, 226
  experiencing presence of, 22–27, 207
  finding within, 23–25, 40
  future generations and, 20
  Hebrew and English names for, 23, 227, 231
  love from, 35, 43

God *(cont.)*
love of, 52, 107
modern view of, 207
as One, 2, 13, 223, 227
personal relationship with, 19–20,
  26–27, 47–48
receipt of Ten Commandments from,
  17
resources for understanding, 21–25
shared views of, 22
soul and, 231
taking name in vain, 2, 60, 65–70,
  76, 223
tragedies and, 20–23
understanding ways of, 20–22
waiting for, 40
See also First Commandment; Third
  Commandment
Goethe, Johann, 76
Gold, Michael, 145
Golden Calf, 37–42, 48
Golden Rule, 107, 189–90, 191
Gonnif (thief), 171, 227
Good deeds, 28–29, 140
Gossip, 3, 183–201
  curbing, 189–98
  Hebrew term for, 228
  reasons for, 187–88, 200
Gossip: The Power of the Word
  (Wylen), 195
Gottlieb, Lynn, 23
Greeley, Andrew, 41–42, 159
Green, Arthur, 91
Greenberg, Irving, 85
Gregorian Chants, 53, 227
Group bonding, 188
Growth, personal, 28
Guard Your Tongue (Pliskin), 194, 198
Guilt feelings, 125
Gur Aryeh ha-Levi, 121
Gurdjieff, G. I., 40

Habits, overcoming, 175–76
Halakhah, 227
Harrelson, Walter, 147–48
Hasidism
  defined, 227
  traditional stories of, 53–54, 185–86
  wordless melody of, 229
Hathout, Hassan, 21
Havdalah prayers, 103
Havurot, 227
Hayyim ben Moses Attar, 66
Health and healing
  appropriate anger release and, 72–73
  for caregiver, 125
  effect of past hurts on, 132–34
  for older population, 121
  parent-child relationship and,
    111–12, 113, 121–25

psychological/spiritual links and, 6,
  30
unblocking of spirituality for, 28,
  30–31
women's rituals and, 217
See also Illness
Heart attack, 72
Heart connections. *See* Relationships,
  interpersonal
Heart of Stillness, The (Cooper), 42
*Hebrew and English Lexicon of the
  Old Testament, The* (Brown,
  Driver, Briggs), 130
Hebrew language, 6–7, 17, 78
Helping organizations, 122–23
Henning, Kris, 151
Hillel (rabbi), 189
Hinduism, 227
  ancient breathing techniques and,
    155
  awakening spirituality and, 42, 94
  inner intentions and, 195
  Islamic relations with, 70
  Karma and, 190, 228
  moral action and, 29
  yoga and, 50, 228
Hirsch, Samson Raphael, 84, 168
Hite, Shere, 159
Hofetz Hayim (Kagan), 194
Holiday celebrations, 27, 41
Holmes, Ernest, 230
Holocaust, 5, 6, 22, 227
Holy Letter, The, 146
Holy One. *See* God
Holy places, 27
Holy Spirit, 50
Homelessness, 178
Honesty. *See* Integrity
Honoring parents. *See* Fifth
  Commandment; Parents
Honoring relationships. *See* Third
  Commandment
Horney, Karen, 209–10
Hot Monogamy (Love and Robinson),
  153
Hughes, R. Kent, 150
Humanism, 227
Humanity, 67–70
Humiliation, 130–31
Hunger, 178
Hunt, Morton, 159
Hurtful talk. *See* Talk, hurtful
Hymns, 99

Idols, false, 223
  breaking away from, 45–46
  modern equivalents of, 2, 34–38
  See also Second Commandment
Iggeret Ha-Kodesh (The Holy Letter),
  146

ABOUT THE AUTHOR

Leonard Felder, Ph.D., is a licensed psychologist in private practice in West Los Angeles whose six books have sold over 850,000 copies and been translated into eleven languages. His books include *Making Peace with Yourself, A Fresh Start, When a Loved One Is Ill, Does Someone at Work Treat You Badly?,* and the best-seller *Making Peace with Your Parents,* which won the 1985 Book of the Year Award from *Medical Self-Care* magazine.

A widely requested speaker nationwide, he has appeared on *The Oprah Winfrey Show, Sally Jessy Raphael, CNN Newsnight, NBC Nightly News,* and more than 150 radio and television programs, along with being invited to give lectures and workshops at colleges, churches, and synagogues in fifteen states. Dr. Felder is active in several volunteer activities and won the Distinguished Merit Citation of the National Conference of Christians and Jews for his many years of facilitating dialogues between people of different races and religions.

Originally from Detroit, Michigan, he currently lives in Mar Vista, California, with his wife, Linda Schorin, and their son, Steven.